Spelling Rules, Riddles and Remedies

Advice and activities to enhance spelling achievement for all

Sally Raymond

Routledge
Taylor & Francis Group

LONDON AND NEW YORK

First published 2014
by Routledge
2 Park Square, Milton Park, Abingdon, Oxon OX14 4RN

and by Routledge
711 Third Avenue, New York, NY 10017

Routledge is an imprint of the Taylor & Francis Group, an informa business

British Library Cataloguing in Publication Data
A catalogue record for this book is available from the British Library

Library of Congress Cataloging in Publication Data
Raymond, Sally.
Spelling rules, riddles and remedies : advice and activities to enhance spelling achievement for all / Sally Raymond.
pages cm
1. English language--Orthography and spelling--Study and teaching (Elementary) I. Title.
LB1574.R28 2014
372.63'2--dc23
2013034440

ISBN: 978-0-415-70999-6 (hbk)
ISBN: 978-0-415-71000-8 (pbk)
ISBN: 978-1-315-81448-3 (ebk)

Typeset in Arial
by Saxon Graphics Ltd, Derby

Image credits: © Shutterstock 2013.
Additional illustrations by L. Collard.

Printed and bound in Great Britain by
CPI Group (UK) Ltd, Croydon, CR0 4YY

Spelling Rules, Riddles and Remedies

Spelling Rules, Riddles and Remedies is for anyone supporting learners who are struggling to understand the world of English spellings.

This book engages both learners and their learning by using practical and dynamic resources to reveal the cause and effect of spelling confusions. By posing opportunities for understanding memory-related applications, learners and their spelling tutors are then empowered with the knowledge and resources required to amend, improve and proliferate spelling success.

Using a range of unique and very accessible 'Spelling Detective' and 'Learning Application' activities, best-selling author Sally Raymond:

- shows how to engage a pupil through use of meta-cognition;
- highlights reasons why spelling abilities might fail;
- explores and resolves the impact of English spelling irregularities and deviations through informed discovery;
- uses mnemonics and story-lines to link tangible prompts to confident spelling ability;
- provides structured game-play and challenging practise lessons;
- boosts pupils' achievement through the strategic use of multiple processing abilities.

Clearly presented and highly illustrated, this book encourages creativity and shows teachers how to adopt and adapt a variety of learning strategies to suit different needs.

Targeting learners in Key Stage 2 upwards, *Spelling Rules, Riddles and Remedies* brings a wealth of ideas to stimulate spelling success.

Sally Raymond has worked as a school SENCo, a dyslexia tutor and a dyslexia course manager delivering SpLD teacher-training courses, and has also run courses for parents of dyslexic children and provided dyslexia consultancy advice to schools, colleges and the workplace.

Also available from the same author:

**Supporting Key Stage 2 and 3 Dyslexic Pupils, their Teachers and Support Staff:
The Dragonfly Worksheets**
Second Edition

2014 – 144 pages

Paperback: **£19.99**
978-1-138-77462-9

Hardback: **£90.00**
978-1-138-77461-2

**Extending Support for Key Stage 2 and 3 Dyslexic Pupils, their Teachers and
Support Staff: The Dragonfly Games**
Second Edition

2014 – 80 pages

Paperback: **£19.99**
978-1-138-77460-5

Hardback: **£90.00**
978-1-138-77459-9

To Tia, Tazmin and Robert.

Contents

Introduction:
The Impact of Spelling Difficulties

Who Needs This Book and Why Do They Need It?

Spelling Rules, Riddles and Remedies has been developed using 15 years of experience of supporting and developing literacy confidence and skills. It targets the needs of learners who find English spellings confusing; is designed to be used as an adaptable resource for spelling tutors (adults with or without academic training); and is presented in a style which allows for flexibility and variation according to need.

- An index of spelling families and words enables spelling tutors to tailor lessons to suit individual lessons and learners.
- Section headings highlight specific topics of interest.
- Materials focus on spelling patterns encountered during Primary education years. These also support older learners needing to master key spelling patterns, and can be extended to embrace new vocabulary.
- The use of verbal discussions and detective investigations are also employed to use observation, discovery and ideas to enhance personal engagement and participation. *Spelling Rules, Riddles and Remedies* aims to *empower learners* with information and skills. By understanding the nature of English spellings, along with methods to enhance memory storage and recall, a variety of different routes into learning are available to interest, inspire and entertain learners.
- Sample spellings are used in different activities to provide examples for immediate use. However, spelling tutors and learners are positively encouraged to adapt materials to suit their needs. This could include the addition of curriculum-based and personally-relevant spellings; repeating an activity with new spellings to widen access to further learning opportunities; duplicating an activity yet changing the topic to allow the exploration of new material within a familiar setting.
- Some activities require the advanced preparation of materials.

Spelling ability is, like any skill, easier for some learners to acquire than others. Some individuals will absorb spelling patterns just through the reading and writing of words to create spelling memories which are easily and accurately recalled and applied. Others have to work harder to identify which spelling patterns relate to which sounds; which words are attached to which spellings; and which words ignore all the rules to display a cacophony of letters that challenge both memory processing and common sense.

There is no doubt that English spellings are fraught with idiosyncrasies and that additional barriers to learning can develop if confusion, error and frustration become linked to the spelling experience. However, by actively exploring and defining spelling vulnerabilities, inquisitive minds can be guided and engaged in a topic which some learners find easy, others find difficult, and everyone else falls somewhere in between.

Ultimately focusing on memory storage and recall, this teaching resource provides a variety of adaptable methods and materials to enhance engagement and learning; understanding and ownership; motivation and success. Championing learner-empowerment, this book encourages the learners themselves to explore and identify the many features of English spellings which infuse it with opportunities for confusion and error. Practising methods which utilise different coping strategies also fosters independence and triumph to boost a learner's skills and confidence in their own ability.

Despite an initial need to introduce the role of letter-to-sound rules in written text, a failure to help learners move beyond the use of their ears when spelling will lead many into trouble. English spellings must engage the eyes as well as an understanding of word meaning and spelling structure to help the brain register where and why letters appear in the patterns that they do.

- English spellings lack the regularity of many other languages. 'H<u>erd</u>', 'h<u>eard</u>', 'b<u>ird</u>', 'w<u>ord</u>', 'p<u>urred</u>', 'st<u>irred</u>', 'c<u>urd</u>' and 'det<u>erred</u>' all share the same sound, but not the same spelling.
- Alphabetic letters can be seen to perform different roles as shown by the letter 'c' in 'cat', 'chair', 'ice', 'machine', 'magician', 'ocean' and 'sock'.
- Letters can share the same spelling but not the same sound as in 'h<u>ead</u>' and 'b<u>ead</u>' / 'p<u>ear</u>' and 'h<u>eart</u>' / 'h<u>eard</u>' and 'b<u>eard</u>'. (Additional variations arise borne of accent; pronunciation; clarity of hearing and speech.)
- In a transparent language (such as Spanish) one grapheme (letter or letter-group) is generally used to represent that one sound in all the words in which it appears. If this was so in English, spellings would become far more regular: 't<u>oa</u>d' / 'bloa' (blow) / 'goa' (go) / 'noat' (note).

English is full of irregularities and choices.

The Impact of Spelling Difficulties

When individuals are failing to achieve success at the rate of their peers, they can feel a sense of inadequacy, low self-esteem and disappointment.

- Measures of success (including failure) often influence identity, expectation, performance levels and goals.

Spelling skills (alongside reading, writing and numeracy) are commonly used as benchmarks of success and achievement within educational settings. If singing abilities were subjected to similar levels of scrutiny, a different group of learners would be struggling to access the stimulating and inspirational effect of achievement and acclaim.

- In modern society, literacy skills have great value and importance. Spelling accuracy is considered a reflection of educational and learning expertise, intelligence and attainment.

Faced with high expectations, learners who struggle to succeed often experience anxiety and stress. These emotional responses can themselves present barriers to learning. They may also trigger additional behaviours such as avoidance strategies, self-deprecation and disinterest, further impeding access to progress and positive outcomes.

- Adults with good spelling skills are often unaware of the potential for many English spellings to trigger spelling errors, and how deeply demotivating the cause and effect of spelling difficulties can be on individuals. Exploration of potential barriers to learning encourages spelling tutors to identify where and why difficulties have arisen. By exploring a variety of accessible routes into learning, both tutors and students can discover the rewards of strategic application.

The use and expression of language forms part of everyone's social identity. Commercial gimmickry; vernacular vocabulary (such as 'doh!', 'innit', and 'L8'); and American-style spelling patterns, are indicative of modern times.

- Youngsters often use (and enjoy) text-speak spellings. For those who find conventional spellings difficult (along with those who don't) the recent spelling revolution which has brought new, fashionable and largely phonically-based spellings into everyday life can be easier for them to learn and remember. Whether these trends will retain their popularity, is, as yet, unknown. However, unless we increase the access to spelling success, the tendency for many learners to adopt an alternative, easier, spelling system will prevail.

There are an estimated 185 spellings for the 44 sounds found in English, with 69 spellings having more than one sound.

Consider the following common words and their spellings to see how easy it is for confusions and errors to arise.

thr<u>ough</u> / f<u>ew</u> / tr<u>ue</u> / b<u>oo</u> / wh<u>o</u> although / s<u>ew</u> / s<u>o</u> / s<u>ow</u> / t<u>oe</u> b<u>ough</u>t / c<u>augh</u>t / c<u>our</u>t / t<u>au</u>t / s<u>or</u>t dr<u>ough</u>t / ab<u>ou</u>t / d<u>ou</u>bt / n<u>ow</u>t b<u>ough</u> / c<u>ow</u> / th<u>ou</u>sand tr<u>ough</u> / o<u>ff</u> / qu<u>aff</u> r<u>ough</u> / st<u>uff</u>	<u>kn</u>it <u>n</u>ice <u>gn</u>ome <hr> m<u>u</u>ch h<u>u</u>tch t<u>ou</u>ch	<u>ch</u>oose lo<u>se</u> brui<u>se</u> bl<u>ue</u>s sn<u>oo</u>ze ne<u>w</u>s vie<u>w</u>s <u>f</u>u<u>se</u>	allowed aloud road rode rowed piece peace scene seen bean been steal steel mince mints sighed side sight site flower flour write right rite their there they're wait weight grown groan

d<u>oor</u> dr<u>aw</u> dr<u>awer</u> p<u>our</u> <u>oar</u> st<u>ore</u> s<u>ure</u> w<u>ar</u> s<u>aw</u> f<u>or</u>	b<u>oa</u>t n<u>o</u>te gr<u>ow</u> s<u>o</u> s<u>ew</u> <hr>f<u>ie</u>ld m<u>ea</u>l gr<u>ee</u>n rec<u>ei</u>ve	h<u>er</u>d abs<u>ur</u>d b<u>ir</u>d h<u>ear</u>d w<u>or</u>d st<u>irr</u>ed <hr>clo<u>ck</u> loo<u>k</u> magi<u>c</u>	<u>l</u>augh ha<u>lf</u> gira<u>ffe</u> <hr>magi<u>c</u>ian revi<u>s</u>ion addi<u>ti</u>on cu<u>sh</u>ion	<u>p</u>e<u>t</u>al <u>k</u>e<u>tt</u>le <hr>clou<u>d</u> clow<u>n</u>	<u>c</u>en<u>t</u>re en<u>t</u>er <hr>ri<u>ch</u> pi<u>tch</u>

English has more homophones than any other spoken language

SAME LETTERS – DIFFERENT SOUND
<u>h</u>eard / <u>b</u>eard   l<u>or</u>d / w<u>or</u>d   b<u>ea</u>d / h<u>ea</u>d   lo<u>se</u> / do<u>se</u>   s<u>o</u> / d<u>o</u>
w<u>ou</u>nd (injury) / w<u>ou</u>nd (wrapped up)   <u>minute</u> (small) / <u>minute</u> (time)
m<u>oo</u>n / b<u>oo</u>k / p<u>oo</u>r / fl<u>oo</u>d   c<u>a</u>rd / w<u>a</u>rd   cr<u>ea</u>ture / cr<u>ea</u>tive
jump<u>ed</u> / call<u>ed</u>   t<u>a</u>ll / sh<u>a</u>ll   aw<u>a</u>ke / f<u>a</u>ther / h<u>a</u>t   <u>ow</u>n / d<u>ow</u>n

Many spellings do not match the sounds of the words they represent. They might have done in the past, but not any longer.
    important – "importurnt" / different – "diffrent" / many – "menny"
    properly – "proply" / nothing – "nuthing/k" / damage – "damidge"

Sound variations between words can lead to many spelling errors. To reduce these, learners need to understand and be aware of the spelling choices and irregularities which lurk amongst English spellings waiting to trip them up.

For example, the letters 'ea' make one sound in 'pl<u>ea</u>se' but a different sound in 'pl<u>ea</u>sant'. This can explain why the following words are often misspelled:

> tr<u>ea</u>sure, d<u>ea</u>lt, h<u>ea</u>lth, inst<u>ea</u>d, d<u>ea</u>th, m<u>ea</u>sure, r<u>ea</u>dy, f<u>ea</u>ther.

See page 102: Spelling Riddles

Silent letters in English spellings can lead to errors:

le<u>i</u>sure, cou<u>l</u>d, g<u>u</u>ard, com<u>b</u>, <u>w</u>rist, s<u>c</u>issors, autum<u>n</u>, cas<u>t</u>le, fu<u>d</u>ge, bis<u>c</u>uit, c<u>o</u>urage, s<u>c</u>hedule, r<u>h</u>yme, ans<u>w</u>er, temp<u>e</u>rature, <u>i</u>sland, <u>k</u>nit, fo<u>l</u>k, ta<u>l</u>k, <u>g</u>nome, h<u>ea</u>rt, hous<u>e</u>.

See page 105: Silent Letters

Many spelling errors surround the incorrect use of single or double letters in words such as:

> a<u>cc</u>o<u>mm</u>odation
> emba<u>rr</u>a<u>ss</u>
> exa<u>gg</u>erate
> re<u>c</u>o<u>mm</u>end
> di<u>s</u>a<u>pp</u>ointed
> ne<u>c</u>e<u>ss</u>ary

Many learners benefit from the use of learning strategies which enhance the memory storage and recall of spelling patterns.

Words from other languages often bring with them unfamiliar spelling pronunciations and patterns: rendezvous, Ferrari, café, fiesta, Venice, vermicelli, déjà vu, faux pas, chow mein, en suite, ballet, rouge.

The plural form of words can be made by adding an 's':

> cat > cat<u>s</u>   chair > chair<u>s</u>

However, the ending -es is also used to denote the plural form, with or without additional letter-changes:

> lady > lad<u>ies</u>
> tomato > tomato<u>es</u>
> leaf > leav<u>es</u>
> knife > kniv<u>es</u>
> mass > mass<u>es</u>
> wish > wish<u>es</u>
> beach > beach<u>es</u>
> box > box<u>es</u>
> quiz > quiz<u>zes</u>

See page 70: 'Suffixing Quiz'.

Many American-English spellings often appear in texts:

colour / color
honour / honor
neighbour / neighbor
humour / humor
centre / center
metre / meter
defence / defense
realise / realize
recognise / recognize
catalogue / catalog
traveller / traveler
jewellery / jewelry

See page 97: History of English Spellings.

Txt speak demonstrates how language evolves over time:

B4, w8, LOL, GR8, 2day, BTW, BFN, 1der, U.

Targeting Spelling Performance

Spelling Rules, Riddles and Remedies brings novel, varied and engaging approaches to learning which explicitly target spelling performance and skills.

It provides opportunities to deliver both alternative and complementary materials to either replace, or boost, existing programmes of study.

Topics can be delivered sequentially as they appear in this book, or ordered according to need. (See page 131 for list of key topics.) Lessons are designed to specifically acknowledge and explore the ways in which English spellings have the potential to confuse and bemuse learners of all ages.

Spelling Detective Activities

These activities present investigative challenges which learners can explore on their own, in pairs, or with their spelling tutors.

They typically provide the opportunity to introduce a spelling rule, riddle or remedy by exploring the nature of the topic in hand.

As learners hone their logical and creative reasoning skills they become more familiar and skilled in the use of detective questioning as a means of exploring English spellings.

Interest and purpose is engaged through self-discovery which reveals details the brain might otherwise have overlooked.

Learning Application Activities

Opportunities to apply, consolidate and rehearse learning is vital.

Learning Application Activities over-learn and reinforce lessons in the use of morphology (how words are made up of different units which go together to convey meaning); phonology (how the sounds of words are expressed within different spellings); graphemic representations (the look and shape of spellings); irregular patterns and expressions; and, most importantly, the use of words through an understanding of their meaning and context.

Having investigated an activity together, they can be used to practise and enjoy the use of a topic between formal lessons.

A Sample of Spelling Rules and Riddles

A Spelling Detective Activity

For each of the following pairs of words can you identify:

(a) How the words differ in spelling?
(b) How the words differ in sound?

	bead	head
(a) Difference in spelling:	....	
(b) Difference in sound:	....	

	curtain	certain
(a) Difference in spelling:	....	
(b) Difference in sound:	....	

	whole	hole
(a) Difference in spelling:	....	
(b) Difference in sound:	....	

	gem	gum
(a) Difference in spelling:	....	
(b) Difference in sound:	....	

	hoping	hopping
(a) Difference in spelling:	....	
(b) Difference in sound:	....	

	tripped	trimmed
(a) Difference in spelling:	....	
(b) Difference in sound:	....	

Check your answers on page 134.

The role of Spelling Detective allows learners to actively participate in exploration and discovery.

Why Do Some Learners Find Spelling Difficult?

Many learners pick up spellings with relative ease. However, some learners experience barriers to learning for one or more of the following reasons:

Auditory (sound-based) and visual processing skills

If the brain cannot easily identify units of sounds within words and/or match them to the correct lettered displays, then spelling memories and coding ability is going to be weak. In English, it is not enough to know that 'ea' makes an /e/ sound (as in 'h<u>ea</u>t'), there are other patterns which need to be identified and understood, such as those in 's<u>ee</u>d', 'b<u>e</u>', '<u>e</u>ve', 'f<u>ie</u>ld', 'man<u>y</u>' and 'h<u>ea</u>d'.

Furthermore, an over-reliance on either the audio or visual aspects of words leads to errors due to the unpredictable nature of English spellings.

Confusion, frustration and failure

Making errors such as 'wurry' and 'importurnt' when attempting to match letters with sounds; not remembering the difference between 'their', 'there' and 'they're'; confusing 'were' with 'where' and 'two' with 'tow' can cause embarrassment, frustration and failure.

Lack of positive outcomes

All learners make initial errors, but when failure persists it erodes confidence, interest and motivation. Achievement levels influence the attitudes and behaviours of learners, their teachers, parents and peers. Avoidance strategies are often adopted to hide failure.

Memory storage and recall

There are many factors which influence memory processing, storage and recall. This book explores many of them including external features (such as the environment in which learning takes place) and internal factors (such as an individual's processing weaknesses and strengths, confidence and engagement).

Shortage of practice

With limited time available to exercise spelling ability (without a spell-checker to hand), learners often have few opportunities to practise and extend their spelling vocabularies.

Different Ways to Learn Spellings

## <u>Write a spelling out a number of times</u> *through* *through* *through* *through* *through* *through*	For some learners this activity works well by helping their brains link the visual pattern of letters alongside the physical act of moving their pen across the page. For many, this might bring them success in the following spelling test, but, when using the word three weeks later within a piece of mainstream writing, the memory trace of the spelling may well have been forgotten. 'Good spellers' may only need to see and write a word a few times before mastering its spelling. However, spelling aptitude (just like musical or artistic abilities) varies between individuals. It is unwise to measure the success of this method through the results of a few when, for many, frustration and failure results if no additional learning opportunities are provided.
## <u>'Look, say, cover, write, check'</u> **Read the word** **Say the word aloud** **Cover the word** **Write the word** **Check your spelling** **Repeat daily for a week**	This approach is used in many schools to add sound, sight and muscular actions to the learning activity. By engaging the ears, eyes, mouth and hand to complete this daily learning routine, a variety of neurological processes are involved. This is called 'multisensory' learning as a number of senses are used to enhance the spelling input. This method works well for some learners, whilst for others it only brings short-term success. 'Look, say, write, cover, check' uses short-term memory processes. There is no incentive for the brain to transfer the spelling trace into long-term memory. Nor is there any connection made between the word's meaning and its spelling at the time of learning, and no use of a memory prompt to trigger the accurate recall of the spelling's lettered display at a later date. This reduces the links between short and long-term memory, word meaning and spelling, reducing its efficiency. Spelling success must be measured over time, and provide building blocks for future spellings.

letter-to-sound rules to learn spellings

Long e: /e/

thr**ee**, s**ee**, tr**ee**

m**e**, w**e**, h**e**, sh**e**

happ**y**, part**y**, bab**y**

cl**ea**n, b**ea**ch, st**ea**m

k**ey**, mon**ey**,

p**ie**ce, f**ie**ld, sh**ie**ld

c**ei**ling, rec**ei**ve

Phonics is the term used to describe the links between alphabetic letters and the sounds (phonemes) that they make. There is no doubt that the brain benefits from early letter-to-sound tuition to help it understand that there are links between the squiggles of letters and different sounds.

However, unlike transparent languages (such as Spanish and German which have fewer letter-to-sound irregularities and choices), English is not a phonetic language. Words such as 'some', 'enough', 'through', 'pleasure' and 'purpose' demonstrate the lack of regularity between many letters and their sounds. We also use a lot of homophones (such as 'towed', 'toed' and 'toad') whose sound alone does not confer meaning.

Furthermore, everyday speech does not always match the lessons we are taught. For example, the word 'certain' often appears in speech as 'certun' or 'cer'n'; 'important' as 'impor'nt'; and 'something' as 'sumthin' or 'sumfin' or 'sumthink'! The sounds of words can be affected by accents too, as well as the speed and clarity of speech, background noise and by the ability of the individual to accurately process auditory-based information.

Well-designed phonic programmes provide a structured introduction to literacy, but an over-reliance on phonics can, for some, hamper progression when moving beyond materials tailored to match specific teaching programmes.

Some learners find auditory processing difficult. Others 'perform' but fail to develop accurate and secure spelling memories over time.

Phonics play an important role in English spellings, but additional attention to the visual structure, shape and representation of different spellings is needed for most learners.

I'm not a poor speller, the English language is difficult to spell!

Multiple-processing activities to enhance spelling memories

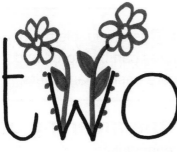

Sally **A**nne **is d**ead <u>said</u> the vet.

The teaching techniques explored in this book are based upon the principles of:

- Varied and practical activities which enhance the storage and recall of spelling memories.

- Learner engagement through discussion, ownership, knowledge and skills which stimulate personal participation and meta-cognition (thinking skills).

- Multiple processing activities which promote creative and constructive opportunities for positive learning outcomes.

Learning takes place when the brain is engaged, motivated and equipped with the ability to learn.

Learning the spelling of 'does'

<u>DOES Ollie Eat Snails? – Yes, he does!</u>

A **memory prompt:** <u>Does</u> <u>O</u>llie <u>eat</u> <u>s</u>nails? provides a meaningful and memorable aid which enhances memory storage and recall.

The **emotions** of disgust, horror and gleeful surprise also strengthen the input.

The letter-to-sound rules of 'does' do not match the sound of the word – the brain needs something to **nudge it** away from 'dus'.

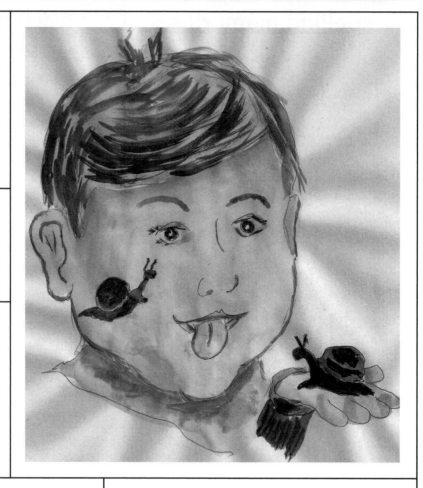

As 'does' is a common word, there are **repetitive opportunities** to practise this memory prompt.

A **picture** is a valuable memory store. Pictures can be stored and recalled more easily than letters.

Linking a word's spelling to a phrase **relating to the meaning of the word** helps to transfer spelling lessons into mainstream writing.

Drawing your own picture promotes **ownership of learning**. It also boosts visual memory and recall and uses kinaesthetic (muscle) skills which increases the number of neurons being fired in the brain.

Amusement, novelty and purpose all stimulate interest, motivation, confidence and success.

Vital Ingredients of Spelling Success

<u>Using the strategies explored in this book</u> **Ownership of learning** **Memory prompts** **Pictorial links** **Multiple processing activities** **Emotions** **Over-learning and practice**	To support long-term spelling memories, this book uses a variety of activities and strategies. Learners are provided with opportunities to achieve ownership of their learning. For example, becoming a 'Spelling Detective' (see page 31) stimulates thinking skills whilst personalising the use of different spelling prompts and aids. Drawing your own pictures which link to your own interests and ideas, makes learning more effective, engaging and meaningful. Pictorial links are vital. Not only do they provide an image which the brain stores and recalls more easily than letters or words, but pictures also provide memories which last longer over time. By drawing your own picture you are engaging visual processing along with both thinking and muscular movement, all making that memory-prompt pathway even stronger. Memory is very closely linked to emotions. We notice and remember things which stimulate feelings such as surprise, humour, revulsion and fear. By creating memory pathways that link spellings to pleasurable, amusing, appealingly repellent, and/or surprising events or stories, the memory is enhanced. Learners also enjoy the fun of devising these links as it makes the task exciting, personal, relevant and engaging. No matter how good the memory pathway, it needs to be practised. Only by putting it into use can the learner discover if their chosen learning strategy will work, or if any changes are required. Furthermore, every time that information is rehearsed, it strengthens neurological pathways which promotes memory storage and recall. This book provides ideas, activities and challenges, often in the form of game-play, which engage and inspire application and success.

Using This Book

Once spelling tutors have been introduced to *Spelling Rules, Riddles and Remedies* and explored the topics covered in different chapters, they can link application to suit the needs of their learner(s).

Activities can be used for one-to-one focused study and/or small group discussion and exploration, providing there is equality of opportunity for access and inclusion amongst different learners in the group.

Time must be provided to allow for preparation, talking, thinking, exploration and application to take place. The principles of this book centre around guidance leading to self-discovery, understanding and the security of memory traces. Learners are offered varied examples of strategic applications to develop their own learning skills but most will need guidance and experiential materials to achieve success.

The under-utilisation of an activity through the exclusion of key elements (such as discussion, artwork and practise) reduces access to understanding and success. For learners already struggling with English spellings, further examples of failure are to be avoided.

Anyone needing to develop their spelling confidence and skills will find this book useful. Spelling tutors (especially those who are unfamiliar with spelling difficulties) will also find the advice and resources helpful in providing them with both an understanding of different learning strategies, and an insight into some of the rules and riddles of English spellings they may not have previously noticed.

As with all teaching and learning materials, it can never suit all of the people all of the time. This book is intended to demonstrate key features to inform and empower readers with the ability to explore, adapt, extend and enjoy the intriguing nature of English spellings.

Having utilised materials, spelling tutors and their learners should take ownership of their work to produce individualised folders recording their progress and achievements. This allows for the easy extension of vocabulary and topics according to need.

By providing a firm foundation of understanding and skills, individuals have the confidence and ability to further investigate the English writing system (also known as orthography). Reading skills are enhanced, vocabularies are inspired and an interest in the evolution and use of written language is fuelled and ignited.

Chapter One:
Varied and Innovative Learning Opportunities

For spellers who have established errors (such as 'sed' in place of 'said'), a strong memory trigger is needed to overcome their inaccurate habits.

Creating a spelling prompt for 'SAID'

<u>s</u>now <u>a</u>nd <u>i</u>ce <u>d</u>ay	This spelling prompt is not effective because it is too bland. It does not relate to the word 'said' so it is unlikely to be triggered when the word 'said' is needed in mainstream writing.
<u>S</u>ally <u>A</u>nne <u>i</u>s <u>d</u>ancing	This spelling prompt is more interesting, particularly if the learner likes dancing. HOWEVER, it lacks drama, and also lacks any relation to the meaning of the word 'said' reducing its ability to be triggered when using the word in mainstream writing.
<u>S</u>ally <u>A</u>nne <u>i</u>s <u>d</u>ead, <u>said</u> the vet. Turn to page 31 to see how to practise this spelling prompt	This spelling prompt attracts attention due to the drama of something being dead (toned down by the report being made by a vet). The two capital letters (S and A) have the potential to impact on the spelling, of 'said', but don't appear to do so. The learner is involved with their learning and aware that the prompt is there to help trigger their spelling memory. The engagement of their thinking skills probably accounts for the brain's ability to use lower-case letters when writing 'said'. <u>Learners should draw their own picture</u> to increase the strength of neurological pathways to and from long-term memory.

Turn to page 31 to see how to practise this spelling prompt

Creating a spelling prompt for 'THEIR'

T̲heir h̲amster e̲ats i̲ced r̲ings	This spelling prompt contains the key word, helping to trigger its recall at the point of writing 'their' in mainstream text. It also uses the word in a sentence that helps identify the use of 'their' (rather than 'there' or 'they're'), reducing confusion between these homophones. HOWEVER, it is relying on a lengthy mnemonic where every letter of the spelling is contained in the phrase. For some, this may be necessary, but for many, all they need is a reminder of which 'their/there/they're' to use when referring to ownership.
their cat *their car*	This spelling prompt achieves the same effect as the one above, but in a more concise fashion. It also demonstrates how helpful it can be to (a) avoid the necessity to create mnemonics for every spelling, and (b) identify where the spelling mistake is commonly made, and focus the memory prompt just at that point. Learners should copy this prompt to add visual and muscular activities to their memory pathways, adapting it to suit their individual interests. (For example, choosing a drawing that depicts 'their bike', or 'their dog' instead.)
t**here**	Identifying the spelling of 'there' by asking "Is it <u>here</u>, t<u>here</u> or everyw<u>here</u>?" helps provide a memory prompt for other spellings too.
They are playing volley ball, and they're losing! *they're*	Often, learners do not realise that 'they're' is a contraction of 'they are' as the latter is not used in speech as often as it used to be. Shifting the focus of spelling to *meaning* (rather than sound) can be very helpful to a novice speller, especially when faced with multiple spelling choices.

Turn to page 31 to see how to practise these spelling prompts

Creating a spelling prompt for 'WHAT'

What help are toes?	This spelling prompt contains the key word, helping to trigger its recall at the point of writing 'what' in mainstream text. HOWEVER, it is an example of how the challenge of creating a mnemonic out of the letters available has resulted in a prompt that lacks interest and is easy to forget.
 **What an amazing hat!**	For this prompt, FIRST ask the learner(s) to draw a hat of their own invention which you will be able to look at and say "What an amazing hat!" Once this is done, write the word 'what' and ask them what the connection is between the picture they have drawn, your expression of "What an amazing hat!" and the spelling of the word 'what'. This spelling prompt is created by guiding the learner through a process which reveals purpose and discovery. For the learner to identify for themselves the appearance of 'hat' within the word 'what' is far more effective than for them to be told this by someone else.
When the hen ...	Having introduced 'what', then encourage the learner(s) to decide how to apply the same idea to the spelling of 'when'. Remember that the prompt must link to the meaning of the word so you would expect their memory prompt to begin: When the hen ... Drawing their own picture of whatever the hen is doing, helps to consolidate their thoughts.

Only use spelling prompts if the learner is misspelling the word. Applying these activities when they are not needed will promote disinterest and boredom.

<u>Linking memory prompts to personal errors</u>

<u>WERE</u> We <u>we</u>re ... We <u>were</u> really <u>e</u>xcited to see .... N.B. 'We were really excited **when** ...' is **not** appropriate as the wh- of 'when' could encourage the brain to use 'wh-' when spelling the word 'were'.	If a learner spells 'were' with an 'h' (i.e. 'where'), then a memory prompt which emphasises the 'we' beginning would be appropriate. If the error is something else (such as 'were'/'wer'), then extending the memory prompt would be necessary. As always, give learners time to draw (or doodle) their own picture which illustrates the memory prompt.

<u>PLEASE</u>
 	
'Please <u>e</u>at <u>a</u>pples <u>s</u>aid <u>e</u>lephant, (waiting at end of the word, hoping you'll feed him the cores!)

	'Please' can be misspelled in a number of ways, most commonly as:
	
	   'ples'
	   'plese'
	   'pleas'
	   'plees'
	
	As the final 'e' is a 'useless e' it has no links to the sound of the word.
	
	Use whatever elements of a prompt are necessary for the individual learner.
	
	Provide examples of pictures (such as an elephant) for them to use, which are easy to copy if they wish.

<u>PEOPLE</u>
All the "pee-o-ple"...

This memory prompt uses a mispronunciation of the word to emphasise the letter 'o'. This uses a 'spelling voice' to help link letters to sound.
	'People' is often misspelt as:
	
	   'peple'
	   or 'pepul'
	
	If there is an error with -le, then a spelling-family activity which focuses on 'the troublesome -le' (page 62) can be useful, as the -le pattern appears at the end of many English spellings.
	
	Having a 'spelling voice' can help some learners ... but it won't suit everyone.

Spelling-family Story-links

Knowing that the letters 'ee' create an /e/ sound, as in 'tree', is all very well, but spelling tee (tea), mee (me), feeld (field), receeve (receive) and eev (eve) with the 'ee' pattern, is no good at all.

Some languages (such as Spanish and German) have very transparent links between sounds and letters. This means that if the word 'toad' is spelled with an 'oa' then most other words containing the /o/ sound will also be spelled using the 'oa' letters.

But the English language does not have these transparent links between its words and their spellings. English has an opaque orthography, meaning that choices and oddities are found when matching the sound of words to the letter-strings of their spelling.

By linking <u>a spelling pattern</u> to a memory prompt, the variations of sound are less able to have such a devastating effect on spelling:

'He made a <u>noise</u> like a tortoise blowing its <u>nose</u>.'

Grouping words into spelling families is also very useful for those learners who struggle to decide between different spelling choices:

boat, bote or bowt?

A storyline and picture are needed to anchor the spelling pattern to the memory to ensure recall is achieved with confidence and accuracy. By linking spelling families together in this way, a robust spelling anchor is available to support the learner's needs.

The following spelling-family activities strengthen memory storage and recall by using pictures, stories and meaningful associations.

The Goat-in-a-Boat Story

As a spelling tutor, draw a picture to illustrate a storyline which includes a number of words found within the 'oa' spelling family. I have provided an example of the storyline below, but do adapt it to meet your needs making sure that no competing spellings (e.g. 'n<u>o</u>te') appear in your story.

> Here is a g<u>oa</u>t in a b<u>oa</u>t. Here is a t<u>oa</u>d in the b<u>oa</u>t with the g<u>oa</u>t, eating s<u>oa</u>p (silly t<u>oa</u>d!). The t<u>oa</u>d is m<u>oa</u>ning and gr<u>oa</u>ning. The b<u>oa</u>t is afl<u>oa</u>t. It is near the c<u>oa</u>st. There is a r<u>oa</u>d and a tree ... what sort of tree do you think it might be?

This final question identifies whether the learner has realised that the words share the /o/ sound. If so, they may well suggest 'oak'. If not, direct their attention back to the key words to help them identify the link.

Highlight the fact that not only do the key words share an /o/ sound, but that their spellings also share the same way of spelling /o/ (using the letters 'oa').

Now put your picture out of sight.

Learners are then challenged to doodle their own picture of the goat-in-a-boat from memory. When completed, they (verbally) recount the story to see how many key words they have remembered.

It is likely that some words have been missed out. Why might that be?

Encourage learners to suggest answers – involve them in the learning activity.

One answer might be that words which lack a distinctive visual impact on the picture (e.g. 'afloat') make a weaker impact on the memory than clearly visible 'concrete' images (e.g. 'goat' and 'toad'). Adding a cl<u>oa</u>k fl<u>oa</u>ting past the boat would provide a stronger link between the picture and spelling of 'fl<u>oa</u>t'.

As the brain remembers things it hears, sees, manipulates and understands, better than things it experiences in less detail, the use of different processing opportunities is vital. However, they may have had so much to remember, some words just didn't get registered very well. Encourage a light-hearted approach and praise application and achievement. Most learners enjoy these spelling-family story-links, and benefit from spending time drawing pictures.

Later, test their verbal word recall again. They will probably now remember more of the words. Then get them to write a list of 'oa' spellings from the goat-in-a-boat story to check the 'oa' pattern has been registered, correcting any mistakes by referring back to the purpose of the picture.

Add further 'oa' words to the picture as and when they are needed.

The Sound of 'er'

The /er/ sound in words can be spelled in different ways:

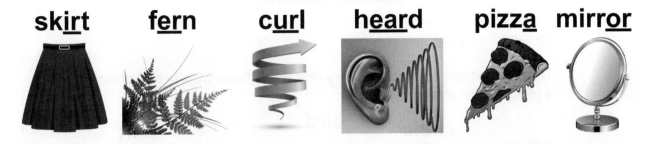

sk<u>ir</u>t   **f<u>er</u>n**   **c<u>ur</u>l**   **h<u>ea</u>rd**   **pizz<u>a</u>**   **mirr<u>or</u>**

This can lead to errors when the speller cannot remember which pattern of letters to use in the word they want to spell.

Their ears can tell them there is an /er/ sound, but their visual memory, along with links to the word's meaning, is needed to select the correct letters.

Putting letter-families together into an interesting and meaningful story illustrated by a picture provides more information to help the brain remember and recall which pattern to use.

Common patterns such as 'er', 'ur' and 'ir' can be grouped and linked through story lines which are related to a target spelling prompt.

Less familiar spelling patterns can be linked to individual story lines which allow the brain to register and engage with spelling.

He shouted in his ear: "Can you **hear d**ragon?" ... the dragon <u>heard</u> the troll's voice, and let out a terrified scream!
 	
Discuss / invent a story to match this prompt. Draw and label a picture to match it.

	p<u>i</u>zz<u>a</u>
	   t
	   e

	<u>I</u> <u>a</u>te pi<u>zz</u><u>a</u> *slowly/quickly**
	
	**Learner submits own ideas.*

		He looked in the mirror and saw to his horror a ....
		
		He shouted with terror "There must be an error!"

bird tales

Write out the following words and read them with your learner(s).
Be sure they know the meaning of each word.

Then invite them to create a story that uses these words, and draw
a picture to illustrate it.

shirt **circle** **bird** **skirt**

birthday **first/third/thirteenth**

girl **fir**

thirst/thirsty **circus**

dirt/dirty

'The girl was given a magic skirt for her birthday.
She wished she was a bird, then flew away to join the circus.'

'The boy climbed the fir tree to try and catch a bird. It flew off in a circle then
dropped a dirty mess on his shirt.'

More 'ir' words can be added at a later date.

Do not overload the brain by giving it too much information to handle at one time.

Avoid exploring the 'ir' and 'ur' stories at the same time or your learner(s)
will get confused ... pace different activities out over time.

<u>Curiosity (almost) killed the cat</u>

The cat sat watching the candle burn. He purred with pleasure as the burning flame curled sideways each time he disturbed it with a flick of his tail.

Suddenly, he jumped up with surprise when the flame turned purple and started spurting bright sparks across the room.

"My fur is getting burnt! I'm getting hurt!" meowed the cat.

He hurled himself across the furniture and up the curtain furthest from the burning flame.

Ursula hurried into the room and quickly tipped the blackcurrant yoghurt she'd been eating, onto the flame to put it out.

Luckily, the cat wasn't injured by the candle's outburst, but he wouldn't come down from the top of the curtain for four days!

Ursula never left a burning candle unattended again.

1. Read this story aloud to your learner(s) as they follow the words.

2. Discuss the story and the purpose of this activity ... it is vital to empower learners with understanding and clear goals. This activity helps them identify that English spellings contain different ways of creating the /er/ sound in words, with this story grouping 'ur' words together.

3. Learners underline all the 'ur' patterns. (Replace the word 'four' to 'three' if you want to begin by only exploring spellings representing an /er/ sound.) N.B. Discuss the pronunciation of 'currant'.

4. Learners then draw a picture of their choice relating to the story.

5. Read each sentence aloud, one at a time, and ask them to write down all the 'ur' words which they can recall and/or hear under their picture.

6. Review work, adding in any missed words.

7. Revisit over time. More 'ur' spellings can be added in the future.

Alternatively, collect words of your choice which contain the 'ur' spelling pattern and use them to create a different story line with pictures.

Circle or Curve?

Spelling game using 'ir' and 'ur' spellings.
Game for two players

After creating 'ir' and 'ur' spelling-family stories (see previous pages), this game strengthens the new memory pathways.

To prepare for this game, cut out, read through and discuss the playing cards (see below) with the learners. Add new words as and when you extend the stories (e.g. the cat's adventure happened on a Thursday). Shuffle the cards and place face-down on the table.

Provide each player with a pen and one of the game templates. Players have either the circular or curve template each, changing to use the other one when repeating the game.

- The aim of the game is to be the first one to complete a circle of 'ir' spellings or a curve of 'ur' spellings.

- Read out each playing card. Repeat the key word(s) which have been underlined. Whoever believes they hear a word which belongs on their template, writes it down. If a player incorrectly enters a word on their playing board, their opponent is allowed to enter an additional word of their choice (that contains the right spelling pattern) onto their template.

Circle or Curve? Examples of playing cards:

He drew a <u>circle</u> in the sand.	His <u>shirt</u> had shrunk in the wash.	The soup was so hot it <u>burnt</u> my mouth!
She was hot, hungry and <u>thirsty</u>, and lost in the desert.	I would be very, very <u>surprised</u> if my ears <u>turned</u> yellow.	He <u>hurled</u> a <u>fir</u> cone which hit the giant on the nose.
The dog ran away to join the <u>circus</u>.	The <u>bird</u> could fly at <u>thirty</u> miles an hour.	"I didn't <u>hurt</u> him on <u>purpose!</u>" she cried.
The <u>girl</u> was wearing a <u>purple</u> jumper.	He <u>turned</u> and fled when he saw the tiger.	<u>Dirty</u> grey <u>curtains</u> covered the windows.

Read a sentence from the card, then repeat the target words on their own.

Circle or Curve? game templates

circle the b<u>ir</u>d

Players can make their own game templates.
Increase the number of circles / rectangles if you wish.

s<u>ur</u>f the c<u>ur</u>ve

The *schwa* is the term used to describe an unstressed vowel sound (often pronounced 'uh') which frequently appears in English words. (Its sound can vary according to accents.)

the schwa sound

For example, the 'a' in words such as 'a̲bout', 'a̲sleep', 'a̲way', 'a̲llow', 'a̲rrived', is different to the sound of the letter 'a' expressed in 'a̲nt', 'a̲pple', 'A̲lison' or 'a̲naconda'.

It is sometimes confused for, and spelled as, an 'er' sound.

To identify the schwa sound, read and discuss the words below. Use the words to create sentences which are linked to an anaconda snake. Note how the first letter of 'anaconda' is expressed differently to the letter 'a' appearing at the start of the other words. This activity helps remind the brain that 'anaconda' and 'asleep' etc. both start with the letter 'a'.

asleep, awake, afraid, aware, attack, appear, away, arrive, about, around, again

(An ant can be used in place of an anaconda, but it makes a far less interesting, and therefore less impressionable, impact on the brain.)

Other examples of the schwa sound include:

- the 'e' in 'tak*e*n'
- the 'i' in 'penc*i*l'
- the 'a' in 'postm*a*n'
- the 'u' in 's*u*pply'
- the 'o' in '*o*ccasion'

<u>O</u>h <u>u</u> greedy <u>h</u>orse ...
you've eaten right thr<u>ough</u> the gate!

The use of the letter 'u' to represent 'you' doesn't appear to confuse the learner – they are involved with the learning of the memory prompt, so their brains are aware of the link between the 'u' prompt and the 'ough' spelling.

Having introduced this prompt, print out the following picture on the bottom of a sheet of paper. Help learners link other words containing the **ough** spelling pattern to create a story around the horse in a field. As the story grows, they then add (and label) pictures to the page.

For example:
- I have <u>brought</u> you some carrots I <u>bought</u> for 20p.
(Discuss links between '<u>br</u>ought' and '<u>br</u>ing' – Make the 'bo' of '<u>bo</u>ught' into two coins)
- The field is <u>rough</u> where it has been <u>ploughed</u>.
(Discuss meaning of 'rough answer' and 'played roughly' too.)
- Is there <u>enough</u> water in your <u>trough</u>?
- Oh U greedy horse, you've eaten right <u>through</u> the gate even <u>though</u> it was <u>tough</u>.
- The hedgehog has got a terrible <u>cough</u>.

This activity emphasises the use of *meaning* to link a spelling family.

William's Wall of Words

One day William was playing with a football.

He was kicking the ball against a wall. He was trying to hit a small red dot on the wall, but he kept missing it.

Suddenly, William heard a small voice coming from the wall. "Stop! Oh please stop," called the small voice. "Please stop or you will knock me off the wall."

William looked all around, but he couldn't see where the small voice was coming from. He started kicking the ball against the wall again.

Suddenly, William heard the voice calling out his name again.

"William, please don't knock me off the wall," it begged. "I don't want to fall."

William went closer to the wall and then he saw that the small red dot was moving. He saw that it wasn't a red dot at all, but a small ladybird.

"Hello, ladybird," said William. "I won't knock you off the wall with my football. I'll move you somewhere safe."

So William picked up the ladybird, and because William was tall, he could reach above the wall to put the ladybird safely onto a branch of a fir tree.

"Thank you," called the small voice as the ladybird hurried away out of sight and away from the dangerous football.

– Creating a personalised story engages interest and pleasure.
– Short passages also provide an attractive length for the struggling reader.
– Read through together. Learner then repeats it alone. Then ask them to identify and circle spellings matching the spelling-family group of -all. Learner writes words onto the wall below, adding more until all the bricks are labelled.

Using spelling-family story-links avoids the need for letter-patterns to share the same sound.

The memory pathways are developed by using visual information derived from pictures and letter shapes which are linked to a variety of memorable and meaningful prompts.

In addition, the multiple processing learning experiences found in different activities increases the nature and range of learning opportunities available to the individual learner.

The following rhyme about a bear wearing teardrop earrings illustrates the variety of sounds available to the 'ea' spelling pattern.

Pace the input so that the learner hears, then sees, then reads and explores the ditty, before grouping words according to sound. Achieving the ability to write this rhyme out correctly practises a number of very useful spellings.

<u>The Bear with the Teardrop Earrings</u>

The bear wears earrings in his ear,
And a teabag on his head.
He eats a feast of beans and peas ...
Spreads cream upon his bread.
"I was a beast that creatures feared,
That really was displeasing.
So pearls and tea leaves mean instead,
I bear kind-hearted teasing."

Chapter Two:
The Storage and Recall
of Spelling Memories

| hearing | seeing | writing | drawing | thinking | emotions |

All these activities fire neurons in the brain.

However, sometimes, even though the brain has been stimulated and focused on learning, it fails to transfer that learning into long-term memory in a manner that allows for accurate recall at a later date.

I learn my spellings every day,
Before I go outside to play.
But now I want to scream and shout ...
They're in my head, but won't come out!

To help spelling memories move from short-term to long-term memory and back again, a number of supportive strategies can be employed such as:

- Making the target spelling more significant, interesting and dynamic to heighten its impact on attention and memory.
- Providing memory-tabs which act as a link between a word and its spelling to support accurate recall over time.
- Using multiple processing activities which stimulate a variety of responses including those of interest, ownership, competition, novelty, surprise and understanding.
- Remove memory overload by focusing lessons on specific topics.
- Promoting the use of deep (rather than shallow) thinking.

Dicey Spellings

– a novel and amusing multiple-processing activity which develops the use of effective memory prompts.

- Write out spellings on individual cards

> *forest*

- The learner, as a 'spelling detective', identifies where a spelling error might be made. This promotes thinking skills and allows for a variation of errors between learners.

For example: forest (forist / forrist)

- Devise a memory prompt which links the word's meaning to the correct spelling. For example:

Where has the <u>rest</u> of the <u>forest</u> gone? or

The deer is having a <u>rest</u> in the <u>forest</u>.

- The spelling tutor should prepare ideas for memory prompt(s) before a lesson begins.

- Personalise the prompt and make it more significant by adding more details ... Where might the forest be? Where might the rest of the forest have gone? Do you think the deer is having a rest alone in the forest? Discuss the meaning of 'rest'.

- Discuss the purpose and design of the memory prompt, and, as learners become familiar with the game, encourage them to contribute their own ideas for prompts.

- The player then doodles and labels their own picture.

REMOVE EVERYTHING FROM SIGHT.

Then play the following dice game.

Playing Dicey Spellings

After creating a memory prompt to help your brain link the correct spelling to a word, draw a picture then move all your writing and drawing out of sight.

Throw a dice and follow the instructions below.

1	Write the word with your opposite hand
2	Speak the spelling with your eyes closed
3	Draw a doodle of your spelling prompt
4	Write the word with your eyes closed
5	Write the word in capital letters
6	Write a word with a similar meaning

After checking your answer, move on to the next word you are learning to spell. Repeat this game a number of times over a week, revisiting the memory prompts you have created for each spelling. Soon you will find each spelling and memory prompt are firmly lodged in your mind. (If one of your prompts isn't working, then think how it could be changed to be more effective.)

Spelling prompts must relate to the meaning of the word.

Encourage learners to recognise how amusement, repetition, variety and purpose are all features which help bring them spelling success.

Also help them to explore and question the reasons for spellings errors. The role of the memory prompts is to avoid the pitfalls and traps which often lurk within English spellings ... understanding why they have been tripped up helps the learner avoid repeating the error.

Create a book of spelling prompts and pictures.

See the gallery of spelling prompts (page 34) for more ideas.

Understanding Dicey Spellings

Dicey Spellings is designed to incorporate factors which engage both learners and learning. It is particularly effective for use with **individual words with irregular spellings.**

It makes the brain think

Adopting the role of 'Spelling Detective' actively promotes thinking and reasoning skills. Memory prompts provide additional material which captures interest and thought. Creating a picture further embellishes the input through the action of drawing directed by personal choice and expression. Recalling the spelling through the use of different activities positively entrenches the memory links activated above. It also provides a rewarding outcome to boost satisfaction in one's own personal learning achievement.

It motivates success

The unusual, accessible and multiple processing design of Dicey Spellings attracts learners by its focus on variety, amusement and game-play. It demonstrates access into learning which may well have previously eluded them. It offers ownership, choice and variety of learning opportunities to target different learning and memory needs. This in turn raises confidence, engagement and ability to retain and display spelling success.

It incorporates repetition

Learners enjoy repeating this game as it gives them routes into spelling success. Dice-play employs chance and variety. Tasks also lack performance judgements (writing with your opposite hand is not supposed to be neat).

It links to mainstream writing

When using a word within a sentence, it is the *meaning* of the word which is foremost in your mind. Therefore, if the spelling's memory prompt has a connection to the word's meaning, the brain is encouraged to trigger the spelling prompt too.

Empowering learners with strategies they can understand, adapt and use for themselves promotes independence and self-esteem.

GALLERY OF SPELLING PROMPTS

- The key word MUST be included in the spelling prompt to attach it to meaning.
- It is not just the prompt that helps learners remember a spelling, it is also the exploration and discussion of the prompt, personal adaptations, and the drawing of <u>your own</u> picture which engages the brain in developing strong memory traces.
- The memory prompt (whether it is one from this gallery or one you have created yourself) MUST be practised to rehearse and reinforce new memory traces.

Spellings in italics represent common spelling errors

accident *axident* *axsidernt* *acident*	There's been an a**CC**ident! a r r a s h	Add extra material as and when required: "There is a <u>dent</u> in the car." "It was an accident**al** mistake," said A**l**, the non-judgement**al** dent**al** nurse. "I a**cc**ept it was an a**cc**ident," said Rebecca. Learners draw own picture, then label it.
all *awl* *orl*	<u>All</u> **all**igators **l**ike **l**egs!	The dramatic impact (and resulting pictures) helps imprint this prompt in a manner which helps to over-rule alternative spelling possibilities. Use colour and drama to engage learners.
animal *animul* *anml* *anerml*	**An** insect **m**unching **a** leaf is an <u>animal</u>.	Use all, or part, of this prompt, depending on need. Encourage learner to identify how they might adapt this prompt to suit themselves.
are *ar*	**A** rabbit's **e**ars <u>are</u> ... or <u>ar e</u>ggs dangerous?	Devise prompts which link to learner's existing habits. Encourage them to embellish a prompt to make it personal to them.
bear / bare *bare*	The <u>bear</u> is w**ear**ing **ear**rings in his **ear**s. You <u>hear</u> with your **ear**.	The trees **are** <u>bare</u> in winter.
because *becos*	**B**ig **e**lephants **c**an **a**lways **u**nderstand **s**mall **e**lephants <u>because</u> they speak the same language.	Remember to always include the key word within the spelling prompt otherwise learners remember the phrases but not the words they help to spell!
bridge *brij*	bridge hedge	Exploring the drawings, and creating your own, helps to reinforce the pattern of letters in these and other '-dge' spellings.

caught / court *cawt* *cort*	I **c**augh**t** an **u**gly **g**rey **h**erring **t**oday. I **c**aught my n**aught**y d**aught**er laughing in a way I never t**aught** her!	courtroom / courtyard / courting / royal court / tennis court / court favour – **our** team is next on <u>court</u>
complete/ly *compleet* *compleatley*	An ath**lete** called **P**ete compe**t**ed in the **E**xeter **t**o **E**astbourne race ... he comp**lete**d the distance, but was comp**lete**ly exhausted by the end of it!	
despair *dispair* *dispare*	**Des** <u>despair</u>s when his h**air** is **des**cribed as having an un**des**irable **des**ign.	Des despairs ... helps to avoid the error of 'dis-' when it is not required.
dinosaur *dinersaw*	What a **din**! **O**h **s**uch **a**n **u**gly **r**oar! A train, a plane, a bear in pain? No – it's a prehistoric <u>dinosaur</u>!	Spelling interesting words encourages learners to apply spelling memory strategies to words they want to use. They may find the exploration of the prompt is enough to highlight the spelling pattern.
don't *dont*	Many learners do not know that 'don't' is a contraction of the words 'do' and 'not'. This weakens their memory of the required apostrophe.	"<u>Don't</u> forget **Don** has only got one tooth!" (Draw the apostrophe as one big sharp tooth.)
eye *eiy*		Also have fun with
fir and fur fire		e (draw a fir tree on fire)
four / our *for / ower are*		 Can't you stand still? No! <u>Our</u> <u>four</u> legs **o**nly **u**nderstand **r**unning!
furious/fury *fyuryous/furrey* buried/bury *berried/berry*	She was <u>furious</u> when I bought a real **fur** coat ... so I **bur**ied it. (B<u>ur</u>ied on Th<u>ur</u>sday or Sat<u>ur</u>day?)	Play around with spellings and prompts to help the mind focus on the nature of the task in hand.
go *gow* going / gone *gowing / gon*	<u>go</u> <u>go</u> with your **yo yo**. **go** **n**ow Ellen and then you'll be <u>gone</u>!	Spelling 'gow' instead of 'go': in this case, the spelling tutor found a two-lettered word ending with -o which was already known by the learner, then linked it to 'go'. The prompt was then practised: "I'm going to get my yo yo."

horse *hors*	"Hey, look at me!" Shouted the **e**lephant as it followed the <u>horse</u>. The elephant didn't want to be missed out.	The **e**lephant also follows a 'mouse', 'house', 'bruise', 'noise' and 'voice' ... any word which has a useless 'e' at the end of its spelling (an 'e' which doesn't appear to do anything), which is being left out.
immediate/ly *imediurt,* *imejurtly* appropriate appreciate	"**M**ore **m**unching, <u>immediately</u>!" he ordered as **i ate**. Did **P**ompous **P**ercy not app**reciate** that eating fast was not app**rop**r**iate** when ...	Double letters in longer words can trip many spellers up. Attach spellings to sayings which help prompt the right letters.
know *no / now*	Did you <u>know</u> that **k-now** (pronounced ker-now) helps you **k-now** (pronounced ker-no) the right spelling?	Some people find it very helpful to use 'a spelling voice' to mispronounce words in a way which highlights their spellings.
laugh *larf*	<u>l</u>augh **a**nd **u g**iggle **h**elplessly.	Get learners to giggle helplessly whilst practising this prompt.
many / any *menny / eny*	<u>M</u>**a**ny **a**nts **n**ick **y**oghurt. Yoghurt or yogurt? – both spellings appear in the UK	Also link to <u>any</u>: At **any**time, **any**where, **any**one can find **m**any **a**nts **n**icking **y**oghurt.
occasion separate	On one <u>occasion</u> I saw **two c**ockroaches and **one s**lug, on a <u>separate</u> occasion I saw **a rat**!	Encourage the use of emotionally-charged scenarios to make them more memorable.
our *are owr*	<u>O</u>ur **O**ld **U**ncle **R**obert ... is y<u>our</u> fav<u>our</u>ite neighb<u>our</u>.	Create a story line around 'our old uncle Robert' to make him interesting and memorable. Does he often go <u>out</u>?
science *siens*	Can you see <u>two 'c's</u> in **science**? (<u>see cc in</u> – is an anagram of 'science' – it also reminds us there are two letter 'c's).	A s**cie**ntist hides the letter 'c' – and discovers he can follow the i (eye) with an e.
sight *sit site*	A **g**reen **h**airy **t**ongue is a horrible s<u>ight</u>! This distinctive description strengthens the memory.	Collect other '-ight' spellings into a story linking them with a 'horrible s<u>ight</u>'.

sure and sugar *shor shore* *shuger* *shooger*	Make <u>SURE</u> **U R E**ating <u>sugar</u> not salt!	'Sure' and 'sugar' are easily misspelled. Offer learners some salt or sugar to enhance learning (!)
teeth *teef*	When children lose their front teeth, they find it difficult to make the sound of 'th'. To help them connect the tongue to their tee<u>th</u>, give them a mirror so they can watch <u>their own mouths,</u> instead of copying someone else's. Practise other 'th' words too – learner reads them off a card.	
they're, their and there.	They are playing volley ball – and they're losing! they're	Their house ...	Here, there and everywhere ... **here** and t**here**
thumb *thum*	thum**b**	Also collect other words with silent 'b' such as 'climb', 'limb', 'comb' and 'bomb' – see Silent Letters page 105
peace / piece *pees pis pice* **war** *wor*	peace	The **pea** made <u>peace</u> (not w<u>ar</u>) with the c**ar**rot. Use colour and fun to emphasise memory prompts.	piece A <u>piece</u> of **pie**.
peculiar *peequlier,* *peculer*	If I speak in a **pe – cu – li – ar** way, I can sound out the syllables of this <u>peculiar</u> word.	It is only a pe-cu-li-ar spelling because it is an un-fa-mi-li-ar pattern of letters.
weary *werry whirry*	The bear was <u>weary</u>. She'd been up all night with earache which was very **wear**ing (tiring) then got woken up early by baby bear wearing a tea pot!	Discuss the roots of spellings and how they link to the meaning of the word even if the root-word is no longer in popular use.
weight *wait* **height** *hite*	The .... weighed in with a <u>weight</u> of **eight** tons! But **he** only had a <u>height</u> of **eight** ...., so could hardly lift an eight kilogram weight.	Learner invents something around the memory prompt, to help register meaning, then draws their own picture and labels it.
whole / hole *hole / howl hol*	A <u>whole</u> pile of **wa**ffles just for me! **Wh**at! You ate the **wh**ole lot!	whole	How did that <u>hole</u> happen? ho le

Collect a folder of your own memory prompts over time.

Memory Recall

The more often you recall something, the stronger you make its impression on the brain, improving the ease with which that memory can be triggered and accessed in the future.

Familiarity with a topic leads to confidence and habitual responses which reduce the demands on working memory. This allows more space for thinking, exploring and enjoying successful achievement.

Slow processing speed and working memory overload are both made worse when the brain is handling unfamiliar and difficult things. By providing illuminated pathways (eg using a spelling prompt to learn a spelling), the challenges faced by the brain are made easier.

Improving memory storage	Improving memory recall
<ul><li>Use multiple processing activities – ones which stimulate different senses, actions and meaningful links along with interest, purpose and reward.</li><li>Increase 'size' of input (eg adding a prompt to a spelling pattern) to make it a bigger, brighter, target for memory storage and recall. But then use a picture to capture and store that information effectively.</li><li>Avoid overloading the working memory. Pace inputs carefully over time. Remember that additional factors such as background noise, anxiety and stress will also be making demands on working memory.</li><li>Add new material to existing memories (e.g. create a spelling-family story with a few words, then add more at a later date).</li></ul>	<ul><li>Practise recall soon after input has been delivered. (This helps the brain identify the need to store the new material, not erase it after initial use.)</li><li>Use a variety of activities to recall information over following days to strengthen multiple memory pathways.</li><li>Recall the memory prompts alongside spellings to encourage their paired sites of storage and recall (which also helps to 'crowd out' earlier established errors).</li><li>Promote the ownership of learning by involving learners in their own exploration of creative ways to trigger memory recall and revision.</li><li>Provide opportunities for learners to demonstrate rewarding success.</li></ul>

Involve learners in discussions about memory.

Developing Robust Memory Pathways

Spelling memories (letter patterns, rules and memory prompts) need to be rehearsed to help create strong pathways to and from long-term memory.

Some learners will have established spelling errors which need to be over-ruled by the correct memory prompt.

If there are any specific learning difficulties (e.g. those caused by weak audio or visual processing skills), the learner will take longer to develop accurate and rapid links between long-term and short-term memories. Firstly, their specific areas of difficulty will add additional burdens to working memory at the time of learning, and secondly, relying on a sole route for recall (e.g. relying on the sound of a word when the audio-processing modality is weak), increases the incidence of failure and frustration.

Using the multiple-processing methods described in this book therefore helps to target a number of spelling-memory needs.

Once initial learning has taken place, the practise of these lessons is vital. As every act of recollection makes a stronger and clearer pathway between long-term and short-term memory, and every memory prompt or aid adds more significance and 'brightness' to the spelling pattern, it is clear that for those learners for whom spelling memory storage and recall is difficult, they need more practice.

Of course, doing lots of writing where the spellings are being used accurately in context would provide the best application of practice. However, with the many demands presented by a complex educational curriculum and alternative forms of entertainment, learners struggling to learn their spellings rarely embrace this option with the enthusiasm and commitment necessary to bring them worthwhile levels of results. In addition, the demands of creative writing which includes the production and application of ideas, grammar, punctuation, penmanship etc, as well as spelling, can lead to working memory overload and failure.

Therefore, examples of a variety of games provide examples of how spelling lessons can be practised and consolidated; rehearsed and applied; shared and enjoyed; by using a number of different activities.

- Keep games simple and fun.

- Adapt games to meet your needs.

- Revisit to revise and extend learning.

Spelling Danger

– a spelling revision game

- Create a pack of cards containing words whose spellings have been previously targeted.
- Create a monster playing piece.
- Create playing piece for the speller.
- Make your own game board (template opposite).
- The spelling tutor reads out a word, and repeats it in an appropriate sentence.
- The speller writes the word down.
- A correct spelling allows the speller to move forward two spaces. An incorrect spelling reduces this movement according to the number of errors.

For example: 'forest'

'forest'	correct spelling	no error	move forward two spaces
'forist'	'i' instead of an 'e'	one error	only move forward one space
'forrist'	extra 'r' and 'i' instead of an 'e'	two errors	no movement on that go
'forst'	the 'e' is missing	one error	only move forward one space

- The monster's playing piece is moved (by the spelling tutor) two spaces (in either direction) during their go. If, at any time, the monster and the speller lands on the same space, the monster wins and the game is over.

This game does encourage the occasional conscious misspelling of a word (to avoid capture). This unusual twist may appear inappropriate, but to misspell a word, the correct spelling needs to be known.

Allow thinking time. Encourage the rehearsal of memory prompts to aid memory recall and spelling success.

- Short games invite repetition.
- Games make good homework activities.

Spelling Danger

Player starts from here	1	2	3	4	5
					6
12	11	10	9	8	7
13					
14 Monster starts from here	15	16	17	18	Player is now safely home

- Learners can create their own playing board and playing pieces to personalise the game. Copy instructions onto back of playing board.

- Playing the game regularly to revisit past spelling lessons helps to reinforce memory pathways.

- Update the pack of playing cards, but do continue to rehearse previous spellings (and their spelling prompts) to help secure robust memory pathways (and remove any habitual errors).

Homophone Matches

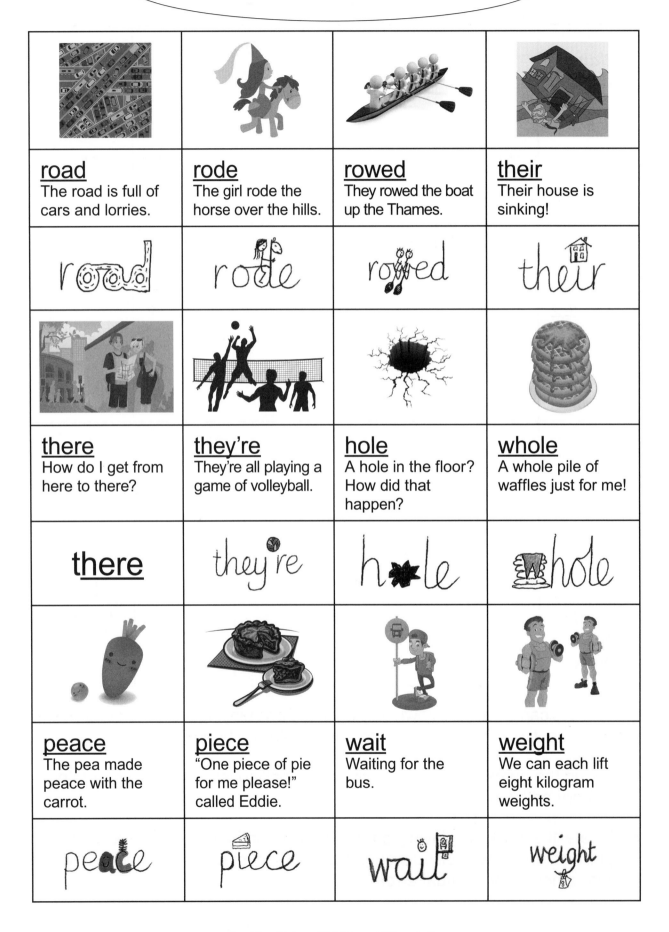

road
The road is full of cars and lorries.

rode
The girl rode the horse over the hills.

rowed
They rowed the boat up the Thames.

their
Their house is sinking!

there
How do I get from here to there?

they're
They're all playing a game of volleyball.

hole
A hole in the floor? How did that happen?

whole
A whole pile of waffles just for me!

peace
The pea made peace with the carrot.

piece
"One piece of pie for me please!" called Eddie.

wait
Waiting for the bus.

weight
We can each lift eight kilogram weights.

Homophone Picture Matches
– matching meaning with spellings

In this activity, the learner is shown all the information – pictures, the words and sentences demonstrating their use, along with a spelling-memory prompt to highlight key features of the different spellings.

1. Start with the pictures and meaningful sentences scattered, face-up, on a table. Read each word and accompanying sentences aloud with the learner, then match to the right picture. This stimulates thinking and learner-engagement.

2. Then add the memory prompts. Discuss how they link to the spelling pattern (and help to prevent common spelling errors).

3. Turn all the cards face-down and shuffle them about. Learner turns them over and matches them together. (Help them if and when they need it.)

4. The learner then practises writing each of the words using the spelling-memory prompt.

5. Remove everything but the pictures. Turn them face-down and shuffle them about. Learner turns one over.

6. The spelling tutor then reads aloud the key word followed by the meaningful sentence. (In other words, the learner *sees* the picture; *hears* the word and its accompanying sentence; and *recalls* the spelling memory prompt.) The learner then writes down the key word (not the full sentence).

If their spelling-confidence is low, allow them another look at the spelling prompt before removing that from sight.

Repeat this activity over time. Future games can be started at (5).

Help learners identify the purpose and processes employed by this game.

Three-in-a-row Spellings

– a game to revisit and revise spelling topics.

- Create a playing board based on the template.
- Use four different colours of card to create FOUR piles of spelling cards. Three piles match each of three colours on the centre of the playing board, plus an extra pile ('green' in the table below).
- Allocate a spelling category to each of THREE colours. A category could be a letter-to-sound spelling pattern or choice; a spelling rule; a group of curriculum topic words ... anything which links spellings to a spelling topic which has been previously explored by the learner(s).
- On each card, write the word to be spelled along with a sentence to make sure the learner understands which word is being used.

(explain to players the topic of each pile of spelling cards) For example:		
blue card	yellow card	pink card
words which contain either an 'ir' or an 'ur'	words containing the spelling pattern 'ough'	words containing the suffix -ful
example of card: <u>shirt</u> His rugby shirt is covered with mud.	example of card: <u>brought</u> We have brought you a bag of straw.	example of card: <u>careful</u> Be very careful with my expensive glasses.

The fourth pile of cards contain spellings which do not fit these categories.

green card	ERROR ESCAPE CARD	If you wish, give each player three of these error-escape cards. Players can choose when they want to use them.
additional words		
example of card: <u>road</u> They are building a new road to the airport.	This card can only be used once. It allows counter to be placed despite a spelling error.	

- Pens, paper, a playing board (see template opposite) and dice are needed.
- Players need sixteen coloured counters (or similar) each, and one playing piece that they move around the outside track of the board.
- Gold stars, smiley faces, paperclips or other prize tokens are also required. These are awarded to players who achieve a row of three of their coloured counters in the board's central block.

How to Play the Three-in-a-Row Spellings game

- Players take turns to move their playing piece around the outside track of the board. After throwing the dice, they can decide whether to move in a clockwise, or anticlockwise direction.

- Having landed on a coloured square, somebody else reads a card out to them from a pile of cards of the matching colour.

- If they spell the word correctly, they place one of their coloured counters onto any of the matching coloured spaces in the centre of the board.
(A counter can be placed in any empty space within a coloured column.)

- If they land on a green square (the colour of the 'additional words' pile), and spell the word correctly, they can choose to place their counter on ANY of the other three colours in the centre of the board.

- When a player has completed an uninterrupted horizontal or vertical line of counters, they receive a prize token. The three counters on the board can then be removed or retained – decide this house rule yourselves.

- Players can choose to try and stop other players making a row of three counters. This encourages tactical play which stimulates engagement.

Place piles of spelling cards, face down, ready for use.

BLUE – ir or ur?	YELLOW – ough	PINK – suffixes	GREEN – spelling mix

START	Y	P	B	Y	G	Y	P	B	G	Y	G	P
P												B
G												Y
Y												G
B												P
P												B
Y												Y
G												P
B												G
P	Y	B	P	G	P	Y	B	P	G	Y	Y	B

THREE IN A ROW SPELLINGS GAME

blue card spellings   yellow card spellings   pink card spellings

THREE IN A ROW SPELLINGS GAME

- Change the spelling topics over time to provide variety and revision.

Spelling Piles

This game allows you to revisit a past spelling pattern using a quick game. Either use it to reinforce a recent lesson, to assess learning outcomes and/or to introduce new words which share a previously-explored spelling pattern.

One player turns over a card displaying a word containing one of the spelling patterns (e.g. spellings containing either an 'all' spelling pattern or an 'ir' spelling pattern). They then read the word <u>aloud to the other player, and put it into a meaningful sentence</u>. The other player then decides in which pile that word and its spelling belongs, and writes it in.

The first player shows them the card so that the spelling can be checked. Discuss any errors, and correct them.

There is no penalty for spelling a word incorrectly in this game. Errors inform learners where they are making errors and encourage discussions about the use of memory prompts. As a revision exercise, this game provides the opportunity to re-visit a memory prompt, and to be reminded of aspects of spelling found between different words. For example, the word 'called' ends with the letters -ed, not just 'd'; the word 'circus' contains two clowns (who put on a performance for 'us'); 'tallest' contains the suffix '-est' despite sounding like '-ist'; and 'thirsty' begins 'th' not 'f'. Practice helps to consolidate learning.

The first player to fill up a pile of five words is the winner.

player one: Tia		player two: Tazmin	
'all'	'ir'	'all'	'ir'

Games based on chance remove links between losing and failure.

Switch Off Your Ears

Because so many spelling patterns in the English language are confusing, it can be very helpful for learners to be directed towards the use of visual and meaningful clues to spelling rather than relying solely on their ears.

Whilst phonics (the letter-to-sound relationships within words) is an important and necessary aspect of spelling, an over-reliance on just one route into spelling (whatever route that might be), is never going to be successful for most spellers. In languages such as German and Spanish where their spellings usually share the same letters for the same sound, the ears can be used to support spelling skills much more easily.

If we were to use the same letters for the same sound, we could have:

'oo' Using the letters 'oo' to make the sound we find in 'moon' ...	true	troo	But then many people would need to find another way of spelling (or pronouncing) the word 'book'.
	through	throo	
	who	hoo	
	flew	floo	
	you	yoo	
	two	too	
	fruit	froot	

To help learners identify between spellings which share the same sound, but not letters, use 'Spelling Piles' (see previous page) but use two (or maybe three) different groups of spellings which have been previously studied.

ci<u>r</u>cus On Shirley's thirteenth birthday we all went to the circus.	t<u>ur</u>n Please turn off the lights and don't disturb the neighbours when you leave.	<u>ger</u>bil Robert has a perfect pet. It is a gerbil called Nibbler.

There are many strategies available to support memory storage and recall. Learners need stimulating activities to engage thinking skills. They enjoy using materials which apply different types of game-play to promote success.

Chapter Three:
Exploring the Rules of English Spelling

Spelling rules can be very helpful for those who find English spellings confusing. By understanding *why* certain spelling patterns occur, spellers have additional information to work with when engaging with a variety of different spellings.

Whilst many English spellings do not follow the rules, having an understanding of why some letters are arranged as they are, helps to explain some of the peculiarities we find in English. By explaining some of the spelling rules, we can add another layer of information, interest and support to strengthen spelling memories, engagement and application.

Test your knowledge of English spelling rules by answering the following questions:

clo**ck** loo**k**	Why does -ck appear in 'clock', but -k' in 'look'?	see page 56 to check your answer
measur**e** / measurable chang**e** / changeable	When -able is added to 'measure' and 'change' why does the 'e' disappear in one but not the other?	see page 140 to check your answer
kitten, **k**ey **c**at, **c**old	Why do 'kitten' and 'key' begin with a letter 'k' but 'cat' and 'cold' begin with a letter 'c'?	see page 59 to check your answer
e**d**ge fu**d**ge bri**d**ge	What is the purpose of the letter 'd' in 'hedge', 'fudge' and 'bridge'?	see page 75 to check your answer
pu**dd**le mi**dd**le	Why are there two 'd's in 'puddle' and 'middle'?	see page 62 to check your answer
ra**bb**it ca**b**in	Why are there two 'b's in 'rabbit' but only one in 'cabin'?	see page 74 to check your answer

Spelling rules help those who find them useful.

The Role of Vowels

The vowels (a, e, i, o, u and sometimes y) play an interesting role.

A number of useful spelling rules depend on the sounds made by vowels so it is useful to know how they work.

When on their own (standing away from other vowels) they make a 'short' vowel sound …

c<u>a</u>t egg w<u>i</u>nk s<u>o</u>ck m<u>u</u>g

Practise listening to words containing short vowel sounds and hearing the difference between them. Sorting words into groups which share a short vowel sound can be useful (e.g. '<u>e</u>gg words': 'peg', 'step', 'men' but not 'man'.)

However, the term 'short' vowel sound can be very confusing.

I can say the two words 'cat' ('short a') and 'cake' ('long a') at the same speed, or make either word sound shorter or longer than the other. If I don't understand (or remember) the meaning of the term 'short vowel sound', it is very difficult to work it out.

For some, a memory trigger such as 'short s<u>o</u>cks' helps them to recall the meaning of the term 'short vowel' sound and match it to ŏ.

The sound 'ā' (as in 't<u>a</u>ke') is then either referred to as a 'long' vowel sound, or, 'the letter's name'.

⬭ Short vowel fillings

Using the short vowel sounds, how many words can you make using the following collection of consonants?

(The term 'consonant' refers to the letters which are not vowels).

c_t b_t m_d t_g l_d p_d

_nk _mp s_nk b_ng s_ng

Two vowels together will make just one sound:
'N<u>et</u>' becomes 'n<u>eat</u>' and 'b<u>o</u>nd' becomes 'b<u>ou</u>nd'.
One letter apart and you'll still hear one name,
'H<u>o</u>p' becomes 'h<u>ope</u>' and 'T<u>a</u>m' becomes 't<u>ame</u>'.

r<u>ai</u>n	c<u>a</u>k<u>e</u>
b<u>ea</u>ds	sc<u>e</u>n<u>e</u>
t<u>ie</u>	<u>i</u>c<u>i</u>ng
c<u>oa</u>t	p<u>o</u>n<u>y</u>
T<u>ue</u>sday	c<u>u</u>t<u>e</u>
pl<u>ay</u>	b<u>a</u>b<u>y</u>

Two letters which make one sound, can also be called a 'digraph'.

The word 'm<u>a</u>k<u>e</u>' contains a 'split digraph', as, in this case, the 'a' and 'e' are split by the letter 'k'. The first vowel (a) is now making a 'long' vowel sound (also sometimes known as 'the sound of its name').

Accents often affect the sounds of vowels within words. Some people hear and identify sounds within words more easily than others.

When two, or more, consonants stand in the way,
The vowels are then left to have their own say:
'Diner' and 'dinner'; 'competing go-getters',
Show that vowel sounds are ruled by their
                                neighbouring letters.

buttons   shopping   package   kitten

Two letters stop the two vowels from affecting each other.

Explore vowels in action only after learners have learnt basic rules.

Vowels in Action

Read through the following passage. Then return to the underlined words. If they contain a 'short vowel sound' highlight them with a yellow highlighter pen. If the words contain a 'long vowel sound' highlight them in blue.

Now examine the spellings: Are the vowels following the spelling rules outlined above?

Ruby Rabbit was in the habit of hopping into Peter's garden for a tasty feast. She would nibble away at lettuce leaves, carrot tops and raspberries. But last Tuesday, she bit into a chilli. Wow! The taste was hot! Quickly, Ruby headed for a puddle of water, running as fast as her legs could take her. She licked up every drop of the rainwater to wash away the stinging taste of chilli. It took a while to recover, but Ruby had learnt her lesson. Chillies are not for bunnies!

Check your answers on page 135.

The Rules (and Riddle) of -ING

When -ing is added to the end of a word,
one of three things will usually happen:

either (a) The last letter is doubled to stop the 'i' of -ing
changing the sound of a 'short vowel sound'.
sk<u>i</u>p/skipping; r<u>u</u>n/running; st<u>e</u>p/stepping; st<u>o</u>p/stopping

or (b) The 'i' of -ing will replace the letter 'e'. If the 'i' can
do the same job as the 'e', then the 'e' is no longer needed.
ING eats the 'e'
slope/sloping; take/taking; complete/completing

or (c) No changes need to be made to the base word's
spelling ... -ing is just added onto the base word.
walk/walking; keep/keeping; wink/winking; cook/cooking
However ...
(establish an understanding of the three rules above
before moving onto these -r plus -ing spellings)
Some words ending in -ar, -er, -ir, -or, -ur (r-controlled vowels) need to
have an extra 'r' added before the -ing.
war/warring; transfer/transferring; stir/stirring; occur/occurring

Spelling Detective Activity

Discuss the comments above. Then complete the following:
a) Use each of the words below in a spoken sentence.
b) Add -ing to each word. Write it down. Speak a new sentence.
c) Then can you now work out how you should spell each word if the suffix -ed was
added to each of the words instead of -ing?

drop	flap	invent	rave	tease
train	occur	stir	transfer	star
limp	repeat	please	regret	scar

Check your answers on page 137.
(As with all activities, adapt to match relevant spelling patterns)

Nightmare Spellings

Word-catcher cobweb template

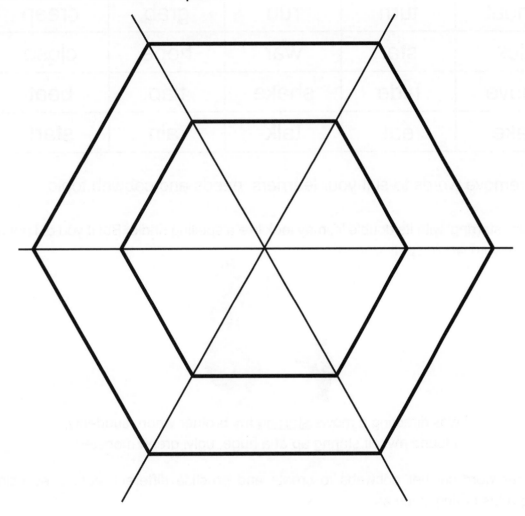

- Player turns over a key word (see examples below), adds -ing, then writes the word onto their word-catcher cobweb.
- (Discuss and correct any spelling errors.)
- When each new word is added, the player SPEAKS an event which could occur in a nightmare which contains that word.
- When the dream-catcher cobweb is full, the player then SPEAKS a nightmare story made up of events which contain each word. They can repeat an event they thought of earlier, or change it if they wish.
- Player then draws one picture relating to their nightmare story.
- Remove cobweb from sight.
- How many -ing words can be recalled and written around the picture?

Use this word-catcher cobweb for other activities too.

<u>Examples of key words</u> – copy out onto cards

try	lose	stir	scream	slip
glare	stop	chase	stare	fight
shout	turn	run	grab	creep
tick	star	war	hope	close
move	hide	shake	flap	beat
take	eat	talk	rain	start

Add / remove words to suit your learners' needs and cobweb topic.

The word 'starring' with its double 'r', may look like a spelling riddle. But if you did not double the 'r' the word would spell 'staring'.

I was directing a movie <u>starring</u> my brother when, suddenly,
I found myself <u>staring</u> up at a huge, ugly, green monster!

Use other word-catcher cobwebs to create and practise different story lines using the spelling rules of -ing, such as:

- 'A Day in Ant City' cobweb
- 'Underwater Adventure' cobweb
- 'A World Without Words' cobweb

Word-catcher cobwebs can be used in other ways too:

By using cobwebs as a method of trapping words and ideas which flutter into working memory, they can be used to capture key sounds, feelings or events which appear when planning a forthcoming story line. A different cobweb might display synonyms for 'said' or a range of interesting adjectives. Cobwebs can also be used as a note-taking tool to enhance listening skills.

Pitching in with a -tch

<u>fetch</u> wr<u>etch</u> p<u>atch</u> c<u>atch</u>es w<u>itch</u> st<u>itch</u>ing h<u>utch</u> cr<u>utch</u>es h<u>otch</u>p<u>otch</u>	When the /ch/ sound follows a 'short vowel sound', the letters -tch are used. 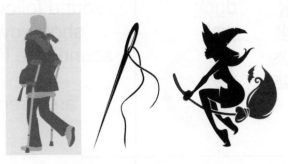

HOWEVER, the addition of a 't' does not affect the sound of /ch/, nor does it appear to play any significant role.

To demonstrate this point, explore the sound of the words:

rich / pitch   such / hutch   much / crutch

For those who can 'hear' the 't' in -tch, their eyes are influencing their ears. The sound of the word 'huch' is no different to the sound of the word 'hutch'.

Common words which ignore the -tch rule include:

rich, such, much, which, touch, attach and sandwich

The history of the sandwich

Historical information adds depth of information and interest to help make a stronger memory trace.

In 1762, the Earl of Sandwich was believed to have invented the idea of placing a filling between two slices of bread when he wanted to eat roast beef whilst playing cards. The bread stopped his hands from getting greasy.

'Wic' comes from the Latin word 'vicus' meaning hamlet.

'Sandwic' therefore meant 'sand village' or 'place on the sand.' The modern spelling of 'Sandwich' has evolved over time.

Create a spelling-family story linked to the word 'sandwich' if any of the other words <u>not containing</u> 'tch' are being misspelled.

The Rules of /k/

pack　rack clock　sock luck　duck slick　pick peck deck 	When the /k/ sound follows a 'short vowel sound', the letters -ck are used.	<u>note</u> This -ck rule applies to single-syllable words.
park　mark look　book seek　week wink　blink bank　thank	When the /k/ sound follows <u>any other sound</u>, the letter -k is used. 	

See page 57 for an activity (Take Your Pick) to apply these rules.

Having explored and practised the ck/k rules, move on to explore the -ic ending of longer words.

Don't panic in the attic!

'Pick' is a short word with one syllable ... and ends with -ck.

'Panic' has more than one syllable ... and the final 'k' is missing.

Search for other words with more than one syllable ending in -ic.

However, in the following list of words ending in /k/ (all of which have more than one syllable), some end with the letters -ck, and others with -ic. Why might this be?

comic　magic　seasick　frantic　topic　broomstick

traffic　sidekick　drumstick　panic　lipstick　attic

Check your answers on page 138.

Look out for other spellings containing -ck to see if they are also following the rules, or not. (Not all spellings follow the rules even when they are supposed to!)

Take Your Pick

Write in a word (or words) which match the pictures below.
Use words whose spellings contain either 'ck' or 'k' to make the /k/ sound.

Information:

- In most short words, if a /k/ sound comes after a 'short vowel sound', then the letters 'ck' are used.

  pick, tick, luck, lucky, tickle, sock.

- In words where the /k/ sound comes after *any other sound* then the letter 'k' is used.

  bark, think, book, week, lake, talking.

1	2	3	4
5	6	7	8
9	10	11	12

Check your answers on page 138

More News about the Sound of /k/

doctor or actor or tractor

(These words end with the letters -or even though we often say these words as if they end -er)

They do not use -ck to make the /k/ sound, only a 'c' despite following a short vowel sound.

There is no simple reason for this, but if you find the /k/ sound **does not** come at the end of a morpheme (a unit which conveys meaning within a word), it is often just a 'c'.

Look out for other words making a similar use of the letter 'c'.

At the time when Samuel Johnson's famous dictionary was printed in 1755, the -ck ending was present on the end of many of words we now spell with -ic.

Samuel Johnson used the spellings 'musick', 'elastick' and 'arithmetick' in his dictionary.

We still need to follow this pattern when adding 'ing' to words ending with -ic such as 'panic' (which becomes 'panicking') and 'picnic' (which becomes 'picnicking').

The reason we add -king and not -ing to these spellings is to prevent the influence of 'soft c' (see page 59).

'Reebok'

Commercial brand names often ignore spelling rules.

anora<u>k</u>

Words which have been adopted from other languages are called loanwords.

Often they are adapted to match a familiar style of spelling, but may well retain unusual patterns.

The word 'ánorâq' (from the Inuit language of Greenland Eskimos) has been absorbed into English as the word 'anorak', which uses the letter 'k' on its own following a short vowel sound.

Pick one of these spelling oddities and draw a picture to help your brain remember it.

Hard and Soft G

leg, bag, gold, ghost, glee, ground, angle.	The letter 'g' usually makes a /g/ sound. This is called the 'hard g' sound.
giant, gem, gypsy, hedge, edgy, ageing, staging.	However, if the letter 'g' is followed by an 'e', 'i' or 'y', it makes a /j/ sound. This is called the 'soft g' sound.
Spelling riddles: As with any spelling rule, you will almost always find exceptions such as: girl, get, gift and baggy.	

Spelling Detective Activity

Given the information above about 'hard and soft g', look at the following words and their spellings. What is going on?

guide, argue, guy, catalogue, tongue, guess.

Check your answer on page 139.

Hard and Soft C

cat, cry, clip, cliff, cut, magic, recall, actor, uncover.	The letter 'c' (unless used to make /ch/) usually makes a /k/ sound. This is called a 'hard c' sound.
ceiling, city, icy, decide, circus, ice, cycle, circle, mice.	If the letter 'c' is followed by an 'e', 'i' or 'y', it makes a /s/ sound. This is called the 'soft c' sound.
kitten, key, king, kiss, kind, sky.	The letter 'k' often appears in places where a 'c' would make a /s/ sound.
Spelling riddles: As with any spelling rule, you will almost always find exceptions such as: 'kosher' (from Hebrew), 'kangaroo' (believed to have originated from an aborigine word) and 'kudos' (from the Greek word 'kydos' meaning glory and fame).	

Hard and Soft C Bingo

Create some playing cards using spellings which contain either a 'hard' or 'soft c' sound along with some matching word-clue cards.

some example spellings

bicycle	music	face	price
camping	circus	nice	space
Arctic	decrease	success	accident
circle	cartons	mice	December
exciting	prince	dance	receive

word-clue cards:

There are two wheels on a	The opposite of 'failure' is ....
Jazz, Hip Hop and Reggae are all types of	I didn't mean to spill the milk. It was an ....
Eyes and nose are on your	A letter 'o' is the shape of a ....
The cost of something is its	Milk comes in bottles or ....
You need a tent to go	The plural of 'mouse' is ....
Clowns are often found in a	November is followed by ....
The opposite of 'horrible' is	The opposite of 'boring' is ....
The moon, the planets and the Milky Way are all found in	The princesses' brother is called a ....
A large area around the North pole which has long cold winters	The Jive, the Moonwalk and the Tango are all types of ....
The opposite of 'increase' is	The opposite of 'deliver' is ....

Hard or Soft C Bingo
– the game's purpose and design

This game can be played by giving each learner a Bingo card displaying a selection of target words. 25% of words should be unique to that card.

Read words aloud together before the game begins.

One of the word-clue cards is then read out. Players are given time (and support, if required), to find the appropriate word and circle it.

When one player circles a horizontal line of words, the game stops.

Players then work out their scores by counting up the value of all the hard and soft Cs they have in the words they have circled. The highest score wins.

hard c = 1 point
soft c = 2 points

FOR ONE PLAYER
Present the player with a playing card, and place the clue-cards in a shuffled pack face-down on the table.

After a horizontal line of encircled words has been achieved, they add up their score. Can they now beat this score on subsequent games? What is the highest score they achieve?

RATIONALE
Single-word reading relies solely on visual and audio decoding clues present in a lettered display. This can present a challenge for struggling readers, especially those whose audio (sound) and/or visual memories are weak.

However, providing a meaningful clue allows the brain to use priming and prediction to aid reading success. This is called a 'top-down' approach.

By reducing the stress and demands on the brain through the aid of clues, it has a greater capacity for processing, registering and remembering additional information (such as the role of the letter 'c' within different spellings).

This game provides an opportunity to practise and over-learn a topic. As words become more familiar, the demands on working-memory are reduced, improving the ability of the brain to process and consolidate details.

Learners are also given a reason for the varied spelling patterns surrounding 'c', 's' and 'k'. This empowers them with confidence borne of knowledge, encouraging them to have ownership and control in their spelling lives.

The Troublesome -le

apple bubble circle dangle eagle fumble giggle huddle idle jungle kettle little middle nibble obstacle people quibble riddle saddle table usable valuable wobble x y z	Many spelling errors are made by the misleading sound of the '-le'. *puddul, sircul, middul, kettul.* In Old English, the word 'middle' was spelled 'middel' which explains the appearance of the two letter 'd's in the word. Without two consonants between the two vowels, the word 'middel' would have been pronounced 'midel' (rhyming with modern-day 'idle'). (See the role of vowels on page 49) A few spellings share the same sound as those words which display the '-le' pattern but they use the letters 'el' instead.

Spelling Detective Activity

Look at the shape of the letters which come before the '-le' and '-el' letters below, and see if you can identify a pattern.

little	camel
castle	towel
kettle	cancel
wriggle	barrel
puddle	parcel
ripple	funnel

Check your answers on page 139.

Spelling Detective Activity

If you are able to break something, it is a breakable object.

The morpheme (unit of meaning) '-able' means 'is capable of'.

Examine the following spellings to see what happens to the base-word's spelling when the suffix of '-able' is added to the word. There are different patterns. Can you explain why?

renew	renewable	comfort	comfortable
believe	believable	notice	noticeable
recharge	rechargeable	remove	removable
inflate	inflatable	accept	acceptable
collect	collectable	afford	affordable
change	changeable	desire	desirable
excite	excitable	adjust	adjustable
Check your answers on page 140			

The 'i' before 'e' rule

Many people have heard the phrase 'i' before 'e' except after 'c'. What they often do not know is the second half of this rule which says:

When it makes an 'ee' sound.

Read through the words below and listen to the sound of their 'ie' / 'ei' letters:

'i' before 'e' (when making an 'ee' sound)	'e' before 'i' when following 'c' (when making an 'ee' sound)
I <u>believe</u> the answer is 64. There were thirty cows in one <u>field</u>. Would you like a <u>piece</u> of this pie?	Did you <u>receive</u> your prize? The opposite of 'floor' is '<u>ceiling</u>'. They were <u>deceived</u> by the forgery.

Exceptions: 'protein' and 'seize'. (Also ignore this rule when 'ie' is being used to add a suffix to a word such as 'vacancy > vacanc<u>ie</u>s'.)

Collecting Valuable Spellings

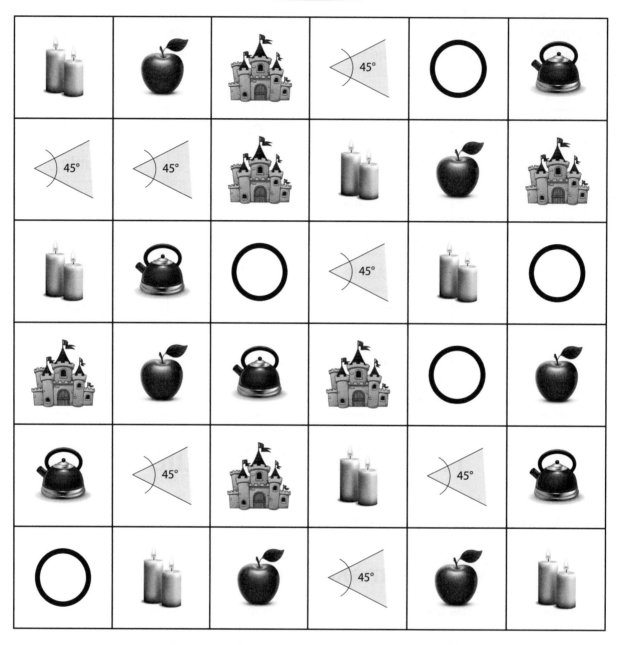

Players place their playing piece on any picture on the board.

All pictures relate to a spelling containing the 'troublesome -le': candle, castle, circle, apple, angle and kettle. Move pieces (in any direction including diagonally) according to the throw of a dice, making a 90° turn when meeting outer edges. Write down the word the turn ends on. Game stops when one player has collected all six words, but continue until everyone has had an equal number of goes. Allocate the numbers one to six to the pictures across the top of the board. Throw the dice. The word which corresponds to the dice throw is now your 'valuable word' and is worth two points. All other words are worth one point. Work out your score by adding up the value of the words you wrote down during your game. The highest score wins.

Oh Y is Y Different?

Nouns ending in 'y'

Many English spellings add the letter 's' to the singular meaning of a word to make it into its plural form. For example:

The <u>pirate</u> woke up the other <u>pirates</u> with his snoring.

However, when a root word ends with the letter 'y' the suffixing rules are not always straightforward.

singular	plural
one cowboy	two cowboys
one day	two days
one monkey	two monkeys
one guy	two guys

singular	plural
one baby	two babies
one story	two stories
one lady	two ladies
one party	two parties

Spelling Detective Activity

Read through the words above, and look at their spellings.

Some root words ending with the letter 'y' just add the suffix 's' to make it into its plural form, but other spellings follow the rule:

Change the 'y' to an 'i' then add '-es'.

Can you work out why there are two different spelling rules?

Check your answers on page 141.

Spelling Rules, Riddles and Remedies

Oh Y is Y Different? (continued)

After looking at the spelling of nouns ending with 'y', the next challenge is to see if the same rules apply to the spellings of words when they are being used as verbs.

A verb is a doing word: 'visiting' and 'viewing' are both verbs.

The fly wanted to <u>fly</u> faster than the other flies.

-ies verbs

Spelling Detective Activity

What happens when the letter 's' is added to a verb whose root spelling ends in the letter 'y'?

I play	he plays	I spy	she spies
I buy	she buys	I cry	he cries
I obey	it obeys	I carry	it carries
I betray	it betrays	I reply	it replies

Is this the same, or different from, the suffixing rules which were applied when singular nouns ending in 'y' were made into plurals on the previous page?

Check your answers on page 141.

Revisit the terms 'nouns' and 'verbs' according to need.

Oh Y is Y Different? (continued)

The spellings of verbs tell us 'when' an action happened. The suffix '-ed' is (usually) added when the action has already happened (i.e. in the past).

Today I play ...	Yesterday I play**ed** ...
He must stay ...	Last week he stay**ed** ...
I will enjoy ...	Yesterday, I enjoy**ed** ...
He will reply ...	Yesterday, he repli**ed** ...
I can carry ...	I carri**ed** it ...
They copy ...	They copi**ed** ...

Spelling Detective Activity

Read through the verbs above, and look at their spellings.

What can you say about the spelling of words ending with the letter 'y' when the suffix '-ed' is added?

Do the same rules apply when the suffix '-ing' is added?

Check your answers on page 142

She stays ...	She is stay**ing** ...
He will buy ...	He is buy**ing** ...
I can destroy ...	I am destroy**ing** ...
She will try ...	She is try**ing** ...
They might cry ...	They are cry**ing** ...
I want to fly ...	I am fly**ing** ...

Investigate other words which end with -y + ed / ing, to see if you can find any spellings which do not follow the rules.

Exceptions to the Rule

The past tense of the verb 'to play' is 'played': Yesterday, I **played** football.
The past tense of the verb 'to cry' is 'cried': I **cried** when I hurt my toe.

But there are three common spellings which do not follow these two spelling rules you discovered on the previous page:

If 'play' becomes 'played' then why does 'pay' become 'paid'?
"He <u>paid</u> me five pounds."
Why does 'lay' becomes 'laid'?   "She <u>laid</u> it down on the grass."
Why does 'say' become 'said'?   "They <u>said</u> it wouldn't rain."

'Paid', 'laid' and 'said' are spelling riddles.
They do not follow the rules.

Riddles in the Past

– a game reinforcing the -y + ed spelling rule and three exceptions.

If a word ends with a vowel digraph (e.g. -ay) add -ed.
If not, change the 'y' to an 'i' then add -ed ...
unless you land on a spelling riddle which might catch you out!

	1	2	3	4
START →	play	satisfy	obey	cry
13 fry	12 say	9 enjoy	8 lay	5 destroy
END	11 reply	10 toy	7 try	6 pay

<u>How to play</u>
Throw a dice. Odd number = move 1 space. Even number = move 2 spaces. Write down the past tense of the word being used as a verb. BUT if you land on a spelling riddle, write the past tense down, then move back one space.
The player *<u>with the most words</u>* at the end of the game, is the winner.

Oh Y is Y Different? (continued)

suffixes

Spelling Detective Activity

Read the following story.

What do you notice about the spelling of the words which have been underlined?

Can you identify their base words and suffixes? For example: '<u>carries</u>' = carry + es (change 'y' to 'i' then add '-es')

Harriet Hedgehog loves <u>strawberries</u>. So do the people who visit <u>Fruitiness</u> Farm. During the school <u>holidays</u>, <u>families</u> visit the farm to gather the <u>beautiful</u> berries, <u>merrily</u> filling their baskets and <u>bellies</u> with fruit.

Harriet Hedgehog <u>enjoys</u> <u>spying</u> on these <u>activities</u> from her hedgerow den. She <u>envies</u> the sun-hats worn by the <u>babies</u> and would like one to keep the sunlight out of her eyes. She listens <u>worriedly</u> in case a human comes too close with their <u>playful</u> <u>friendliness</u>, but their <u>berriful</u> feast keeps them too busy.

Suddenly, Harriet <u>spies</u> her chance. A basketful of fruit is left nearby and unattended. Harriet <u>scurries</u> up to the basket and heaves herself <u>clumsily</u> over the brim. She <u>hurriedly</u> curls into a ball, then rocks and rolls around with glee. A few minutes later, safely back under the hedge, Harriet <u>greedily</u> sets about the <u>business</u> of eating all the <u>goodies</u> her prickles have spiked.

Check your answers on page 143.

Suffixing Plurals (-s or -es endings?)

Spelling Detective Activity

A Suffixing Quiz: How much do you know already?
Write down the SINGULAR spelling of the following PLURALS.
If you're not sure of the answer, have a guess.

PLURAL	SINGULAR	-s or -es?
The <u>cows</u> are in the milking shed.	cow	-s
Both the <u>babies</u> are crying.	baby	y/i + -es
They have finished building six <u>houses</u>.		
The sky is filled with little white <u>clouds</u>.		
All her <u>dresses</u> need ironing.		
I don't like <u>tomatoes</u>.		
I need some new coloured <u>pencils</u>.		
<u>Knives</u> and forks are in the top drawer.		
There are no <u>buses</u> running today.		
The tree has lost all of its <u>leaves</u>.		
There are wonderful <u>beaches</u> in Cornwall.		
Henry VIII had six <u>wives</u>.		
Please could you wash up the <u>dishes</u>?		

Check your answers on page 145.

tomatoes   knives   leaves   babies

Suffering Suffixes!

– a game for two players to practise the addition of suffixes

START	1 stay	6 please	5 sleep	
	2 grip	7 cry	4 shop	
	3 carry	FINISH	3 trip	
	4 hum	7 walk	2 smile	
	5 care	6 wonder	1 play	START

- Each player places their playing piece on opposite START squares. They will also need pens, paper and a dice.
- Throw the dice. Both players then move their playing pieces:
  - even number = move two spaces forward
  - odd number = move one space forward
- Players then write down the root word they have landed on, and then write down as many additional words they can make with the use of suffixes.
- For example: 'take' could create: 'taking', 'taker', 'takes'.
- Provide a list of suffixes to help players if required.
- When making your own board, add words of your choice.
- When the game reaches the middle of the board, turn the board around and repeat. This gives each player an equal chance to land on the same words.
- The player with the most (correctly spelled) words at the end is the winner.

Suffixing Plurals

Spelling application activity

start   finish

-es	-s	☀	-ies	-es	-s
☀	-ves	-ies	-es	☀	-ves
-s	☀	-ves	-s	-s	-ies
-ves	-ies	-es	☀	-ves	☀
-ies	-es	-s	-ves	-ies	-es

- Turn over a card, and read the phrase containing an underlined word.
- Place your playing piece in the left-hand column above, on the suffix which would turn the underlined word into its plural form.
- Turn over the next card. Identify which suffix is used to turn the underlined word into its plural form. Move your piece to another square ONLY if the suffix you need is in a square touching the one you are in.
- You can move your playing piece horizontally, vertically, or diagonally.
- If you land on the same square as an opponent player, their playing piece is moved back to the left until it lands on a suffix.
- The first player to reach the right-hand column is the winner.
- When making your own playing board, use colour and create larger word cards to make it inviting and easier to handle.

PLAYING CARDS *(reproduce on larger cards, adding additional words as required)*

fresh <u>tomato</u>	sandy <u>beach</u>	newborn <u>baby</u>	baked <u>potato</u>
short <u>story</u>	bread <u>loaf</u>	friendly <u>donkey</u>	foot <u>x-ray</u>
cupboard <u>shelf</u>	Autumn <u>leaf</u>	Labrador <u>puppy</u>	little <u>alleyway</u>
sports <u>injury</u>	friendly <u>elf</u>	packed <u>lunch</u>	spider <u>monkey</u>
butter <u>knife</u>	email <u>address</u>	thin <u>paintbrush</u>	curry <u>dish</u>

The Apostrophe Catastrophe

Often, learners are not aware that words such as 'don't' is a contraction made up of two words (do + not). They therefore miss out the apostrophe needed to indicate the absence of one, or more, letters.

The following story has two parallel strands. The left/right sentences do not always duplicate each other's meaning, but share key words.

Read through the sentences together. Discuss the use of the apostrophes.

Print out and cut up into sentence-cards. Learner recreates the story line, writing down the contracted words to practise spelling and punctuation.

He did not get up early.	He didn't hear the news.
He could not find his shoes.	He couldn't find his hat.
He should have worn his boots.	He should've ditched the slippers.
"I can not find my keys."	"I can't drive my car."
He knew he had to walk to town.	He knew he'd better hurry.
He had not expected it to rain.	He hadn't got his coat.
The rain is not stopping.	The sun isn't coming out.
He does not hear the warning.	He doesn't hear the shout.
He has not seen the rush of water.	He hasn't seen the flood.
He is quickly swept away.	He's quickly lost his footing.
He should have learnt to swim.	He should've stayed indoors.
"I do not know what I should do!"	"I don't think I will survive!"
Then he sees there is a tree that is filling up with rubbish.	And then he sees there's a branch that's close enough for him to grab.
"I will hold on!"	"I'll soon be rescued!"
Soon they have pulled him into a boat. "I am saved!" he shouted.	They've got him safely back to land. "I'm so grateful!" he cried.
"I will not forget you saved my life!"	"I'll be prepared next time it rains!"

THE END

Spelling Rules, Riddles and Remedies

Using the Rules

By exploring and uncovering spelling rules, learners are empowered with information to aid and engage their spelling memories.

- An understanding of different spelling rules gives learners another lens through which to view spellings.

- Different rules provide a framework of understanding for those who find English spellings confusing.

- Spelling rules can explain the role of different letters (including the apostrophe), phonemes (sounds) and morphemes (units of meaning) within different words.

- If a spelling contains a spelling irregularity, and doesn't follow a rule, the brain has this additional piece of information to help define and register a spelling memory.

- An understanding of rules helps learners discover more rules and riddles for themselves. This fuels interest, engagement and thinking skills.

Thinking stimulates pathways into learning.

For example, compare the spelling of 'cabin' with 'rabbit'.

Knowing that 'cabin' does not follow the spelling rule which should require it to be spelled 'cabbin' (the role of double consonants, page 51), flags up a possible need to employ a spelling memory prompt such as:

<u>B</u>ill lived alone in his ca<u>b</u>in.

(Only use a spelling prompt if a spelling error is made.)

'Cabin' is following the spelling conventions of Latin which does not use a double consonant to keep vowels apart. Instead, it usually used a mark (an apex) above the vowel if it represented a long-vowel sound.

Understanding -dge

- Consider the spelling of 'hedge'.
- Can you explain the role of each letter?

> See 'hard and soft G', page 59 and the role of double consonants, page 51 to help you if necessary.

Answer:

The 'g' followed by an 'e' creates the /j/ sound. (Good)

'Hege' would rhyme with 'siege' (hege). (Not good)

Therefore a second consonant is needed to keep the two 'e's apart to protect the 'short e' sound.

'Be**tt**er', 'se**nd**ing' and 'ye**ll**ed' demonstrate this pattern.

'Hegge' would add in a 'hard g' (heg-ge). (Not good)

By using a 'dg' the vowels are kept apart. (Good)

The /d/ and /j/ blend together to make one sound. (Good)

If you close your eyes and focus on the position of your tongue when making a 'd' and then a 'j' sound, you'll find they are very similar.

For those grappling with the rules and riddles of English spellings, this type of detective exercise provides another layer of stimulating thought to further register the spelling pattern present in many '-dge' words.

- Collect as many '-dge' words as you can to see how often this pattern appears in English spellings.

Chapter Four: Promoting Creativity and Ownership

Learning by rote or mimicking responses modelled by others, can often produce 'shallow memories' which are easily forgotten. More effective memory traces are achieved when personal thinking and ownership is involved. Firing more neurons makes a stronger network of links in the brain.

Linking a spelling to the meaning of the word is vital.

When the brain is stimulated to consider the meaning of a spelling, it is adding more information to the shape and sound of the word.

might – might Imogen get home tonight? provides a memory prompt which places the string of letters in order, but also attaches the spelling to the word's meaning. In addition, the spelling prompt triggers an emotional concern – why? What might happen to stop Imogen getting home tonight?

There might be a storm, snow or a long way to travel. Imogen might be a snail, a penguin or an old woman. Using 'might' and 'night' that share the same spelling pattern within the prompt is also good, and weaving in 'sight', 'light' and 'plight' builds up multiple spelling attachments and links too.

When the word 'might' is required in mainstream writing, it is chosen because of its meaning ... 'We might see a ghost.' As the spelling memory prompt is linked to meaning, the brain is triggered to recall the spelling prompt of 'might' at the same time as it is thinking of using 'might' in a sentence.

If the learner wants to use 'Isobel' or 'Imran' in place of 'Imogen', this creative personalisation adds a further opportunity to add ownership to their learning.

Creative activity

Discuss the use of this (or alternative) memory prompt and talk about the value of it containing personalised and creative elements.

Then invent your own background story and picture to add depth, breadth and ownership to the memory prompt.

Who, or what, might Imogen be? Why is she away from home? Why might it be difficult for her to get home tonight?

Drawing a picture boosts memory storage and recall.

The creation of a picture provides learners with personal involvement, choice and application. The picture itself provides a strong visual input to aid memory storage and recall, and the TIME engaged with drawing a picture helps different processing channels interact with the topic in hand. This increases opportunities for the input to be rehearsed and consolidated.

The visual processing, muscular movement and thinking skills used whilst drawing all fire neurons in the brain. This increases the imprint of learning.

The act of drawing a picture and labelling it with words can help to develop the links between words sharing a spelling pattern (such as 'ough' spellings collected on page 27) or a theme shared by different groups of words (such as in the 'Odd-Bod Gatherings' on page 114).

The spelling of 'orange'

1. Where (and why) might someone make a spelling mistake when they are writing the word 'orange'?

2. Ollie <u>rang</u> Eddie on his <u>orange</u> phone makes a spelling-memory prompt that helps the brain remember how to spell 'orange'. Explore the prompt to see how it links to the spelling of 'orange'. Adapt it if you want.

3. To make it more amusing, Ollie could be an octopus with orange tentacles and Eddie could be an eel with orange stripes. The phone may or not be on the Orange network.

4. Why do you think Ollie rang Eddie on his orange phone?

5. Draw a picture to illustrate the spelling-memory prompt:

    <u>O</u>llie <u>rang</u> <u>E</u>ddie on his <u>orange</u> phone.

    Use the colour orange as much as you can in the picture.

6. Now play Dicey Spellings (see page 31) to practise this spelling using different brain-stretching activities.

7. Store picture away for later reference.

8. The picture will soon be in long-term memory to prompt the correct spelling of 'orange' when it is needed.

Understanding purpose expands capabilities.

The majority of learners who display ongoing difficulties with English spellings are often confused, frustrated and disappointed. Their poor performance in front of their peers, their teachers and parents can lead to anxiety, avoidance strategies and low self-esteem. These emotional barriers to learning can further impede their ability to engage, achieve and progress.

By equipping learners with the understanding and skills that help them overcome their spelling confusion and despair, their ability to take ownership of their learning is increased. By owning their learning they can achieve a sense of power, authority and independence.

Learners often blame themselves for failure.

Therefore, displacing the cause of their difficulties away from themselves by explaining the oddities and irregularities found within English spelling, raises self-esteem and confidence.

Exploration and discovery helps to identify the nature of the confusions they face, along with the opportunity to spell the vocabulary they want to use.

"I know that the sounds of words can be made with different letters. English words come from different languages and are spoken by lots of people which can change the way they sound, but not their spelling. I like using stories to join them together. I have sayings in my head which help me spell. 'When the hen laid an egg it whistled!' On special days I have crisps, ice-cream and lemonade!' When I grow up I want to be a scientist."

(Natalie aged 9)

sc- 🧍 -en -tist

How can I help my brain remember spellings?

Helping learners' understanding of how memory pathways can be enhanced using different strategies and activities provides them with a variety of tools to support their own learning.

It also offers opportunities for them to extend their ability to explore and test out different routes into learning.

"I like playing games. I made a game to help my brain exercise and revise wise spelling endings! Games are fun. I like to play them with my brother."

(Charlie aged 12)

creature – I would like to see a creature who could eat up raging elephants.

brother – my mother and my other brother were bothered by a moth.

Active engagement stimulates learning.

Providing opportunities for learners to actively engage in discovery and understanding enhances the impact of the learning input.

Presenting learners with words out of context (such as in a spelling list) greatly reduces the stimulation of existing memories relating to meaning. However, if you use a preparation activity which uses target words within a story or sentences, this checks that the meaning of the words are understood. The brain is then activated and primed to absorb more information about the words: their sounds, shape and construction of spellings.

A follow-up activity which applies a new spelling pattern or rule provides the valuable active engagement needed to consolidate learning.

For those learners who struggle to establish spelling confidence and skills, activities which provide them with time to revisit and apply new learning is vital. They need opportunities to practise the use of new memory pathways and to celebrate their success.

Introduce every spelling session with an activity that uses the word(s) in context. Make these activities accessible and easy. Actively remove any challenging barriers (such as reading or initial comprehension). If the brain is immediately overloaded with difficulty it is not able (and quickly becomes less willing) to consider and absorb other information.

Talking About Spellings

Draw lines to join up these words to make four sentences.

1. I wouldn't like to <u>walk</u> ...   without moving your lips?
2. A flower is usually found ...   to school in bare feet.
3. The picture drawn with <u>chalk</u> ...   at the top of a <u>stalk</u>.
4. Can you <u>talk</u> ...   got washed away in the rain.

Then look at the words which are <u>underlined</u>. What spelling pattern do they share? How might you describe the sound of the letters spelling each word?

Draw <u>a picture of each word</u> which links the meaning of each word with this spelling pattern.

See page 146 for examples.

Encourage decision making and thought.

A spelling prompt for 'decided'

Read the following to a learner (without them seeing the text).

As the two cars completed the race in exactly the same time, the judges **decided** to have a **decider**-lap so they could **decide** who was the winning driver.

If and when the learner is happy with the meaning of the word 'decided', they can complete the following activity:

1. Speak another sentence on any topic that includes the word 'decided'. Write the word down and then compare it to the spelling of 'decided' in the sentence above.

2. Are there any spelling errors? If so, why do you think they were made? (If no spelling error has been made and you are happy with the spelling of the word 'decided' then there is no need for a spelling prompt.) Making spelling prompts when you don't need them is both unnecessary and boring.

3. Would any of the following memory prompts help you to spell the word 'decided' correctly?

<u>C</u>olin <u>decided</u> to write 'ice' backwards.
He <u>decided</u> to side with the <u>C</u>omanche Indians (**not** the <u>S</u>ioux).
Hi! I've <u>decided</u> <u>e</u>ating <u>c</u>ockroaches <u>is</u> <u>d</u>isgusting, <u>Ed</u>.
The <u>C.I.D.</u> (the Criminal Investigation Department) were involved in a <u>deed</u> they <u>decided</u> called for undercover agents.

4. Copy down one to use. Or create one of your own.

5. Draw a picture to illustrate your memory prompt.

6. Then play Dicey Spellings (page 31) to strengthen the memory prompt by practising the spelling AND the picture which captures the link into the spelling of 'decided'.

As learners grow in confidence they become better at recognising how they can help develop their own memory prompts and story lines.

Consider different learning styles and needs.

There are many different ways to approach learning and many different topics and personal view-points which call for a variety of routes into learning.

Empowering learners with opportunities for them to explore and express creative means by which to help them understand, remember and recall spellings, provides them with chances to experiment and research different ways to support their own style of study.

Sometimes those with very inventive skills lack the experience of anchoring their spontaneous ideas onto structured foundations. Similarly those who thrive on analytical logic can fail to explore the impact of emotion and artistry on their carefully fashioned approach. By positively placing the topic of English spellings on a platform for discussion, examination and discovery, learners are given opportunities to practise and reflect upon a variety of routes into learning; adaptable and transferable skills they can employ as and when they are needed.

A creative use of 'ridiculous' spellings.

Spelling family – ous words (<u>O</u>pen <u>U</u>p <u>S</u>esame)

<u>O</u>pen <u>U</u>p <u>S</u>esame are the magic words which open up a secret door. Behind this door is an enorm<u>ous</u> cave full of cur<u>ious</u> things. Using the following words, *and exploring different ways of learning any misleading aspects of their spellings*, describe your choice of things that might be found inside the cave.

'Open Up Sesame ... please describe these things for me' ...

gorgeous	hideous
ridiculous	dangerous
delicious	poisonous
enormous	curious

Create your own pictures to emphasise the memory prompts which might be needed to avoid spelling mistakes.

Invite involvement and invention.

Creating a game to play or a practical activity which applies and consolidates spelling patterns can be hugely enhanced by personal involvement. This invites the use of different materials to support individual learning needs.

Create Your Own Game: Stepping Out.

Draw a numbered pathway and decorate the route however you want.

Add any penalty or reward squares which players must observe when they land on that square, such as:

- 'have another go'

- 'miss a go'

- 'move an opponent's playing piece instead of your own'

- 'move backwards on your next go'

Create a pile of playing cards according to the spelling topic in hand. They could be:

- A pile of target words. These target words might be written on the cards which are then read out to players for them to spell, or are described in a clue on the card which the player has to solve (e.g. The opposite of 'floor'). Instruction cards (such as writing word with eyes closed; write on somebody's back; write in 'spidery' letters). These would be turned over after the spelling word is revealed.

- Activity cards could be turned over when landing on a particularly marked square on your playing board. It could be a bonus card if a word is spelled correctly, or a penalty card if a letter is missed out or misrepresented. Paper-clips make excellent scoring chips which players could gain or lose depending on their spelling activity OR on which playing squares they happened to land on.

If a word is spelled correctly, the player moves forward the number of letters in the word.

The first player to reach the end of the pathway is the winner.

Players should always test out their games in draft form before committing to the final design. Sharing games and reviewing the learning engagement and outcomes adds even more value to this activity.

How to play Stepping Out

1. Throw dice and move playing piece.

2. Turn over a triangular, square or round card from the piles of cards provided. Read word aloud then use it in a spoken sentence. Remove card from sight.

3. Throw the instruction dice and follow the instructions below:

Use sticky labels to add letters to the faces of the instruction dice.

A: sing word's spelling as you write it.

B: write spelling in the air.

C: write spelling on paper with your eyes shut.

D: draw a spelling box,,,

for example:

$\square\square\square\square$ = thumb

E: starting with the last letter of the word written on right–hand side of paper write word backwards.

F: spell aloud missing out alternate letters.

4. Check spelling. If correct, move on one space.

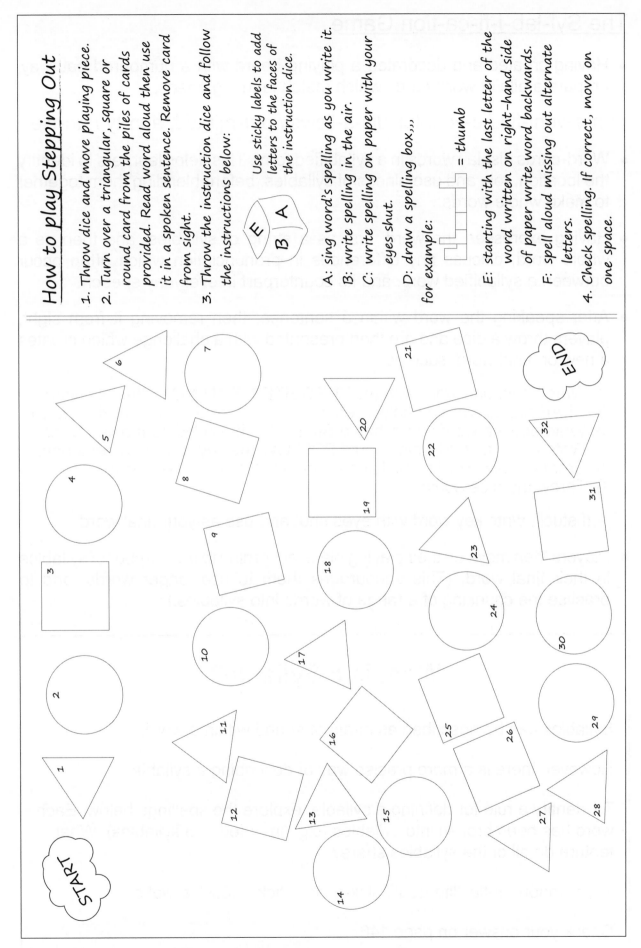

One sample version of Stepping Out game.

Spelling Rules, Riddles and Remedies

The Syl-lab-i-fi-ca-tion Game

- Having created and decorated a playing board with a numbered pathway, prepare a pile of word-cards which match learning needs.

  un-e-vent-ful / e-vent-ful, dis-a-llows / per-mit-ted, aun-ty / un-cle

- Word-cards display words in a syllabified form. This helps learners to identify the location, role and usefulness of syllables, before blending them together to make whole words.

- Having expressed the word, first as a string of syllables, and then as a whole word, discuss any differences in pronunciation which often occur between a syllabified word, and its counterpart in everyday speech.

- After speaking the word within a sentence, then removing it from sight, players throw a dice and are then presented with a challenge which creates a new or 'final word' such as:

  1. Write down one word with an OPPOSITE MEANING to the key word.
  2. CLAP hands whilst speaking each syllable. Use this as your final word.
  3. Write down a word which has a SIMILAR MEANING to the key word.
  4. Write down a word which could FOLLOW the key word in a sentence.
  5. Create a new word by building on the ROOT of the key word.
  6. Throw the dice again.

  – If stuck, write key word with eyes shut and use as your final word.

- Players then move on their playing piece according to the number of syllables in their final word. (This encourages them to use longer words, and to practise the chunking of a range of words into syllables.)

What is a Syllable?

Syllables can be described as beats of sound within a word.

However, there is a more precise way of describing a syllable.

To identify a rule for defining a syllable, explore the spellings below. Each word has been broken into syllables (e.g. 'in-vi-ted' = 3 syllables). What feature do all of the syllables share?

'li-on' 'moon' 'lit-tle' 'life-boat' 'sick-ness' 'stick-i-ness' 'a-wake'

Check your answer on page 146.

A Very Practical Activity

The sound of /shun/

1. Draw lines to link up words which express opposite meanings:

pay attention	southerly direction
a factual account	subtraction sum
northerly direction	notice a distraction
make a correction	a fictional account
addition sum	make an error

Many of these words contain the letters '-tion'.

2. What sound do the letters '-tion' make in these words?

3. Why do these letters often lead to a spelling error?

4. Repeat the activity with the following words:

an old television set	a small bang
a loud explosion	ending a discussion
a quick decision	a sad expression
a happy expression	a delayed response
starting a conversation	a new television set

Many of these words contain the letters '-sion'.

5. What sound do the letters '-sion' make in these words?

6. On separate pieces of card, write down terms containing '-tion' (plus a picture) and terms containing '-sion' spelling (plus a picture).

7. Provide two large <u>different coloured</u> sheets of paper. On one sheet tie on the '-tion' cards and on the other stick on the '-sion' cards:

<u>t</u>ie <u>i</u>t <u>on</u>   or   <u>s</u>tick <u>i</u>t <u>on</u>

(Use garden wire to tie it on)   (Use glue to stick it on)

8. Then practise writing down words from each list.

A competitive element adds an edge.

Spelling Detective Activity

although careful already armful awful always grateful

<u>Question:</u>
What spelling error do the words above often share?
Why do you think these errors are made?

Check your answers on page 147

Then, having explored the role of the letter 'L', playing a short but competitive game helps to rehearse and consolidate understanding and memories.

One 'L' or two?

A game for two or three learners – copy onto a larger board.

START	1	2	3	4	5
					6
12	11	10	9	8	7
13					
14	15	16	17	18	END

Write a selection of words onto cards then read them and discuss meanings, morphemes (the units within words) and spelling patterns before play begins. Players take turns to have a word (and a sentence making use of the word) read out to them. If they identify correct number of 'L's in a spelling, they move forward the corresponding one or two spaces. An incorrect answer puts player back one space. First player to reach the end is the winner.

although	already	almost	always	also
careful	beautiful	final	usual	hopeful
carefully	beautifully	finally	usually	hopefully
called	falling	full	tallest	small

Captivate interest using rewarding investigations.

<u>Guided Study</u>

As an example, uncovering the meaning of a linguistic term (such as 'morphology') invites discovery and detective work which rewards the inquisitive mind with revealing and relevant outcomes.

What Do Morphs Mean?

A morpheme is the smallest <u>meaningful</u> unit within a word.

Identifying a word's morphemes can help to spell a word.

wonderful = wonder + ful = full of wonder

bicycle = bi (two) + cycle (circle) = two round wheels

surprisingly = surpris(e) noun + ing creates a verb + ly creates an adverb

A morph is *the sound* of a morpheme ... one morpheme can have more that one morph (expression of sound).

For example, the morpheme -ed denoting the past tense of a verb makes a different sound in the words 'called' and 'dropped' due to the different tongue-and-palate positions used to sound -lled and -pped. This can lead to the spelling error of 'dropt' if the writer is focusing on the sound of the word, not meaning.

There is much more to be found out about morphology.

By researching this topic, learners are given another lens through which to view spellings.

Topics to investigate could include:

- bound morphemes
- free morphemes
- Greek and Latin morphemes
- allomorphs

Learners can research specific topics like these on their own, or with others. Topics which include unfamiliar terminology are much better explored with others where meanings can be discussed and clarified as study progresses.

Chapter Five:
A Brief History of English Spellings

Within many English spellings as we know them today, are the fingerprints of history. Over hundreds of years, the English language has picked up words, phrases and spellings from all over the world as its people travelled, traded, invaded and explored the depth and breadth of communication afforded by the acquisition of words.

Eager and greedy for power, the seeds of English (which arrived with the Anglo-Saxons) soon took hold and blossomed. Few words survive from the Celtic or Roman times (Christianity and the Norman Invasion would later bring Latin back to our shores), but Old English took hold and embraced, invented, adapted and extended its range of words to meet the many different communication needs of its people.

> Many of our most basic words are based on Anglo-Saxon terms such as faeder (father), moder (mother), sunu (son) and dohtor (daughter). The days of the week are also Anglo-Saxon in origin, each one named after one of their gods. Spellings and pronunciation have changed over time, but their origins can be traced back to the West Germanic languages spoken by the Angles, Saxons and Jutes.
>
> Investigating the root of words demonstrates how words (and spellings) have changed over time.

Surviving written texts from the first century show how Anglo-Saxon runes (straight lines) and letters from the Roman alphabet (the basis of the alphabet we use today) were used to write down Old English (e.g. Caedmon) and Latin (e.g. Bede). However, without an understanding of how these languages worked, it is difficult for us to understand the meaning of many of these words or how they might have sounded if spoken aloud.

The separate kingdoms which existed across England were then further influenced by the invasion and settlement of Vikings who, deriving their language from similar roots to Anglo-Saxon, brought new words into Old English from Old Norse, many of which were soon absorbed into the melting pot of communication and expression.

Sometimes we find more than one word for the same meaning such as 'bairn' and 'child' / 'brook' and 'stream' / 'fell' and 'hill' / 'skin' and 'hide', showing how Old English absorbed additional words from the Viking invaders who mostly settled in the area known as Danelaw.

It is interesting to see how some dialects can be linked to events which occurred in an area's historical time-line.

The use of language to communicate meaning greatly depends on the sounds of words (including the expression of tone and pace). Therefore, it would seem reasonable to agree on a set of conventions to convey these sounds (along with punctuation) when transcribing words onto paper.

Unfortunately, one major difficulty facing those wishing to standardise spoken-to-written codes was the difference in word pronunciation found across the country, and across time. So whilst some people might have included the expression of a 'w' in the word 'sweord' (meaning 'sword'), others, somewhere, must have started a trend for ignoring it. Whatever it was which led to the move from "sword" to "sord" and "answer" to "anser" (which is recorded in Old English as 'andswarian'), the changes were not immediate.

There was also the matter of having more sounds in the English language than letters in the Roman alphabet (adapted from a variation of the Greek alphabet used by the Romans to write Latin). Over the years, letters were changed, and some added, but there remains an underlying difficulty of some letters making more than one sound ('i̱ce', 'c̱hin', and 'c̱at') and, at times, the same sound being expressed by different letters ('g̱iant', 'gra̱dual' and 'j̱ump').

In Old English, the letter 'c' could express both the sound of the letter 'c' in 'c̱old' (the word for 'cold' was 'cald' in those days), and the sound of 'ch' found in 'c̱hild' (the spelling of 'child' at that time was 'cild').

A large number of spelling patterns which existed during the time of Old English were swept away by the arrival of the Normans in 1066. These changes would not have been immediate, but slowly the spread of Norman-French amongst the nobility; the use of Latin for religious and legal purposes; and a creative mix of words spoken by the common people which was undergoing a transition into Middle English, resulted in a medley of sounds and different expressions being used side by side.

As a result of the arrival of words and spellings from different places where they had been designed by different people, some letter-patterns were used to denote different sounds.

For example: the use of 'ch'.

- 'ch' represent the sound of /k/ in '<u>ch</u>aracter' and '<u>ch</u>emist' (words of Greek origin).
- 'ch' also represent the /sh/ sound in words such as '<u>ch</u>enille' and 'ma<u>ch</u>ine' (words rooted in French).
- We also find 'ch' commonly representing the /ch/ sound in words such as 'match', 'thatch' and 'rich'.

To highlight and remember these different 'ch' spelling groups, draw three people and award them with the identities of a 'Greek chemist', 'French chef' and 'English thatcher'. Then surround each one with items which link to appropriate words, using colour to highlight their 'ch' spellings.

The many word pronunciation and spelling changes during the period of Middle English can be seen by the variation of spellings between and within different texts. The word 'name' (which appears in Old English as 'nama' or 'noma') appears in different places as 'nome', 'namen', 'naym', 'nayme' and 'name'. Remember that whilst we might recognise the look of these letters, chances are the words themselves did not sound the way we might read them aloud today.

It also appears that the language expanded to embrace many words rooted in Latin and/or French probably influenced by the Latin and/or French education received by many of the scribes. As English was not favoured in the classrooms it meant that scholars, when they came to write in English, often had to devise a spelling based on educated guesswork. One word may have been spelled in many different ways as the change occurred between Old English, through to Middle English and then on to Early Modern English (which appeared from about 1500 onwards).

The Old English spelling pattern of 'hw' (e.g. 'hwæt') is reversed (leading to 'what'). This also produced 'where' from 'hwaer', 'who' from 'hwa' and 'when' from 'hwenne'. An initial sequence found in some Anglo-Saxon words originally spelled 'cw-' was changed to the letters 'qu-' to conform with French and Latin spellings. This changed the spellings of words such as 'cwen' (via 'quene' and 'quen' during the Middle English period), to become the spelling of 'queen'. In addition to these and other changes, the 'h' in words such as 'miht' (pronounced with a gutteral sound heard in the Scottish 'loch') was replaced with the 'gh' spellings.

> The cacophony of English words built on a language imported by the Anglo-Saxons, embellished by the Vikings and adapted by the Norman-French, had spellings which also became influenced by Greek and Latin, fashion and foible, accent and appearance to create the diverse (and often perverse) selection of letters many of which are familiar to us today.
>
> However, there were still more changes to come.

The Great Vowel Shift which began around 1450, was a gradual move which altered the pronunciations of long-vowel sounds so that the word pronounced "team" began to say 'time'. Words were beginning to sound more like we speak them today.

"Fode" (rhyming with 'rode') changed into 'food', "gayce" into 'geese' and "mowt" into 'moat'. It is these vowel changes which explains many of the differences between the pronunciation and spelling of continental words and English, especially as these changes occurred over many years giving time for variations of sound to affect the spellings which appeared in different texts.

> Exploring the Great Vowel Shift helps to focus the mind on the sound of vowels, and highlights how changeable pronunciation was (and still is) by the alteration of vowel-sounds.
>
> To express words in a different accent, actors find that the study of vowel-sounds spoken in different areas provides them with an effective way of adjusting their speech.

The difference between the language spoken (and written) by Geoffrey Chaucer (1343–1400), and that by William Shakespeare (1564–1616) demonstrates how English and its spelling evolved over those years, not always in a regular and predictable manner.

It is also important to consider the influence of social standing on the choice and expression of language. When those in power were favouring the use of Norman-French, then the fashion to embrace the style of their speech and spellings, is understandable. It has been suggested that the Great Vowel Shift was born of a desire to differentiate the speech and social standing of elite groups once the popularity of French amongst the nobility had subsided. It might have been an invention of the young as an act of demarcation against their elders (plenty of examples of this across all generations), or purely as a result of the increased access to literacy across the population leading to a diversity of dialects influencing written language previously controlled by those with classical educations. Nobody really knows.

Before printing arrived in the late 15th century, scribes could write words using whatever accent and convention they wanted or decided was required, to convey the meaning of their text.

Even once printing arrived, there was still a lack of standardised spelling, not least because of the many choices available regarding pronunciation, word origin and ancestry, conventions, preferences and established habits. Some printers might still have employed an earlier vowel pronunciation when spelling, or chosen spelling to define between words (such as 'great' and 'grate'). They may have favoured the appearance of one spelling over another e.g. 'flute' (rhyming with 'mute') instead of the option of 'floot' (to rhyme with 'boot'), and welcomed the flexibility of spelling to allow for words to create neat lines of text across a page through the addition or removal of odd letters here and there. All these factors contributed towards making English one of the most challenging languages to spell because of the many variations and exceptions to spelling rules that became familiar to the literate masses through print.

The advent of printing in the late 1400s drastically changed the speed and cost at which manuscripts could be produced and used to train even larger numbers of people in literacy. As the dominance of London grew and it became the political and commercial centre of England, the dialect used by the educated people who lived there became the one most often used as a standard in writing. But many of Caxton's printing employees were Flemish. They unwittingly introduced their accent into some of the words they were spelling. This is how the 'h' in 'ghost', 'ghoul' and 'ghastly' are believed to have arisen, and emphasised the use of 'gh' in spellings such as 'light' and 'night'.

In the late 1500s, England became a Protestant country. New texts were needed for the recently-established Church of England, and the norms established by the translators and printers of books such as the King James Bible of 1611 had a huge impact on the transmission of their spelling patterns.

But despite a booming industry responsible for spreading the printed word, spelling variations remained. William Shakespeare himself spelled his own name inconsistently throughout his life. The familiar version of 'Shakespeare' only became settled in the 1860s, with other choices including 'Shakespear', 'Shakespere', 'Shackspeare' and 'Shakspere'.

Shakespeare also invented many of the English words we know today (and others which did not catch on). He used nouns as verbs, added prefixes and suffixes, connected words together and invented new ones. Words he coined include: 'zany', 'rant', 'scuffle', 'ladybird', 'eventful' and 'fashionable'.

> Why is 'Shakespeare' spelled in different ways?
>
> It may have been that there were different ways the name 'Shakespeare' could be pronounced and/or spelled. It may be that in London, one form of address or pronunciation was favoured and thus reflected in one form of spelling, whilst in Stratford another version had been established.
>
> It may be that different scribes spelled his name in different ways due to their preference, accent or training.
>
> Wherever the truth lies, it is true that Shakespeare lived in an era where spellings lacked the rigidity of rules and standards we find today. It is possible that testing out different spellings of a name was quite normal!

Between about 1540 and 1640 there was increased demand for spelling reform in England. Arguments arose between whether to opt for the regularity of Latin versus the preservation of historical influences. In 1582, Richard Mulcaster, in favour of mild spelling reform, published his *Elementaire* which was an early form of dictionary. In an attempt to bring formality and respect to English to bolster its standing amongst scholars, he championed the wealth and diversity of expression afforded by English, and listed over 7,000 'hard words' useful for all professions. These included words such as 'elephant' and 'glitter', along with words we no longer use such as 'flindermouse' (a bat) and 'carpetknight' (a knight who spends his time in the luxury of court rather than on the field of battle). He also established the role of 'silent e' in spellings such as 'bad' and 'bade'; the spelling pattern -tch in words such as 'match'; and removed some of the 'unnecessary' letters which he suspected were sometimes included by scribes who were paid by the line for their work.

The 17th century saw the publication of many texts in English including those on the topics of religion, science, politics, domestic relations and culture. Spelling patterns and word pronunciations continued to be tinkered with, often as a result of scholars deciding a spelling was not correctly attributed to its true historical root. As with any detective story, it is impossible to provide concrete evidence of events which may have been decided on a whim, or for political favour, or by accident, or a reason that has got lost in the mists of time.

Then in 1755, Samuel Johnson's *Dictionary of the English Language* arrived which would become an authority of spelling convention and practice for Modern English for many years to come.

A group of London book-sellers had commissioned Johnson's dictionary hoping it would regularise the spelling and speaking rules which governed English. Johnson quickly recognised that the existing confusion would be impossible to untangle because of the varied history and constantly changing nature of the language, but did his best to research, exemplify and explain the riddles and rules found within English spellings at that time.

Some 250 years later, we can immediately identify some differences between Johnson's entries and modern text. For example, the letters 'ae' still appear as one letter in many of Johnson's entries. Æ or æ, was a letter in the Old English Latin alphabet used in place of a symbol in the runic alphabet called 'ash' which denoted a sound similar to the 'i' in 'fine'.

We sometimes still come across the ash, usually to denote old-fashioned writing, otherwise we find modern spellings use the letters 'ae' or 'a' or 'e', depending on how each spelling evolved from the use of the ash.

> Following the War of Independence (1775–1783), America decided to review English spelling conventions and tidy them up. A recognisable set of American pronunciation features had already developed so the sound of words formed the basis for these spelling changes. The result was a cultural identity that distinguished American pronunciations and spellings from the British, but retained a mutually intelligible language which could be used to communicate with the many other English-speaking groups across the globe.
>
> We can see the effect of this change through the way they have updated spellings which used to contain the ash:
>
>   anemia (American English) anaemia (British English)
>   anesthetic (American English) anaesthetic (British English)
>   archeology (American English) archaeology (British English)
>
> Other spelling changes include the use of -ize instead of -ise; removing the 'u' in the suffix -our (e.g. 'color') which we can see takes away the influence of a French-derived pronunciation stemming from 'colour' (Old French) whose modern French spelling is now 'couleur'; and changing the use of -re in words such as 'centre' and 'theatre' to produce the alternative (and more phonetically accurate) spellings such as 'center' and 'theater'.
>
> See also page 97 (American or British spelling quiz).

But, in 1755, Samuel Johnson established a precedent for awarding each English word a precise form of spelling. His dictionary froze the language in a form that held favour at the time. Despite a few changes, our modern spellings can be seen to be largely based on his version of spelling conventions: conventions which have only recently become to be seriously challenged with the arrival of textspeak (also known as txt-speak, txtese, chatspeak, txt, txtspk, SMS-messaging, and more).

But, as we know, spellings do not always denote pronunciation, as can be seen in words such as: 'f<u>ar</u>m', 'c<u>ar</u>riage' and '<u>ar</u>rived'. Furthermore, accents can greatly affect the spoken pronunciation of a word leading to 'grass' and 'mass' to share a similar vowel-sound, or not; the letter 'r' being clearly expressed in words such as 'c<u>r</u>eam' and 'spa<u>r</u>k', or not; and the letter 't', at times, being noticeably absent in words such as 'little' and 'writer'.

Over time, pronunciations are constantly being modified. Language evolves alongside the ever-changing communities in which it is used to express ideas and information. 'Formalised' language may attempt to define and constrain variation, but societies, and their language, develop and change.

We can never be sure of past pronunciations, even when poetry or sound recordings are available to analyse. The way we express words is dependent on many things not least our audience, education, context and intent. We also adjust our language depending on who is hearing or reading our words. The study of past texts allows us to make informed guesses, but decisions about past expression remains very reliant on the individual context of research materials and settings.

The pronunciation of many words has changed significantly since the 1700s (the date denoting the arrival of Modern English), but rarely have any changes been made to their spellings.

1500	1700	1900	2000
'fern' 'e' = "s<u>e</u>t" and also sound 'r' as separate letter.	'fern' 'er' = 'h<u>er</u>d' vowel-sound changed perhaps to match 'f-eye-rn' or 'f-airn', but still sound the 'r'.	'fern' vowel-sound changed to match 'furn' merge the 'er' together, but reduce the impact of the 'r' sound.	'f<u>er</u>n' now contains a middle sound which matches the schwa often found in '<u>a</u>sleep' and 'm<u>ur</u>m<u>ur</u>'.

The arrival of the r-controlled vowels (e.g. 'ar', 'er', 'air' and 'ear') provide a good example of how letter blends have changed within the sound of words, but often in an irregular fashion with regards to their sound and their spelling.

Whilst 'w<u>or</u>n', 'c<u>or</u>d' and 'p<u>or</u>ter' share one sound, 'w<u>or</u>d', 'w<u>or</u>e' and 'w<u>or</u>ry' do not. Meanwhile the words 'w<u>ar</u>n' and 'w<u>ar</u>d' sound like they should contain the 'or' spelling pattern, but don't, with the word 'g<u>or</u>illa' fluctuating between the sounds of "g<u>e</u>rilla" and "g<u>o</u>rilla", depending upon who you are listening to.

Generally speaking though, the r-controlled vowels produced groups of phonemes (units of sound) created when vowel(s) appear beside the letter 'r' (see page 107). Exploring this, and other aspects of spelling, helps learners to identify the nature of variation (and potential confusion) found amongst English spellings.

The widespread loss of the individuality of the letter 'r' appears to have started in southern England during the 18th century. There is also often the addition of an 'r' sound in terms such as "drawring" (for 'drawing'); "law-<u>r</u>-and-order"; and "he saw-r-a-dragon".

Recognising how English spellings have evolved in ways which explain why the *sounds* of words do not always match the visual appearance of their letters, reduces the disquiet experienced by those who are struggling to understand this discrepancy by themselves. Providing opportunities to explore, question and discover reasons (and riddles) why English spellings might trip up the blameless speller, also enables learners to apply an increased depth of engagement and understanding which empowers their spelling confidence and success.

Listening to recordings of speech from the 19th century shows how much pronunciation has changed.

Royalty, news-readers and politicians usually present a formal version of enunciation, but many variations of dialect and accent are also available to study.

One can only wonder how the English spoken in England and elsewhere will sound in another 50 years from now.

We now find more words sounding similar to each other despite their different spellings, although accents may provide distinguishing features for some.

How many of the following word-pairs do you pronounce as homophones?

'formally' – 'formerly' / 'poor' – 'paw' – 'pour' / 'blood' – 'blurred' / 'stork' – 'stalk'

'our' – 'are' / 'calve' – 'carve' / 'mints' – 'mince' / 'but' – 'Bert' / 'draw' – 'drawer'

Invention and the arrival of the technological age; space travel and fashion; commercial artistry and creative thinking, have all brought new vocabulary into English. Some new words adopt spelling patterns of the past, others adopt new lettered displays, or retain a style popularised by another language. Boundaries appear to be getting less rigid with many modern spellings embracing creativity and invention which provoke disapproval amongst traditionalists.

Another controversial topic is the increasingly visible evidence of American-English spellings found in both reading and writing activities. For some it is a sign of progression within a global economy. For others it is an undesirable loss of national identity. Over time, we can expect some of the distinctions between British and American English to get blurred.

American or British?

Can you identify if the following words are displaying an American English or British English spelling pattern?

If so, can you describe any features of the spelling's journey which has led it to its lettered-organisation of today?

colour	nappy	autumn
skillful	meter	travelling
diaper	honour	defense
connexion	color	fall
honor	organize	defence
advertise	dialog	metre

Check your answers on page 148

As the Spanish language pre-dates English in most of the American southern states, words borrowed from Spanish have now been imported into English. These include: 'armadillo', 'patio', 'rodeo' and 'fiesta'. Similarly, a number of Yiddish words such as 'bagel', 'glitch' and 'klutz', have entered English; Russian words ('cosmonaut', 'mammoth' and 'pavlova'); Japanese words ('bonsai', 'karaoke' and 'origami'); and Indian words ('shampoo', 'bungalow' and 'chutney'), are just a few of the many words and spellings which are now familiar in modern times.

Some spellings have become anglicised, whilst others reflect the original style of its orthography (the conventional spelling system of a language).

The arrival of text messaging has brought significant changes to familiar spelling conventions such as the use of '2moro'; 'JAM' ('just a minute'); 'book' (meaning 'cool' due to predictive text messaging selecting the former when the latter was required); 'L8R' ('later'); and ':)' (representing 'smile'). Further signs of change can be seen in the names of the bands listed in the top 40 chart list (such as 'P!nk' and 'will.i.am'); brand names and logos.

Whether these changes will catch on in mainstream writing will depend on a number of factors, some of which are totally unpredictable. Only time will tell.

It would appear, though, that changes in spelling conventions have arrived, which may, or may not, influence or stimulate spelling reform.

A: C u @ 6. Dnt B L8. Hav gegs 4 T. :)

B: Wt r u on abwt?

A: gegs = scrambled eggs.

B: Oh I C. LOL

The English Spelling Society (established in 1908) is a leading authority in spelling reform in the U.K. Its aims are to raise awareness of the problems caused by the irregularity of English spelling, and to seek remedies to improve literacy, including spelling reform.

George Bernard Shaw (1856–1950) also championed the idea of spelling reform. When he died in 1950, he left funding for a contest to design a new, phonetic alphabet. The contest was won by Kingsley Read, who based his new alphabet on words as they were spoken by King George V. At the time, that pronunciation model (Received Pronunciation) was considered typically British (or rather, typically English), and was held in high esteem. However, 50 years later, the 'cut-glass accent' of the Home Counties has lost some of its favour, and can often fail to match the familiar representations of speech experienced by the general population.

The spread of electronic communication widens the scope for new inventions, conventions and standards. This and the presence of such things as American-British spelling conventions, text-speak and spell-checker foibles, all challenge the status quo. Yet that is how language evolves, and changes: driven by the nature and nurture of its people.

We just have to hope that the protagonists of change are able to balance the rapidity of evolving invention with familiarity of archaic convention to maintain an underlying need for effective communication and expression.

Chapter Six:
Spelling Riddles

Many English spellings do not appear to follow the rules.

There are a number of reasons why spellings can appear to be riddles when they do not follow the standard pattern of letters found elsewhere.

The definition of a riddle is that we do not understand how it works, and as a consequence, we can make an error. Some errors are made because:

- The riddle is, as yet, an unknown rule. If a speller is unaware that 'guide' contains a necessary 'u' to keep the 'g' and 'i' apart to prevent the word saying "jide", they can see the spelling of 'guide' as a riddle.
- The spelling expresses the way a word used to be pronounced. Our speech has changed over time, but spellings often remain outdated as we see with 'knock' and 'knife' where the 'k' is now no longer voiced.
- The style of writing used by medieval scribes used a quill and ink to form joined-up letters. These letters were made up of small straight lines based on the style of the letter 'v'. Some spelling changes occurred to improve legibility such as: 'luv' becoming 'love', 'sum' becoming 'some', and the increased use of 'y' in place of 'i' so that 'bodi' became 'body'.
- The word contains a sound or pattern of which there is a choice of spelling. 'Road', 'rode' and 'rowed' are all 'correct', providing you have attached each spelling choice to the right meaning. 'Noat' and 'note' both spell the right sound, but only the latter is a correct spelling.
- A spelling may be influenced by a different set of spelling patterns, rules, pronunciation or conventions attached to the word's original source. The word 'thyme' is of Greek origin so is spelled with a 'y' whilst 'time' is a Germanic word and contains the 'i'. The difference in spelling may well have been preserved due to the two words being in use with different meanings, or positively chosen to denote a word's background.
- There are also words whose spellings had become established in one form and were then resistant to the changes being made by scholars and printers at times when attempts were made to standardise spellings. 'Match', 'hutch' and 'fetch' for example, contain a -tch pattern which is missing in the more frequently used spellings of 'rich', 'such' and 'much'.

Encourage learners to notice and explore spelling riddles.

Having an idea about why a spelling might be unusual is better than not registering its difference, and then not knowing *why* it might be different. Even if you attribute a reason to a spelling riddle which isn't right, you have avoided the brain struggling to make sense of it.

Double Consonants

Spelling rules (page 51) explain why the word 'dinner' contains two 'n's.

dinner   The double 'n' keeps the 'i' and 'e' vowels apart.
Otherwise the word would say 'diner'.

This rule applies to the spelling of 'rabbit', 'silly', 'cabbage' and 'coffee'.

However, whilst many spellings do follow this rule, many other spellings don't. One reason for this is that words arriving from Latin and French root words did not follow the double-consonant-after-a-short-vowel spelling pattern (they used diacritics instead ... little dots and dashes which have got lost over time):

cabin	habit	body	dragon
solid	limit	vanish	topic
petal	copy	lily	profit

Linking pairs

The following pairs of words are linked together in some way which relates to their meaning. The words are paired so that the first word contains one consonant whilst the second word contains two.

Copy individual words onto cards. Match into pairs, read through together and discuss meanings and spellings. Shuffle cards about before learner matches them back into pairs. Adapt game to target spellings in which the learner is making errors and encourage them to notice the consonant patterns in new words they meet.

cafe – coffee	body – massage	dragon's – egg	magic – dagger
melon – jelly	panic – button	finish – dinner	rapid – gallop
very – narrow	forest – parrot	metal – arrow	solid – traffic
habit – pattern	topic – lesson	salad – dressing	syrup – pudding

Misleading Ed

Many spellers make errors such as:

jumped / jumpt   packed / packt   hopped / hopt   walked / walkt

This is because the -ed at the end of some words sounds like a 't'.

Spelling Detective Activity

Read the words below aloud and decide which ones *sound* like they end with the letter 't'.

Can you identify which letters might be responsible for the -ed making the sound of 't'?

washed	jumped	hopped	tried	called	dropped
smiled	prodded	hoped	played	added	wished

Answer on page 149

Horrible or Adorable Spellings?

It is very poss<u>ible</u> to speak in a manner which highlights the aud<u>ible</u> sound of -ible at the end of words such as 'flex<u>ible</u>', 'horr<u>ible</u>' and 'respons<u>ible</u>'.

It is also understand<u>able</u> to make errors when writing words ending in -ible, when it is notice<u>able</u> that a consider<u>able</u> number of spellings use an 'ador<u>able</u>', 'depend<u>able</u>' and 'guess<u>able</u>' ending instead.

By exploring the suffix of -able (see page 63), meaning can aid the construction of **'adorable' spellings** such as 'enjoyable' and 'changeable' – note the need to retain the 'e' in 'changeable' to maintain the 'soft g'.

By attaching an alternative label of **'horrible' spellings** to those words with a terr<u>ible</u> knack of causing vis<u>ible</u> mistakes, a feas<u>ible</u> way of remembering the differences is made poss<u>ible</u>.

Pick -ible words required by the learner. Add more over time. For example:

horrible <u>i</u>nsects / draw large picture of undesirable insects

It is incred<u>ible</u> how indestruct<u>ible</u> a cockroach is.
Dung beetles make sens<u>ible</u> use of the ed<u>ible</u> parts of dung.

Feathers and Beads

'Feather' and 'bead' have similar letters, but the 'ea' pattern within them both is pronounced differently.

It is as if some words should be spelled with both the 'a' and the 'e' to make the long vowel sound we hear in words such as 'seat' and 'teach' whilst other words should only be spelled with one 'e' (as we find in 'wed' and 'neck').

Sometimes you will find similar words having the same 'ea' spelling patterns making different sounds ('pleasure' and 'please' / 'mean' and 'meant').

It is possible that all 'ea' spellings made the same sound in the past. It might be that some scholars or printers used the 'ea' spellings enough in some words for them to become popular even though the letters did not really match the sound of the words. What is certain is that words have changed in their pronunciation over time, and so it is possible that the word 'wealth' used to be heard as 'wheel-th' and 'bread' as 'breed'. Whilst we cannot be sure of this, and a deeper study into the history of English reveals other factors which influence the story, it is quite a useful tactic for learners to develop a spelling voice to help their brains assimilate the nature of the spelling riddle.

A spelling voice is where a word is pronounced in the way its letters suggest to prompt the appropriate spelling.

Below are a selection of 'ea' spellings. Read them together and discuss their meanings and sounds. Write them onto cards, shuffle and sort them into two groups before using them to create a spelling-family link (see page 19), using the words to label either feathers or beads.

bread, head, meadow, weather, pleasure, treasure, measure, dead, meant, jealous, death, wealth, feathers, steady, ready, tread, deaf

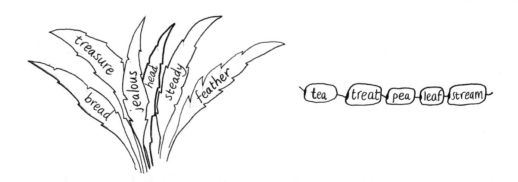

tea, beat, mean, leaf, leak, weak, team, stream, dream, cream, eat, meat, repeat, increase, teacher, reason, please, treat, pea, season

The Sound of OW

The 'ou' digraph can represent a number of sounds:

The gr<u>ou</u>p got into tr<u>ou</u>ble because they w<u>ou</u>ldn't stop sh<u>ou</u>ting.

However, the most common error is confusing the 'ow' for the 'ou' digraph:

You are not all<u>ow</u>ed to talk al<u>ou</u>d when you are miming.

Undergr**OU**nd m**OU**se

round
clock

ticking
sound

An **U**nderground house
for a house-proud mouse

Add more 'ou' words, by linking them to the mouse. For example:

"I've found four pounds!" shouted the mouse.

The mouse could hear a loud sound. It was only a couple of sheep who were munching mouthfuls of grass above her underground house.

Rain poured from the clouds. It pounded on to the ground. It made such a loud sound, the mouse found a scarf and wrapped it around her ears!

"I got lost in the mountains," the mole explained to the mouse. "I shouted and shouted until Uncle Monty came and found me and dug me out."

Wave p**OW**er

Fewer errors are made when the 'ow!' is clearly expressed (as in 'gr<u>ow</u>l').

However, this digraph also appears in 'sn<u>ow</u>' and 'bl<u>ow</u>' so collect and discuss words containing each of these sounds to illustrate their shared spelling pattern.

The town was covered in snow. Power-lines were down, icicles were growing lower, and the wind was howling like an owl.

Slowly, a narrow yellow glow appeared in the night sky. Grown-ups in their nightgowns stood at their windows and saw a jolly fellow in a red coat throwing down showers of gifts while the children lay awake in their beds. Presents fell down the hollow chimneys and into the empty pillow cases below.

Oh how excited the people were! The power-lines were still down, the icicles were growing even lower, and the wind was still howling like an owl, but nobody's face now carried a frown, now that Santa had been to their town.

Historical Evidence

Chapter five highlights key events in the history of English spellings which have fashioned its development and changes over time.

When faced with a choice of lettering (such as the use of 'sc' in 'scream' and the 'sk' in 'skirt') it can be helpful to uncover a reason behind this confusing state of affairs. A reason which can often be traced back to a historical event or influence which affected the choice of different spelling patterns.

Viking <u>Sk</u>irmishes

Spellings containing the 'sk' spelling pattern are mostly found in words which originated from Old Norse (brought over by the Vikings). This compares with the 'sc' spelling pattern more often found in spellings rooted in Old French (introduced into English by the Norman-French).

Collect spellings which contain the 'sk' pattern and then attach them to something which relates to the Vikings.

An alternative picture can then be created on the topic of Norman <u>Sc</u>ribes onto which spellings containing 'sc' are then attached.

Begin with a few words, then add more over time.

How was the word said?

During the period known as Middle English (1100–1500) the word 'said' (spelled 'saide' by the poet Chaucer) probably rhymed with 'maid'.

However, before The Great Vowel Shift (see page 91), the two words were probably pronounced in a way which made them say 'mide' and 'side'.

The pronunciation of many words have changed enormously over time. Often it can help to speak the word in a way they might have been spoken such as:

'waz' ('was'), 'Wed-nes-day', 'hand-ker-chief', 'pi-rate', 'he-art' and 'som-e'.

Better still, match the odd spelling with one which follows the right pattern:

'He s<u>ai</u>d it would r<u>ai</u>n' – '<u>Co</u>me h<u>o</u>me for s<u>o</u>me tea' – 'I h<u>ea</u>r your h<u>ea</u>rt b<u>ea</u>t.'

Silent Letters

Many of the silent letters we see in our spellings today, used to be sounded.

Knock that gnat off your wrist!

Collect together a selection of words containing the 'kn', 'wr' and 'gn' words and utilising their meanings to create story lines. Also practise speaking using a 'spelling voice' (expressing a word in a way which matches its spelling).

Thimbles on thumbs.

Another example of a silent letter is the 'b' in spellings such as 'climb', 'bomb' and 'tomb'. The final -b became silent around the time of the 14th century (which is when many changes in the pronunciation and spelling of English occurred). Identifying them, and registering them, can be helped by noting that the 'b' is usually sounded in words which share a similar root meaning:

bomb – bombardment / climb – clamber (but not 'climber') / crumb – crumble

---

Oh silent b … I want to hear you speak!

Create sentences which use words whose spellings display a silent -b (e.g. 'thumb'), but also hide the spelling pattern within a longer word in which the letter 'b' is sounded (e.g. 'Thumbelina'). See the examples below.

Learners can either compose their own sentences and pictures to help them remember a spelling, or spelling tutors can devise sentences to use as an introductory activity to the topic. Learners would then be asked to find the key words hidden within sentences such as:

Dropping the dumbbell on your foot is a <u>dumb</u> thing to do!

Shake your <u>limb</u>s to limber up before doing the Limbo.

What a great combination of colours used in that range of <u>comb</u>s!

You've dropped <u>crumb</u>s of crumble all over the floor!

Thumbelina was a fairy smaller than the size of your <u>thumb</u>.

Have you ever seen a <u>lamb</u> driving a Lamborghini?!

- Read the sentences aloud. Learners write down key word.
- Do another activity, then return to apply memory recall.
- How many words with silent 'b' can now be remembered?

Riddles Ringing in My Ears

Many spelling errors are made because English uses different letters to make the same sound. Whilst -or might be a common spelling pattern appearing at the end of many words such as 'tractor', 'doctor', 'equator', 'factor', 'alligator', 'visitor' and 'horror', it is not surprising to find the ears misleading the hand into writing -er instead.

Just collecting a list of words which share the -or ending will work for some learners. For many, they need something more robust to overrule their ears.

Discussion, pictures, interesting activities and repetition help to imprint the spelling pattern, and reminds the brain that the sounds of words is only one of the signposts to use when picking the road that links a word with its spelling.

act r — Add your own picture of an actor you are familiar with.	doct r	equat r
tract r	Don't make an err**or** when a word ends in **-or**	alligat r
sciss rs u t	horr r terr r	A metaph r compares the w rld to an range to highlight how both appear solid and strong, but can be easily damaged if not treated carefully.

Introduce this group of spellings ending in -or (adapting the list according to need) and invite your learner(s) to draw their own pictures.

Later, challenge them to test their memories by remembering the pictures, and writing down the words they relate to. Repeat over time to rehearse the links between these words and their spellings.

Attach further 'or' spellings once an initial group of spellings is secure.

Vowel Sound Variations

Having been introduced to the key rules and roles of vowels (page 49) it does not take long before variations become evident within English spellings.

The following few pages focus on this aspect of English spelling by leading the learner through a variety of activities which help to identify and explain where and why vowel modifications occur.

The use of these resources also helps familiarise the learner with a variety of different words and their spellings.

- Read words together and ensure word meaning is clearly understood.
- Create new activities from these templates to repeat investigative challenges within a familiar framework.

Identifying letters which affect vowels

In each of the following rows of words, a vowel sound has been identified which appears in most of the words.

However, the vowel sound is changed in some of the words.

Which letter is responsible for the change in the vowel sound?

the 'i' vowel sound: 'twig' – 'dirt' – 'dip' – 'rim' – 'distant' – 'bird'

the 'e' vowel sound: 'egg' – 'spend' – 'best' – 'verb' – 'netting'

the 'a' vowel sound: 'cat' – 'walk' – 'pattern' – 'flat' – 'called'

the 'o' vowel sound: 'pond' – 'storm' – 'worn' – 'pot' – 'odd'

the 'ea' vowel sound: 'hear' – 'seat' – 'east' – 'cream' – 'beak'

Accents can affect the way words are pronounced too.

Check your answers on page 150.

Discuss the role of spelling patterns which appear in reading material too, but only after focusing on reading-for-meaning. Having read a passage, and discussed its meaning, go back and dissect a few spellings for analysis. If working memory is faced with too many demands to handle at one time it can be tipped into overload which hampers learning progress.

Sentences of Sound

Read the following passages aloud together.

The spelling tutor then moves the passages out of sight of the learners and reads them again, sentence by sentence.

The learner counts how many times they hear the key sound.

Then go through the passage again, underlining and noting down the spelling variations which denote the key sound.

Variations of accent may alter some key sounds.

1. Key sound of /er/

Yesterday, I heard my mynah bird utter his first words: "Murderer under the sofa!" I turned and saw a purple-coloured jumper slither under the sofa ... it was an anaconda undertaking under-cover surveillance of my mynah bird!

2. Key sound of /or/

This morning I walked to the corner shop and bought pork from Cornwall, prawns caught off the shores of Dorset, apple-sauce from North Yorkshire, organic strawberries from Portugal and walnuts from California. As we live in Bournemouth, all this food has been brought 4,000km to the store, then forty steps more, before being gorged (eaten greedily).

3. Key sound of /ar/

Farmer Charles harnessed Ma and Pa (two large cart-horses) to the cart ready for market. The cart was full of jars of marmalade, raspberry tarts and baskets of barn-eggs harvested from the farm. They hadn't gone far when a partridge darted in front of the cart and startled Ma. Farmer Charles spoke softly to calm her, then out of the grass barged a barking Chihuahua, a llama and an aardvark. "We are going to have to start charging the safari park for letting their bizarre animals on our farm," Charles said to Ma, as an enchanting party of marmosets (type of monkey) danced in some branches ahead.

See page 151 and check your answers.

Then play 'Phonetical Allsorts' opposite.

Phonetical Allsorts

– the different sounds vowels can make alongside other letters.

- Throw a dice and place your playing piece on the word in the Key Word List (see page 110) against the number on the dice.

- Read the word out loud and decide which of the following SOUNDS is in that word:

"ar"	"er"	"ir"	"or"	"ur"

- Read the words in column A out loud. Select one with a matching SOUND (not spelling) to your Key Word.

- Score points (1 to 6) for that matching word, depending on which row it is in.

- On your next go, throw the dice and again move your playing piece to land on the appropriate word in the Key Word List. This time, match the vowel sound ("ar", "er" etc) of this word with a word from column B and note down the score depending on which row it is in.

- Continue matching words in the Key Word List with words in each of the other columns by matching their vowel SOUNDS. Then add up your score.

- The player with the highest score is the winner.

For example:

Player One throws a 3, so moves their playing piece down the Key Word List on to the word 'sir'.

Reading the words in column A, the player decides to pick 'curl' as it shares the /er/ vowel sound found in 'sir'.

Player One scores 1 point as 'curl' is in row one.

On their next go, Player One throws a 1, so moves their piece onto the word 'born' in the Key Word List.

Reading the words in column B, the player decides to pick 'lawn' as it shares the /or/ vowel sound found in 'born'.

Player One scores 5 points as 'lawn' is in row 5.

Phonetical Allsorts

– the different sounds vowels can make alongside other letters.

	A	B	C	D	E	F
	curl	germ	verb	caught	circus	straw
	sort	barn	care	scary	furry	burn
	berry	sorry	score	worst	war	very
	word	Mary	carrot	card	girl	party
	marry	lawn	start	arrive	large	August
	shark	thirst	world	talk	bought	calm

Key Word List	
1	born
2	perk
3	sir
4	far
5	turn
6	warm

(Remember that accents may produce different vowel-sounds between different speakers.)

Learning from Doing

- Having introduced the impact of the letter 'r' alongside vowels (page 107), learners are then exposed to more spelling variations so that they are not restricted in their knowledge of alternative letter-strings. This also demonstrates how varied and confusing English spellings can be.

  Whilst this approach might be seen as one which could overload and demotivate learners, it is actually helping poor spellers identify that their errors are not due to their lack of attention, focus or application, but down to the irregular and diverse spelling options which have developed over time.

  By equipping the learner with an understanding of the nature of English spellings, they are better able to apply relevant skills and strategies to support the development of their spelling confidence.

  No one single programme of teaching style or structure of curriculum will suit all. However, for many, providing opportunities for them to discover and explore; test and practise; apply and achieve, enables them to develop their own insights and experiences on which to build further learning.

- The spelling variations of the r-controlled vowel SOUNDS are then witnessed in 'Sentences of Sound' (page 108), first by linking words with their meaning (reading and discussing words presented within a context), then linking them to key sounds, and then matching sounds with the visual appearance of letter-strings.

  Not all spelling patterns appear with equal frequency. Discussions allow spelling tutors and their learners to consider which patterns are most commonly, or uncommonly, used; which may be influenced by the adoption of words / spellings from other languages; and which may be linked to past or present variations in accents or conventions.

- Finally, the use of Phonetical Allsorts (page 109) brings together and practises the use and appearance of different spelling patterns and sounds surrounding vowels. The game provides a template which can be adapted and changed to provide experience of many different words.

  This game can appear difficult (meaning it makes the brain work quite hard to identify sounds). However, the challenges it presents engages thought and experience in a manner which imparts stronger, more memorable impressions upon the mind.

  Keeping a record of spelling activities is vital to ensure that lessons are rehearsed and consolidated, and outcomes assessed. It is also rewarding for learners to identify how and where spelling progress is being made.

Take a Stroll with a Mole

Throughout the history of English spellings, changes have been tried and tested. Sometimes a change caught on, only to be changed again as fashions or rules or pronunciations changed. As a result, English has gathered a variety of words which now share the same sound, but not the same spelling.

It is possible that there were sound differences in the past. Very often the root of the word influences the choice of its spelling, or sometimes a change in spelling is used to distinguish between homophones (such as 'reel' and 'real') but, more often, it appears that some of the spelling patterns caught on with some of the words, whilst others got attached to a different layout of letters.

As a result, we get landed with patterns such as:

mole and stroll

vale and tail

paw and tore

kite and delight

pours and cause

verse and worse

Many 'good' spellers do not notice these confusions because they do not impinge on their spelling ability. But spelling tutors need to identify the range of learning profiles amongst their learners, and recognise that for those who find spelling difficult, the explicit exploration of spelling rules, riddles and remedies will help to demystify their confusion.

For some, the use of spelling patterns may be all that they need to register and secure memory pathways. Others will need more to add depth and strength to the inputs. 'A troll took a stroll with a mole and a vole' (along with appropriately labelled picture highlighting the spelling variations using different colours), provides the opportunity for the spelling riddles to be noticed, discussed, assimilated and applied.

As with other family-spelling stories, once this phrase is secure, additional spellings can be attached as and when they are needed: 'The mole fell down a hole.' – 'The troll ate a jam roll.' – 'The mole was cooked in a casserole.' (!)

Without written application, spelling memories cannot become embedded within the muscular memory of the hand (penmanship or typing), so using a short story, a game or an activity is a necessary element of learning – with some individuals requiring more spelling practice, rehearsal and study than others. Using short phrases which rehearse spelling lessons allows practice to consolidate memory pathways and secure spelling confidence and skills.

Catch Attention with Colour

By emphasising the appearance of a letter pattern by highlighting it using bright colours attracts the attention as it fires more visual neurons in the brain.

Highlight spelling features which are often responsible for errors such as:

- The silent 't' found in 'fetch' and 'catch'; 'fasten' and 'listen'.
- The silent 'n' found in 'autumn' and 'column'.
- The silent 'h' in 'heir', 'ghost' and 'ghastly'.
- The sound of 'al' in words such as 'walk' and 'talk'.
- The use of 'c' in words containing the 'soft c' (see page 59).

Allocating one colour for a 'soft c' can help learners identify and remember its appearance in words where it is often replaced by an 's' by mistake, such as:

circle, certain, ceiling, concentrate, receive, dance, peace/piece and mice

---

Having the choice of a letter 'c' (followed by an 'i', 'e' or 'y') to make the same sound as an 's' is just one more confusing riddle found in English spellings.

The letter 'C' has an interesting history, beginning its days as a letter representing the sound of 'g'.

The Romans adopted it to stand for the 'k' sound and in Old English we find words such as 'cyning' which led to the word 'king'.

When the Norman-French brought their spelling patterns to England, they used the letter 'c' to make an 's' sound when it preceded an 'i', 'e' or 'y'. This meant that the English word of 'cyning' would appear to start with an 's' sound, rather than the sound of 'k'.

Therefore, the letter K became a popular way of showing the appearance of the 'hard c' sound, with spellings such as 'key', 'king', and 'kitten' becoming established in the English spelling vocabulary.

Visual Stress

Some people find that black letters on white paper can appear to swim, dance, swirl or shiver about. This condition is often known as Visual Stress Syndrome. The use of coloured overlays, rulers, lenses and computer-screen background colour, all help to support reading, with a similar attention to coloured paper, pens, etc. being necessary to support written application too.

Odd-Bod Gatherings

Creating pictures which need to be labelled with target spellings helps to reinforce the links between spellings and their meanings. They are also brought together in a form which can easily be displayed and revisited over time.

Irregular verbs

It is useful to have a theme (such as a picture of a Victorian coastal resort to emphasise the past tense of the verbs) to which words such as 'flew' 'swam', 'saw', 'ran', 'caught' and 'sunk' are attached to label actions. Once a picture is created, add more later on.

Treasure map

Making a map on which different features and place-names are labelled is another way of gathering some spellings together once you have identified why they can cause confusion and error.

Words to use could include:

island (not iland); treasure (not tresher); harbour (not harber); 'Firetop Mountain' (not Fiertop Mowtin); pirate (not pirut)

Explore these spellings first and discuss ways of remembering their spellings before using the map as a means of applying and practising their use. By engaging learners in the design of their treasure map, creativity and ownership enhances their learning.

Monster collection

Having designed some monsters, label them with names which describe their features such as 'Hooked-nose Hairy Hopper'.

Words can also be invented which practises the use of familiar phonetic spelling patterns to make names such as 'Oowee'.

Inventive transport

Similar to above, a range of transport vehicles are invented and drawn, then labelled in a manner which highlights their particular features or properties. Provide spellings for copying when needed.

Writing advertising copy for these inventions encourages the use of descriptive terms within a personalised and creative activity. (Use a minimal amount of words for an advert, but ones which grab the reader's attention and interest.)

Solving Puzzles for Fun

Using spellings as a source of entertainment is a good way of practising and experiencing spellings. Not everyone will enjoy the same type of activity, but here are some ideas which can help to stimulate thinking skills as well as drawing attention to the details of English spellings.

Five steps to score a conversion

Starting with word one, change one letter every time you move down a line, creating a new word each time. By the bottom line, every letter will have been changed converting the original word into a completely different one.

1. great

2. _ _ _ _ _   an old coin worth 4 old pennies

3. _ _ _ _ _   a deep mournful sound

4. _ _ _ _ _   got bigger

5. _ _ _ _ _   a colour

6. _ _ _ _ _   past tense of the verb 'to blow'

1. coach

2. _ _ _ _ _   steal rabbits

3. _ _ _ _ _   sheltered area often by the front door

4. _ _ _ _ _   place where a bird sits

5. _ _ _ _ _   boy's name

6. _ _ _ _ _   bright eyed and alert

1. sheep

2. _ _ _ _ _ sound made by a chick

3. _ _ _ _ _ side of face

4. _ _ _ _ _ look again, be sure

5. _ _ _ _ _ throw

6. _ _ _ _ _ sound made by a hen

1. ready

2. _ _ _ _ _ describes small glittering eyes

3. _ _ _ _ _ string these together to make a necklace

4. _ _ _ _ _ make these sounds with a drum

5. _ _ _ _ _ vessels for the sea

6. _ _ _ _ _ makes a quick escape

Let Us Rearrange the Letters

Using the letters of a key word to make other words can be both enjoyable and challenging. If a letter appears once in the key word, it can only appear once in a new word.

For example: 'creature' – tree, eat, act, ear, true, create, rat, etc.

How many words can you make out of the letters of ...
'description' (draws attention to the 'e' and '-tion')
'disappeared' (only one 's' but two 'p's)

Here is another activity to help recognise aspects within spellings which can help to avoid errors.

We do not pronounce the word 'ant' at the end of 'important', nor emphasise the presence of two 'a's in 'separate'. Looking for words within words helps to draw the attention to spelling patterns.

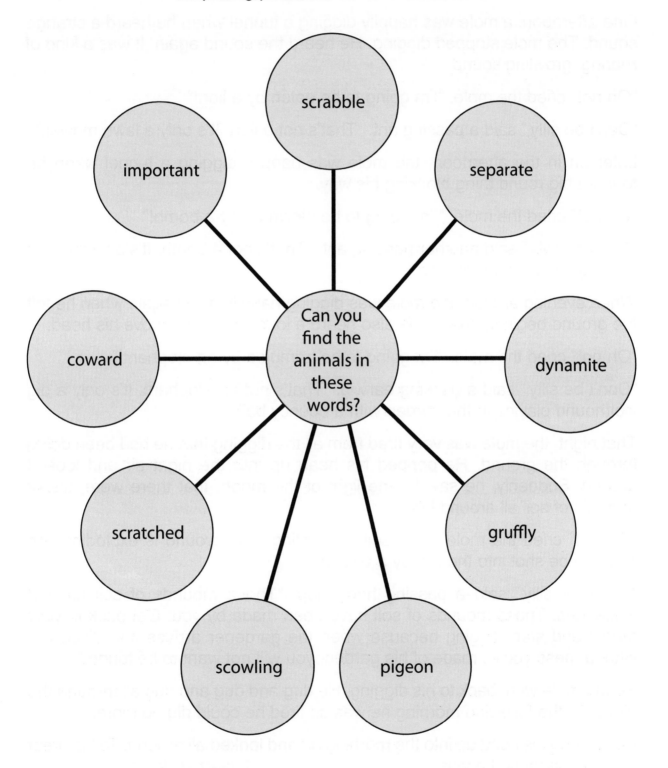

Put spellings into reading activities to utilise words within meaningful contexts. After reading the story together, return to examine the rules and riddles which occur in different words. For example:

<u>The Sound of Ound</u>

One afternoon, a mole was happily digging a tunnel when he heard a strange sound. The mole stopped digging. He heard the sound again. It was a kind of roaring, growling sound.

"Oh no!" cried the mole. "I'm going to be eaten by a lion!"

"Don't be silly," said a passing ant. "That's not a lion. It's only a lawn mower."

Later on in the afternoon, the mole was happily digging a tunnel when he found a big round thing blocking his way.

"Oh no!" cried the mole. "I'm going to be blown up by a bomb!"

"Don't be silly," said another passing ant. "That's not a bomb. It's only a round onion growing in the ground."

When evening arrived, the mole was digging happily away again when he felt the ground begin to shake. He also heard a loud pounding above his head.

"Oh no!" cried the mole. "I'm going to be trampled by an elephant!"

"Don't be silly," said a passing earwig. "That's not an elephant. It's only a big wolfhound playing in the garden with a bouncy ball."

That night, the mole was very tired from all the digging that he had been doing through the ground. He popped his head up into the night air and looked around. Suddenly, he saw by the light of the moon, that there were lots of mounds of soil all around him.

"Oh no!" cried the mole. "The soil is erupting! The ground is exploding. I'm going to be shot into the sky by a volcano!"

"Don't be silly," said a passing hedgehog. "Those mounds of soil are not volcanoes. Those mounds of soil have been made by you! Get back in your tunnel and start digging because when the gardener arrives and discovers what a mess you've made of his garden, you will not want to be found!"

So the mole went back to his digging. He dug and dug and dug all through the night. By the following morning he was so tired he could dig no more.

He popped his head up into the morning air and looked all around. To his great surprise he found he was ....! (*learner decides*)

THE END

Discuss different spellings then draw a mound made of ound words.

Chapter Seven:
Structure and Monitor
Opportunities for Learning

Structuring Delivery

The planning, presentation and monitoring of spelling material should complement associated literacy topics to harness and exercise the interactive aspects of literacy and language.

This chapter offers a range of ideas to support the design and delivery of teaching and learning activities which can be adapted to suit individual needs.

PLANNING AHEAD enables spelling tutors to:

- Link new learning into a programme of needs
- Prepare ideas for effective memory prompts
- Create activities which introduce new topics
- Prepare activities which practise and apply new topics
- Provide opportunities to rehearse and revise past lessons

For example, if the topic of interest is verbs, then the game 'Misleading Ed' (page 101) provides learners with a Spelling Detective Activity which highlights the variation of sound (such as the differences between the endings of 'call<u>ed</u>' and 'jump<u>ed</u>') which is often responsible for spelling errors.

Presenting learners with a selection of cards promotes discussion relating to the role of verbs and their tenses. The degree to which conjugation is explored obviously depends on the age and needs of the learner.

Asking learners to sort a variety of verbs (written out on cards) into groups promotes the use of comprehension alongside an examination of the spelling patterns found within the words.

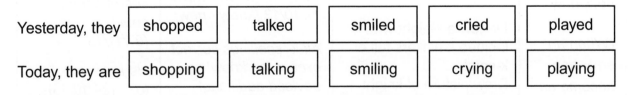

| Yesterday, they | shopped | talked | smiled | cried | played |
| Today, they are | shopping | talking | smiling | crying | playing |

The addition of -ing and -ed (page 52) identifies the occasions on which consonants need to be doubled; the role of -y (page 65) demonstrates the appearance of -ies or -yes endings; 'Riddles in the Past' (page 68) identifies some spelling oddities found amongst commonly used verbs; and 'An Odd-Bod Gathering' (page 114) collects verbs whose irregular conjugation can cause grammatical errors.

Integrating spellings alongside other learning may span a number of lessons.

Example of detailed teaching record: (see index to locate different activities)

spelling	study and memory aids	introduced (date)	applied / assessment (date)
<u>sitting</u> <u>running</u> <u>hopping</u> *ERRORS:* <u>siting</u> <u>runing</u> <u>hoping</u>	Explore the role of vowels and the 'rules of -ing' (see chapter 3). By understanding the role of the doubled consonant, spelling choices can be supported by knowledge.	*01/10/13 – verbs and their common spelling patterns.* *Played Nightmare Spellings adapted to practise the three rules of -ing and -ed.*	*'Three-in-a-row' game; use of dictations; appearance of spellings within mainstream writing during forthcoming term.*
<u>caught</u> *ERRORS:* cawt cort	I <u>c</u>a<u>ugh</u>t an <u>u</u>gly <u>g</u>rey <u>h</u>erring <u>t</u>oday.	*08/10/13 (Played Dicey Spellings)* *Stepping Out game 10/10/13 (correct) 17/10/13 (correct)*	*He caught a cold (24/10/13) They were caught in a trap (07/11/13)*
<u>going</u> <u>gone</u> *ERRORS:* gowing gon	yo yo so so Jo Jo **go go** **go-ing, go-ing** gone **go n**ow **E**mma and then you'll be <u>gone</u>!	*08/10/13 (Played Dicey Spellings)* *Stepping Out game 10/10/13 (gowing) 17/10/13 (correct)*	*We are going to be late. (24/10/13) They were going to the beach when ... (07/11/13)*
<u>know</u> <u>knew</u> *ERRORS:* *no* *new, nuw* *(When an error has become an established habit, it can be harder to overrule it.)*	Did you <u>know</u> that **k-now** (pronounced ker-now) helps you **k-now** (pronounced ker-no) the right spelling? I k-new a k-night who k-nitted k-nickers full of k-nots! Drew picture of knight wearing knitted knickers full of knots.	*08/10/13 (Played Dicey Spellings)* *Stepping Out game 10/10/13 (knew / new) 17/10/13 (knew / new)* *All k- spellings correct except for 'knew' so devised additional prompt: I **k**new OLD (not new) **K**ing Cole stole the painting.*	*How do you know I knew how to swim? (24/10/13)* *By knowing the secret code I could ... (07/11/13)* *He knew the way to ... (24/10/13)* *The pirate knew a good hiding place. (07/11/13)*

Revisit and rehearse the use of these spellings over time to establish secure memory storage and recall. Adjust spelling prompts if they are needed.

GAME-PLAY provides engaging, repetitive and flexible application which is ideal for developing, storing and recollecting spelling memories. For those learners whose memories require additional practice, game-play can be used to rehearse lessons and links by revisiting topics over a period of time. Select and pace inputs to provide a mix of familiarity and challenge.

When players have become competent in their game-play (encourage the discovery and use of tactics), new vocabulary and spellings can be added.

For example, once the rules and riddles of suffixing has been explored, verbs can be used to play 'Three in a Row' spellings (page 44). Designate one of the word-groups as 'verbs' and then the relevant information is provided to the player when they land on that colour.

Alternatively, devise your own game. For example:

Viewing and Visiting Verbs

Having created a playing board, one pile of cards displays a selection of base words and another pile indicating the modification required (such as 'Yesterday they ....' 'Tomorrow, it ....' 'Today they are ....') which is read out to the player at the start of their go.

Players write down the conjugated verb, and speak a completed sentence, then move their playing piece according to the number of syllables in the word they have written down.

For example: 'en-joy-ed' (3); 'ex-plor-ing' (3); 'flies' (1); 'fit-ted' (2)

Syllables can be described as units within a word. Each unit contains one vowel-sound. See also page 84.

By designing a game in which players benefit from handling long words, players soon welcome the arrival of longer spelling strings.

For those who struggle with penmanship and detailed written compositions, a game often offers a welcome alternative route into learning. By reducing the load on working memory, spelling details and discoveries can be recorded.

Planning activities in advance promotes an organised, structured approach – it allows time to devise memory prompts and create activities which introduce and rehearse new topics clearly.

PRESENTATION METHODS will vary according to the topic in hand, but they should be influenced by a number of factors:

- It has been shown that if a <u>word's meaning</u> is not clearly understood, its spelling-memory is weakened. Therefore, the meaning(s) of words must be constantly referred to and applied.

- Encourage <u>ownership of learning</u> through the use of Spelling Detective activities, discussions and explorations; the inclusion of personally-relevant and interesting words; and the active application of learning through game-play. Whilst an over-zealous attention to spelling can impede compositional skills (keep spelling lessons out of creative writing tasks) the appearance of accurate spellings should be acknowledged and praised.

- Develop <u>a proactive questioning approach</u> to spellings:

  ? What is each letter doing within a word

  ? How is each letter contributing towards the word's sound and/or meaning

  ? Does the word display any distinctive visual features

  ? Where might someone make a spelling mistake

  ? Why might they make that mistake

  ? Is a memory-prompt needed to avoid the mistake

  ? If so, what would make a good memory aid

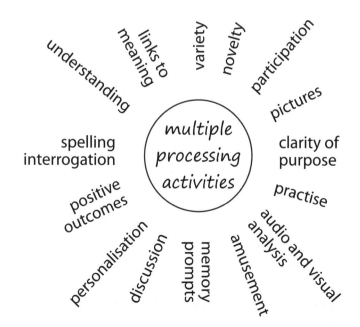

By engaging multiple-processing activities, different areas of the brain are being stimulated at a number of different levels.

Pace activities so that the brain is not over-loaded with too much activity at one time, but attempt to trigger a variety of responses to engage a variety of learning pathways.

IDENTIFY and MONITOR needs and progression to ensure that materials are covered in a manner which supports the needs of the learner(s).

- Collect individual spelling errors to detect personal areas of need. For example, do spelling errors follow any particular pattern?
- Consider different learning profiles. By using observation and feedback, spelling tutors should be able to build up a picture of skills relevant to each learner. By noting areas which display difficulty and ease / weaknesses and strengths / interest and boredom, spelling tutors can fashion effective teaching materials.
- Keeping track of inputs allows progress to be monitored. This is vital if there is any area causing particular concern as any specific learning weaknesses must be identified before the impact of failure, frustration and stress is allowed to further exasperate a situation. There will never be one approach to learning which will suit every individual, so by noting what levels of success are achieved when using different methods and materials, learning support and differentiation can be effectively employed.

If a learner finds it difficult to recall a visual memory of a word's spelling (e.g. struggles to spell a short word aloud backwards – shuts their eyes tightly in an attempt to access visual memory – makes visual rather than audio errors) then investigate the effectiveness of using coloured letters / turning letters into cartoon people, animals and things / writing in the air / attaching spelling to a visually-based memory link to enhance the visual input.	If a learner finds it difficult to identify sounds within words (e.g. misses out key letters – finds background noise distracting – can identify the elements of a word, but cannot string them together – makes audio rather than visual errors) then investigate the effectiveness of removing background distractions / clapping out spelling segments to add additional input / using a sound-based memory link to enhance the audio input.	Discuss the successes and failures of different learning activities with learners to gain feedback.
 The fly was a nuisance at the dance. (nu not new).	No umbrella is a nuisance cried ellen. n u i s a n c e o m b u r l r i i l e i s e e l a d n l n c a e	

SPECIFIC AREAS OF NEED can often be identified by collecting written samples and searching for patterns of accuracy and error.

For example, errors such as 'important/importurnt' could suggest that the learner is using (good) audio-processing skills in an attempt to match each sound within the word with corresponding letters. The visual memory links are missing. Similar errors could include:

'disappointed/diserpointid', 'caught/cort' and 'ambulance/ambulunse'

Alternatively, the pattern of spelling error might reveal a learner's attempt to match spellings to a visual memory of the word. For example:

'measure/meesure', 'particle/partoile', 'fury/furry', 'kung/king' and 'world/wold'

There might be a specific area of processing difficulty which is hampering the effective integration of multiple neurological elements and leading to these spelling errors. For example, visual memory weaknesses can result in an over-reliance on the audio elements within words thus perfecting the experience and habitual preference of audio over visual cues. Audio-processing difficulties can lead learners to rely more on visual-memory clues. Some individuals will have more than one area of processing weakness.

Persistent spelling confusion and errors can then precipitate further anxiety and mistakes along with the repetition of errors developing erroneous habits.

Beware of attributing conclusions on minimal evidence, and discriminate between established errors (habits) and other performance errors.

Areas of strength are also important features to consider when building up an individual learning profile, and the recognition that we all learn in different ways rather than expect everyone to conform to one model of learning. Remember too that a spelling 'difficulty' is not an impossibility. It just means more effort and strategies may be needed to access the road to success.

These considerations highlight the complexity of spelling achievement. Proficient spellers are often unaware of the pitfalls and catastrophes which lurk to irritate and intimidate those in need of savvy spelling support. This can reduce their empathy and lead to attitudes which further hamper amelioration.

Novice learners need the capacity to understand how words are coded into symbolic representations and for that they need to be familiar with the meanings and phonemes of speech. Young learners need time to explore and discover the conventions of letters and sounds, which is a gradual process and, especially with English, not one that should be harnessed to institutionalised time-lines and targets. However, monitor individual progress carefully to avoid a need to wait for abject failure to trigger support.

A MULTIPLE-PROCESSING APPROACH greatly enhances the value and effectiveness of teaching and learning strategies.

Try and ensure that spellings are processed from each of the four angles outlined below, noting any particular difficulties (or strengths) when using different processing channels. Attend to areas of need.

visual (sight)	Explore the shape of letters and words; add colour to emphasise key letters; turn letters into things to fire more neurons e.g. thumb eye bridge sight rowed
audio (sound)	Investigate and practise sound-to-letter rules and riddles; use a 'spelling voice' to highlight oddities e.g. 'knee' could be said "k-nee"; break words into smaller chunks of sound e.g. im-port-ant, dis-a-ppoint-ed, am-bu-lance, man-age; integrate sound with visual links and cues to help the brain recognise where variations and possibilities appear.
kinaesthetic (muscular movement)	Speak, read and write words (exercises muscles of mouth, eyes and hand); write with closed eyes to heighten effort; write in different sized letters (uses large and small muscle movements); typing practice inputs spelling patterns too.
semantic (understanding)	Discover the meaning of root words, suffixes, prefixes and punctuation; explore historical journeys undertaken by words and their spellings; use pictures to link words to meaning which also then trigger spelling-memory prompts at the time the word is being written to express meaning.

APPLICATION of lesson material is vital to develop and consolidate memory pathways. Along with mainstream application, short written activities are often needed which integrate specific spelling vocabularies with focused challenges which apply, consolidate and reward successful outcomes.

- Write a newspaper report of a zoo's latest arrival. Award points for the use of specified spelling patterns (e.g. verb, vowel digraph, plurals, 'soft c', etc.) *Provide a scoring system for up to three different features.*

- Draw one picture displaying a dramatic event in a story line. Surround story with four 'dynamic' words chosen by the learner which are then put through Dicey Spellings if memory-prompts are needed. *Provide a scoring system for those key words when they appear in the subsequent description of the picture.*

A STRUCTURED FORMAT	
Topic introduction	Present an opportunity to introduce a new spelling topic in an easy, relaxed and accessible manner.
Recap previous learning	Memory rehearsal is very necessary to help with the development of strong memory pathways. Recap spelling rules, riddles and memory strategies covered over recent days/weeks.
Return to topic introduced at onset of spelling lesson	The brain has had a period of distraction (the recap of previous learning). This means that revisiting the initial topic is recalling information the brain was recently attending to. The brain is now more receptive to new learning having had a time in which to subconsciously process (prime) and prepare for the new topic.
Employ a Spelling Detective approach so that learners can explore, question and investigate the spelling patterns before them.	By setting up opportunities for learners to uncover and discover lessons, they are far more stimulated and engaged with the topic before them. Beware of overloading some learners with additional demands (reading, writing, word meaning etc) which may result in them lacking the capacity to engage in the focus of the spelling lessons.
Facilitate learner's ownership to enhance relevance and engagement.	Drawing own pictures; creating their own playing boards; linking spellings and topics to areas of interest and need, all help to make learning relevant to individual learners, even if they are working in a group.
Enhance new memory pathways by linking new learning to existing memories. Add memory triggers to enhance storage and recall.	A new memory pathway can be likened to a pathway through a forest – too many brambles, fallen trees and indistinct pathways, and it is easy to get lost. However, remove some of the barriers (reduce working memory overload, anxiety, failure and frustration), and provide some lanterns to spotlight the way, and the pathway soon becomes familiar, easy to follow and available for revisiting and extending in the future.
Record areas of study and revisit over time.	Record-keeping is vital. Progress measures need to be appraised alongside the nature and style of inputs. If there are any specific learning difficulties, assessment of need can be informed by noting responses to different learning materials and tactics over time.

LAYERS OF LEARNING build up to stimulate interest, confidence, familiarity and understanding. The processes required to lay down effective and retrievable spelling memories involves the stimulation of a number of neurological pathways. Not only must the brain establish accurate connections between the sound, meaning, shape and organisation of letters within a spelling, but it must also retrieve and restructure this information with confidence, accuracy and speed when it is required to do so.

As noted before, individuals build spelling pathways with varying degrees of efficiency and speed. For some, background distractions, anxieties and confusions reduce their ability to process new material. Others find it is their memory-retrieval pathways which lack fluidity. The presence of specific learning difficulties / differences is likely to increase the incidence of working-memory overload when processing the coded patterns of spelling, and, for everyone, a lack of opportunity to explore, discover, practise, and develop their spelling vocabularies hampers the growth of achievement and skills.

Spelling tutors must decide which topics of learning to use. Each will adopt different approaches and will greatly benefit from exploring a variety of materials which, as they become further enlightened through the use of reflective responses, acquire the personal, flexible and tailor-made quality necessary to suit different learning and learner needs.

When planning a new topic it can be useful to consider:

- How will this topic be introduced in an accessible and non-challenging way? How will it be linked to existing knowledge? How will the topic be useful, interesting, empowering to the learner?

- What activity could be used to explore the nature of the spelling topic or pattern to allow investigation, discovery and discussion using sample materials? Are their opportunities for confirming past learning as well as stimulating divergent thinking skills? Provide time to support learning needs (e.g. use of memory aids and strategies).

- Having discussed findings, what activity could provide the experience of application (often driven by a competitive element to stimulate engagement, cognitive stimulation and repetition)?

- Return to topic after a brief distraction and recall key elements (either directly or through the application of an activity). Assess areas which require further focus. Reward positive outcomes.

- Consolidate memory pathways through useful / rewarding / varied application in the near future. Revisit, rehearse and reiterate.

- Build on learning by providing extension activities, but beware of progressing too quickly before key topics are understood.

Rewarding Outcomes promote interest and attention. Success breeds success as surely as failure breeds failure. For the individual, this goes beyond the ability to master spelling confidence and skills, it involves knowledge, enquiry, discovery and enlightenment. Use challenges to develop skills which go beyond the spelling test. Provide learners with more interesting ways of exploring and demonstrating their learning. For example:

Spelling Riddles – Accurate or Accidental?

The following words all contain a double 'c'. Having read them through and discussed their meaning and spelling, use the following questions to prompt some ideas as to the role of double 'c' in different spellings:

What is the role of the double 'c' in these spellings?

How might these words cause spelling problems?

Do you know (or can you guess) why the 'cc' rule is not regular?

success	occupied	accurate	accuse
accident	accommodation	moccasin	accept
account	occur	occasion	accelerate

Check your answers on page 152.

The result of this sort of challenge may inform, or assess or apply learning, and does so in a way which empowers, informs and rewards application.

Think Outside the Book to develop further understanding and awareness of features surrounding different English spellings. There are many topics which have not been explicitly covered in these pages, but the principles surrounding engagement, memory and reward apply to whatever additional inputs are required.

Listen to Learner(s) to discover how they view or hear different words. Encourage their feedback and reflection on learning activities, discussions and challenges. What aspects of a memory input has the most engaging effect? Which words would they like to spell correctly with confidence? Also promote shared investigations, problem-solving and the setting of goals to kindle an interest in skills which fuel independence.

TEACHING RECORD name ..G.F.. dob .17./07./04. age .9y. 4m. page .8.

sample lesson plan and record sheet

date / time / location	topic aims and objectives	resources	activity	performance / outcomes	any other comments
07/11/13 11:30–12:15 (10 mins)	The Troublesome -le ending (see page 62) (errors: midil / litul / carsul / buberl) Introduce topic and reason for study.	cards displaying pictures and words ending in -le: kettle, apple, circle, little mouse, puddle, Middle Ages, castle (link to history topic)	Ask M. to name pictures then match them to words. (Support as required) Explore spellings – note letter-to-sound patterns – 'where might spelling trip somebody up?'	_Ticks provide encouragement._ Useful discussion about -le sound – Old English spelling of 'middle' (middel) explaining 'dd'. Added 'giggle' / 'fiddle'.	As this is a visually-based activity, employ listening-based skills to identify -le spellings in future lesson.
(10 mins)	Recap: 'Visiting and viewing are verbs' (-ed not -t / -ing / Odd Bods) Develop confidence in use of prompts and rules.	Exercise book. Activity pictures for labelling e.g. 'Sitting on a horse.'	Write words – G. can add own ideas too. Recap spelling-memory prompts, penmanship and other past spellings.	sitting taking caught going dropped knew walked know said called	To do: 'All' (**all** alligators <u>like</u> <u>legs</u>) – picture, plus 'all' words into a storyline.
To avoid writing an X in presence of learner, when 'called' is spelled 'corlled' the tick is used to cross 'a' and G. is praised for '-ed' ending.					
(10 mins)	Boost self-actuality (ability to achieve success).	Progress Parade cards – page 130.	G. briefly describes a summary of past topics.	post-code mnemonic d.o.b.. 'what' [+ more]	Useful recap of this term's work.
This activity employs spoken delivery to recap (and assess) progress – rehearses terminology and topics – note strengths / weaknesses					
(10 mins)	Apply -le spellings. (Plus '**castle** attackers <u>spear</u> <u>turret</u>' to avoid 'carsul')	'Collecting Valuable Spellings' page 64. Paper to list words.	Play game with M. Take game home to repeat for home-activity.	Enjoyed game. Useful practise in writing 'le' as cursive script.	Explore -able suffix (link to -ing-eats-e rule)
(5 mins)	Draw 'castle' prompt. Add to this week's spellings list	Spelling-record book. Dicey Spellings game.	M. collects pictures and prompts in exercise book.	Good castle picture – speak / write prompt.	Revisit prompt next lesson.

KEEPING RECORDS enables learners and their spelling tutors to track, revisit and extend their studies. In addition, the following two display-methods provide examples of how to present <u>an over-view of spelling topics</u> to monitor achievement and progress.

A Progress Parade

Summarise a spelling topic and then display it on a card to capture the strategy and spellings which have been covered.

As well as building up a picture of achievement, these cards provide a quick means of revising topics (and provide accessible prompts when required).

Place the cards in a prominent position to celebrate progress, and champion the addition of new cards to the Progress Parade as new topics are covered.

Tracking Spelling Topics

The following 'Key Spelling Component' list provides a variety of spelling patterns designed to demonstrate many of the features found within English spellings. Some (such as -tch/ch spelling pattern) exemplify how a knowledge of rules can inform spelling, whilst others (such as 'ou/ow' spellings) familiarise the speller with the lack of easy reasoning to decide between patterns, and the benefit of spelling-family stories and similar memory-enhancing techniques to aid storage and recall.

Many high-frequency words display irregular spelling patterns. These offer opportunities to employ multiple-processing activities (such as the use of Dicey Spelling study techniques boosted by consolidating game-play), to establish secure memory pathways.

Choose topics relevant to your learner(s).

Key Spelling Components

This list is not designed to be undertaken in sequential order although 'the role of vowels' is a very useful topic to begin with. Additional elements (such as 'sh/ch/th') may need to be added, along with other topics included following a review of spelling errors – adapt list to suit individual needs. Use this outline to create your own list, against which study topics can be noted.

<u>The role of vowels:</u> (An introduction to vowels which is extended later on.)

Topic includes 'short' vowel sounds (e.g. 'c<u>a</u>t'); the role of double consonants (e.g. 'b<u>u</u>tter'); suffixing rules (e.g. 'h<u>o</u>pping'); and the influence of short vowels on patterns such as '-<u>ck</u>' and '-tch'.

'Long' vowels sounds can be made with a vowel digraph (e.g. 'tr<u>ai</u>n', 'tr<u>ay</u>', 'st<u>ea</u>m', 'b<u>ee</u>n', 'b<u>oa</u>t', 'h<u>ue</u>') or a split vowel digraph (e.g. 'b<u>a</u>k<u>e</u>', 'b<u>a</u>b<u>y</u>', 'sm<u>i</u>l<u>i</u>ng', 'm<u>o</u>l<u>e</u>'). There are many variations.

<u>Useful spelling patterns:</u> (Make space on this list to add dates when topics studied.)

-ck / -k		-ck / -k / -c	
-tch / -ch		-dge	
'hard g'		'soft g'	
'hard c'		'soft c'	
-le endings		y > i	
prefixes		suffixes	
ite		ight	
-s plurals		-es plurals	
ir / er / ur		contractions	
ou / ow		-tion / -sion	
kn / gn / wr		other silent letters	
ough		i before e for /ee/	
ar / er / ir / or / ur		ear / air / are	

<u>Useful spelling riddles:</u> (Record which sample spellings have been used.)

schwa sound e.g. 'a<u>s</u>leep', 'matt<u>er</u>'		'ea' e.g. 'h<u>ea</u>d' or 's<u>ea</u>'	
single consonant (e.g. 'ha<u>b</u>it')		-or endings e.g. 'doctor'	
rhyming choices (e.g. 'claws' / 'pause')		useless 'e' e.g. 'store'	
more silent letters (e.g. 'lam<u>b</u>', 's<u>w</u>ord')		-ible / -able	
vowel variations (e.g. 'or', 'aw', 'au')		The use of 'r' in different spellings	
more similar sounds e.g. 'sure', 'shore'		American spellings e.g. 'traveler', 'meter'	
high-frequency errors		use of 'spelling voice'	

<u>Other topics:</u>

syllabification of words	homophones
morphemes	phonemes
Change in spoken sound of words over time	historical diversity of spelling patterns

<u>Individual spellings:</u>

<u>Top 200 high frequency words:</u> (add school-curriculum vocabulary)
<u>Dictionary of personal spellings:</u> such as family's names, pets, addresses and post codes, local topics, hobbies and interests, sports teams/players, role models, popular culture etc. (An address book can often be used to create a handy personal dictionary)
<u>Selection of 'interesting words' chosen by the learner:</u> Include in spelling study lessons.

<u>Strategies to enhance the strength and stability of spelling memories:</u>

Spelling-memory prompts linked to word meaning.	Spelling-family story-links matching letter-patterns and pictures.	Memory-enhancing activities (e.g. game-play, fun, repetition).	Recognise and apply the use of alternative routes into learning.
Investigation, discovery, repetition, reward, rehearsal.	Recognise choice of reasons behind many spelling errors.	Recognise impact of English history and ongoing change.	Use of spell-checkers etc. to back-up grasp of key spelling topics.

Create personalised list then use as a check-list to monitor events.

Final Words

The purpose of this book is not just to provide a wide variety of materials and ideas to support the development of spelling confidence and skills, but also to offer a range of stimulating ideas and thought-provoking activities which have the potential to support all areas of learning. It presents materials which place discovery-learning at the centre of teaching and demonstrates how important it is to involve the learner with decisions and choices; personalisation and ownership; proactive activities and practical engagement.

This book is also intended to bring fun into learning. It aims to provoke amusement, interest and understanding in a topic which has the potential to cause so much frustration and despair. By empowering learners with an insight into the nature of the beast, they are hopefully inspired to study ways of reducing its power of confusion and bemusement. They may not conquer every spelling, but will have a range of strategies to use in their attempt to capture the spoken word and pin it down into print.

English spellings are, by nature, full of diversity and historical complexities. Proficiency grows with experience and use, yet the time we spend on writing (especially by hand) is rapidly decreasing alongside the growth of digital aids and applications. There are choices to be made concerning the preservation of tradition (such as excluding American and text-speak spellings from the classroom) and embracing the extension of language offered by the indomitable nature of English to absorb, boost, invent and adapt the use of words, meanings and expression.

English is not new to these discussions. But for as long as we use English as a standard method of composing and communicating ideas and information, we must ensure that learners are given the time and opportunity to become familiar and adept at spelling the key components of its written code.

I am very grateful to everyone who has contributed towards the creating of this book. This includes students, colleagues, family and friends who have encouraged, supported, inspired and tested me over the years. Thank you.

Chapter Eight:
Answers to Literacy Challenges

A variety of literacy challenges appear throughout this book to challenge, entertain, question and explore different features of English spellings. Answers have been listed according to the location of the activities.

Introduction: page 7

A Sample of Spelling Rules and Riddles Identifying how words differ in spelling and sound (pronunciation).
bead   head (a) Difference in spelling: 'b' and 'h' (b) Difference in sound: "b/h" and 'bead' rhymes with 'need' but 'head' rhymes with 'bed' (see page 102: 'Feathers and Beads')
curtain   certain (a) Difference in spelling: 'u' and 'e' (b) Difference in sound: 'cur' sounds like 'ker' but 'cer' sounds like 'sir' (see page 59: 'Hard and soft C')
whole   hole (a) Difference in spelling: 'w' in the first, but not second, spelling. (b) Difference in sound: no difference in sound. (see page 42: 'Homophone Matches')
gem   gum (a) Difference in spelling: 'e' and 'u' (b) Difference in sound: 'gem' starts with a 'j' sound but 'gum' starts with a hard 'g' sound. (see page 59: 'Hard and soft G')
hoping   hopping (a) Difference in spelling: single 'p' and double 'p' (b) Difference in sound: long vowel-sound in 'hoping' and short vowel-sound in 'hopping'. (see page 49: 'The role of vowels')
tripped   trimmed (a) Difference in spelling: double 'p' and double 'm' (b) Difference in sound: "-ippt" and "-immd" (see page 101: 'Misleading Ed')

Chapter three (spelling rules): page 51

Vowels in Action

Having highlighted underlined words in two different colours of highlighter pen to distinguish between 'short' and 'long' vowel sounds, the question was:

Do the vowel sounds in the highlighted words, match common spelling rules?

Answer: Most of them do, but there are a some exceptions.

The passage reads:

Ruby Rabbit was in the habit of hopping into Peter's garden for a tasty feast. She would nibble away at lettuce leaves, carrot tops and raspberries. But last Tuesday, she bit into a chilli. Wow! The taste was hot! Quickly, Ruby headed for a puddle of water, running as fast as her legs could take her. She licked up every drop of the rainwater to wash away the stinging taste of chilli. It took a while to recover, but Ruby had learnt her lesson. Chillies are not for bunnies!

Highlight short vowels sounds in yellow, and long vowels sounds in blue.

short vowel sounds (e.g. căt)

rabbit – Yes – ă protected from the influence of the 'i' by two 'b's.

habit – No – the lack of two letters keeping the 'a' and 'i' apart means this word *should* be pronounced 'haybit'. It is suggested that the word arrived in English during the 14th century from Old French. A lot of French words were derived from Latin which did not use the double consonant pattern to keep vowels apart (but often instead used a mark called an apex above a vowel if its sound was long). See also page 100 for other single-consonant riddles.

hopping – Yes – ŏ is protected by the influence of the 'i' by two 'p's. 'Hop' therefore requires an extra 'p' when -ing is added.

nibble – Yes – ĭ is protected from the influence of the 'e' by two 'b's and an 'l'. 'Nible' would make the same sound as 'nibble' but the double 'b' has become an historical habit left over from the days when words such as 'middle' were spelled 'middel' before the 'troublesome -le' (page 62) arrived.

lettuce – Yes – ĕ is protected from the 'u' by the two 't's.

carrot – Yes – ă is protected from the 'o' by the two 'r's.

raspberries – Depends on how word is pronounced. If 'răsp-' (short vowel sound) the spelling rules are being followed, but if pronounced 'rarsp-', an 'r' appears to be missing. (When familiar with basic rules, move on to page 107: vowel sound variations.)

chilli – Yes – ĭ is protected from the second 'i' by two 'l's.

headed – No – There is an ĕ sound in 'head' which should, according to the appearance of two vowels, be pronounced 'heed'. See also page 102 for other 'ea' riddles.

puddle – Yes – ŭ is protected from the 'e' by two 'd's and an 'l'. 'Pudled' would make the same sound as 'puddled' as in both cases, the 'u' and 'e' are separated by two, or more, consonants.

running – Yes – ŭ is protected from the 'i' by two 'n's. 'Run' therefore has an extra 'n' included in its spelling when -ing is added.

licked – Yes – ĭ is protected from the influence of the 'e' by two consonants: 'c' and 'k'.

stinging – Yes – ĭ is protected from the influence of the second 'i' by two consonants: 'n' and 'g'.

lesson – Yes – ĕ is protected from the 'o' by the two 's's.

bunnies – Yes – ŭ is protected from the 'i' by two 'n's.

---

long vowel sounds (e.g. 'wēek')

Ruby – Yes – The 'y' is acting as a vowel and making the 'u' into its long vowel sound. Compare 'Ruby' with 'rub' to see the effect of the 'y'.

Peter's – Yes – ē is created by the action of the two 'e's. The word 'pet' becomes 'Peter' when the -er is added as the single letter 't' is not enough to stop the vowels affecting each other. Comparing the spelling of 'Peter' with the spelling of 'letter' also highlights the impact of double 't'.

tasty – No – As the 'a' is protected from the 'y' by two letters ('s' and 't') this spelling should mean that the word 'tasty' rhymes with 'pasty' (as in Cornish păsty). It is possible that 'tasty' ('taysty') was pronounced tăsty in Old English, but its pronunciation has changed over the years.

feast – Yes – When two vowels are found together, they usually make one sound: the first vowel speaks its name. The spelling 'feest' would also make the sound of the word 'feast'.

leaves – Yes – When two vowels are found together, they usually make one sound: the first vowel speaks its name. 'Leavs' would make the same sound, but the rule is to replace the -f of 'leaf' for '-ves' when making it into its plural form.

Tuesday – Depends on how the word is pronounced. If the 't' is clearly expressed before the mouth starts forming the 'u' (t-you-s-day) then yes, when two vowels are found together, they usually make one sound: the first vowel speaks its name. However, if the word is pronounced 'choose-day' (as it often is), we have a different vowel-sound to consider. The spelling of 'day' matches the rules with 'y' acting as a vowel to lengthen 'ă' into 'a'. Note how words such as 'tune' and 'tulip' are often spoken with a 'ch' in place of 't' – this has become a recognised speech pattern in recent years.

taste – No – (see also 'tasty' above). According to spelling rules, 'taste', 'paste', 'waste' and 'haste' should all contain a 'short vowel sound' (tăste) as the consonants 's' and 't' are between the 'a' and the 'e' and so stopping them from affecting each other.

take – Yes – Two vowels have one letter standing between them. This is not enough to stop the 'e' influencing the sound of the 'a'.

rainwater – Yes (rain) – When two vowels are found together, as in 'rain' they usually make one sound: the first vowel speaks its name. No (water) – in the case of 'water' the word should be pronounced 'waiter' but has adopted a 'warter' pronunciation over time.

Chapter three: (spelling rules): page 52

Spelling Rules of -ing and -ed

After (a) using words in spoken sentences to demonstrate their understanding of meaning learners were asked to (b) add -ing to the words and create some new sentences.

For (c), the question was: 'How might the words be spelled if the suffix -ed was added to each word instead of -ing?'

This highlights the identical pattern of spelling rules found when -ing and -ed suffixes are added onto root words, namely that the final consonant needs to be doubled if there is a short vowel sound to protect from the influence of the 'i' of -ing or 'e' of -ed; that -ed also 'eats the e' (as, strictly speaking, the final 'e' is removed before the -ed suffix is added on); or, if there is no short vowel to protect, or 'e' to eat, the -ed is just added on.

If -r ending words have been included in the activity, then the same rule applies when adding the suffix -ed as when adding -ing: double the final -r.

ADDING -ING:

'dropping' Protect ŏ sound from -ing	'flapping' Protect ă sound from -ing	'inventing' No change to base word	'raving' Replace 'e' with -ing	'teasing' Replace 'e' with -ing
'training' No change to base word	'occurring' Add extra 'r' before -ing	'stirring' Add extra 'r' before -ing	'transferring' Add extra 'r' before -ing	'starring' Add extra 'r' before -ing
'limping' No change to base word	'repeating' No change to base word	'pleasing' Replace 'e' with -ing	'regretting' Protect ĕ sound from -ing	'scarring' Add extra 'r' before -ing

ADDING -ED

'dropped' Double the 'p' to protect short vowel sound (ŏ) from -ed	'flapped' Double the 'p' to protect short vowel sound (ă) from -ed.	'invented' No change to base word before adding -ed.	'raved' The '-ed' replaces the final 'e' in 'rave'.	'teased' The '-ed' replaces the final 'e' in 'tease'.
'trained' No change to base word before adding -ed.	'occurred' Double final 'r' of 'occur' before adding -ed.	'stirred' Double final 'r' of 'stir' before adding -ed.	'transferred' Double final 'r' of 'transfer' before adding -ed.	'starred' Double final 'r' of 'star' before adding -ed.
'limped' No change to base word as 'mp' is protecting short vowel.	'repeated' No change to base word.	'pleased' The '-ed' replaces the final 'e' in 'please'.	'regretted' Double 't' to protect short vowel sound from -ed.	'scarred' Double final 'r' of 'scar' before adding -ed.

Chapter three (spelling rules): page 56

Don't Panic in the Attic

After identifying the rules concerning the spelling of single syllable words containing a short vowel sound followed by -ck (such as 'clock' and 'duck'), it was then noted that words with more than one syllable ended with -ic, not the -ick which one might have expected (such as 'panic' and 'Arctic').

This revealed the rule that the final 'k' is dropped on words of more than one syllable to produce an -ic ending, not -ick.

A number of words containing more than one syllable were then presented. Some words ended with the -ck spelling whilst others displayed the -ic spelling.

The question was: Why might this be?

comic   magic   seasick   frantic   topic   broomstick

automatic   sidekick   drumstick   panic   lipstick   attic

Answer: Although the word 'seasick' contains more than one syllable, it is actually made up of two separate words stuck together. The resulting word is called a **compound noun**.

The words making up the compound nouns follow the same rules which would apply to the words if they were standing alone (e.g. 'sick' and 'kick').

Chapter three (spelling rules): page 57

Take Your Pick

A selection of pictures are provided for labelling with word(s) containing either a 'ck' or 'k' spelling. Below are some examples of words which could have been used.

1. tank.	2. milk, drink.	3. pockets, broke.	4. fireworks, rocket, sparks.
5. snowflake.	6. crackers.	7. rocking horse, rockers.	8. tickets.
9. shark.	10. skeleton.	11. motorbike, forks, spokes.	12. hockey, stick, puck.

Activities such as these allow a particular spelling pattern to be practised.

They can also be used to practise a group of words (such as adjectives, or words containing the 'ea' spelling pattern) which have been studied recently. The application also stimulates the recall and rehearsal of memory prompts attached to spellings which need an extra trigger to avoid mistakes.

Chapter three (spelling rules): page 59

Hard and soft 'g'.

Having investigated information about 'hard and soft g', the following spellings were presented and the question asked: What is going on?

guide, argue, guy, catalogue, tongue, guess.

Answer: The letter 'u' is shielding the letter 'g' from the influence of the letters 'i', 'e' or 'y'.

Without the letter 'u' keeping these letters apart, the letter 'g' would make the sound of 'j' (the 'soft g' sound) instead of the 'hard g' sound which we find in these words.

"I guess u is not useless after all!" might provide a useful spelling prompt, along with a picture of a proud letter 'u' standing by the letter 'g' keeping it away from the letter 'e'.

Sometimes, the role of 'u' is described as acting as a 'guard' letter to act as a memory prompt. Whilst this works well for the spelling of 'guard' and 'guardian', it must be noted that the 'u' is not actually doing any active service in these spellings.

'Gard' would rhyme with 'hard', 'lard' or 'yard' whereas the lack of a 'u' in 'guide' would suggest a pronunciation of a soft 'g' as in 'jingle' and 'giant'.

Not all spellings follow this rule. 'Get' and 'geese' (whose roots originated in Old Norse rather than Latin) are examples of exceptions, but the point of this activity is to raise awareness of the letter 'u' in spellings where it might otherwise be left out.

Chapter three (spelling rules): page 62

A difference between some -le and -el spellings

The shape of the letters which come before the -le spelling pattern in the words below all display either 'sticks' or 'tails' (e.g. 't' or 'g'). The letters which come before the -el spelling pattern lack a 'stick' or a 'tail' (e.g. 'r' or 'n').

This pattern does not always occur, in fact there are a lot of exceptions, but it does draw the mind into the consideration of this possibility, thus engaging the brain in a deeper processing activity than purely scanning the spelling with the eyes.

As it is easy to establish a habit of attaching -ul to the end of many spellings, so having this additional angle to study adds more information to help register the attention that needs to be paid when hearing 'the troublesome -le'.

little	camel
castle	towel
kettle	cancel
wriggle	barrel
puddle	parcel
ripple	funnel

Chapter three (spelling rules): page 63

Adding the suffix of -able

After identifying the meaning of the suffix -able, a selection of words were listed with a request to observe any resulting influences of the morpheme on the base-word's spelling.

renew	renewable	comfort	comfortable
believe	believable	notice	noticeable
recharge	rechargeable	remove	removable
inflate	inflatable	accept	acceptable
collect	collectable	afford	affordable
change	changeable	desire	desirable
excite	excitable	adjust	adjustable

Different spelling patterns appear on the addition of an -able suffix.
Can these differences be explained? Yes. The differences follow the rules of -able:

'-able' is added to the root word's spelling for example: comfort > comfortable

HOWEVER

If the root word ends with an 'e', -able eats the 'e'
(the 'a' of -able takes over the role of the 'e') for example: excite > excitable

UNLESS

The 'e' is needed to make a 'soft c' or a 'soft g' (see page 59)
- the letter 'a' does not make 'c' or 'g' go soft.
for example: recharge > rechargeable; notice > noticeable,
when the 'e' needs to be retained.

It can be very useful to gather spelling rules (with examples of spellings which follow them), once they have been discovered and discussed.

Having a catchy name for a rule can also help it become more memorable and easy to recall.

The 'rechargeable rule' keeps the electricity left on.

This uses 'rechargeable' as an example spelling, and a saying in which the letter 'e' is represented by 'electricity'.

This saying prompts the addition of an 'e' if a soft 'g' or soft 'c' is required.

Apply a Spelling Detective activity to find which other suffixes also follow the 'rechargeable' rule.

Chapter three (spelling rules): page 65

The Pattern of Plurals (of nouns ending -y)

A selection of words demonstrate how some words ending with the letter '-y' adopt an 's' to denote a plural.

singular	plural	singular	plural
one cowboy	two cowboys	one baby	two babies
one day	two days	one story	two stories
one monkey	two monkeys	one lady	two ladies
one guy	two guys	one party	two parties

Other base words ending with the letter '-y' follow the rule:

Change the 'y' to an 'i' then add '-es'.

The question is why are there two different spelling patterns?

Answer:
When 'y' is part of a vowel digraph (-ay, -ey, -oy, -uy), then these pairs of letters remain together, unchanged, when the word is made into a plural. Their plural is made by adding the letter 's': toy > toys, tray > trays, monkey > monkeys.

However, when the letter 'y' is not attached to a vowel, then it follows the rule:

Change the 'y' to an 'i' then add '-es'.

city > cities, ability > abilities, army > armies, spy > spies,
butterfly > butterflies, penny > pennies, puppy > puppies.

Chapter three (spelling rules): page 66

Adding -s to verbs ending with -y

By investigating the addition of the letter -s onto verbs which end with the letter -y, it can be seen that both nouns and verbs share the same rules regarding the choice of ending.

<u>Either</u> add the letter 's' if the base-word ends with a vowel-digraph
(e.g. -ay): 'He <u>stays</u> with his sister.'

<u>Or</u>: Change the 'y' to an 'i' then add '-es':
(e.g. -ry) 'He <u>cries</u> whenever the train goes into a tunnel.'

I play	he plays	I spy	she spies
I buy	she buys	I cry	he cries
I obey	it obeys	I carry	it carries
I betray	it betrays	I reply	it replies

Chapter three (spelling rules): page 67

Adding -ed to base verbs ending with -y

When -ed is added to base verbs which end with the letter 'y', the same rules apply as those relating to -s, which is:

If the base verb ends with the letter 'y' which is part of a vowel digraph (-ay, -ey, -oy or -uy) then the letters '-ed' need to be added:

stray > strayed   employ > employed

But, if the base verb ends with a 'y' which follows a consonant, then:

Change the 'y' to an 'i' then add '-ed':

hurry > hurried   dry > dried   carry > carried

Phrases which include the direction to:

'change the 'y' to an 'i' then add ....'

are useful ones to learn by rote once they have been used a few times to be sure they are clearly understood.

Chapter three (spelling rules): page 67

Adding -ing to base verbs ending with -y

<u>However,</u> when the suffix of '-ing' is added to base verbs ending with the letter 'y' then THERE IS NO CHANGE to the base spelling.

hurry > hurrying   dry > drying   stay > staying   spy > spying

When adding -ing, keep the 'y' in place.

If, in spellings where the letter 'y' followed a consonant, the letter 'y' was changed to the letter 'i' (as happens in the previous activities), then the words would be spelt:

try > triing and cry > criing

We do not find two letter 'i' together in English spellings. ('Skiing' is one exception).

Some scribes spelling words in early Middle English (see page 88) tried out the use of double identical vowels, but 'ee' and 'oo' was the only ones which really survived although we rarely see 'uu' ('vacuum') and 'aa' ('baa').

Chapter three (spelling rules): page 69

Harriet the Hedgehog (picking up suffixes)

Harriet the Hedgehog loves strawberries ...

By investigating the combination of root words and their suffixes in Harriet's tale, the opportunity arises to explore, revise and consolidate the topic of suffixes.

All the underlined words have base words ending in -y to which suffixes have been attached. This activity is designed to consolidate previous lessons by presenting a range of suffixes which impact on spellings in different ways.

After reading the passage, verbal discussions can be used to discuss the spelling events within the underlined words. Repeat using a short piece of written text selected from a mainstream source to demonstrate the passage has not been 'carefully manipulated.'

strawberries	Strawberry + -es Change the 'y' to an 'i' then add '-es'.
fruitiness	Fruity + ness (relating to the state of being fruity) Change the 'y' to an 'i' then add '-ness'
holiday	In olden times, holy days were days when workers could go to church and worship. The word has changed to become 'holiday', meaning time not at work.
families	Family + -es Change the 'y' to and 'i' then add '-es'. (Note the two 'i's in 'families' ... draw a picture of family members representing the letter 'i's to highlight this feature.)
beautiful	Beauty + ful (full of beauty ... 'full' loses its second 'l'). Change the 'y' to an 'i' then add '-ful'.
merrily	Merry + ly Change the 'y' to an 'i' then add '-ly'.
bellies	Belly + es Change the 'y' to an 'i' then add '-es'.
enjoys	Enjoy + s No change to the 'y' because it forms the vowel digraph 'oy'.
spying	Spy + ing No change to the 'y' because it is followed by -ing. No English words (apart from 'skiing') contain double 'i'.
activities	Activity + es Change the 'y' to an 'i' then add '-es'.
envies	Envy + es Change the 'y' to an 'i' then add '-es'.
babies	Baby + es Change the 'y' to an 'i' then add '-es'.

worriedly	Worry + ed + ly Change the 'y' to an 'i' then add '-ed' (and then '-ly').
playful	Play + ful No change to the 'y' because it is linked to 'ay'.
friendliness	Friendly + ness (relating to the state of being friendly) Change the 'y' to an 'i' then add '-ness'.
berriful	Berry + ful (Full of berry) This word doesn't appear in the dictionary. It has been made up, but it makes sense because it follows a familiar pattern. This flexibility of the English language shows how new words can be created according to need. Can you apply this to a word of your own invention?
spies	Spy + es Change the 'y' to an 'i' then add '-es'.
scurries	Scurry + es (To scamper, to scramble, with haste.) Change the 'y' to an 'i' then add '-es'.
clumsily	Clumsy + ly Change the 'y' to an 'i' then add '-ly'.
hurriedly	Hurry + ed + ly Change the 'y' to an 'i' then add '-ed' (and then '-ly').
greedily	Greedy + ly Change the 'y' to an 'i' then add '-ly'.
business	Busy + ness (Relating to the state of being busy). Change the 'y' to an 'i' then add '-es'.
goodies	Goody + es (An informal term for something attractive and tasty, especially sweets, cakes etc.) Change the 'y' to an 'i' then add '-es'.

What's the Point? (a motivational game)

To highlight the very useful rules associated with the addition of suffixes, learners can be challenged to play games such as Suffering Suffixes (page 71) where different key words are used in different games.

It can also be useful to use a points system for the use of suffixes within a mainstream piece of writing. For example:

one point	two points	three points	
-s -er -ly	-ed -age -ful -ness -less	-able -ible -es (plural)	Add more suffixes as they occur and explore their meaning.

Chapter three (spelling rules): page 70

Suffixing Plurals (-s or -es endings?)

By presenting a number of plural nouns in sentences, then setting the challenge of determining the construction details of each word, the level of knowledge (and deduction) can be assessed. This allows future lessons to target specific topics.

PLURAL	SINGULAR	-s or -es?
The <u>cows</u> are in the milking shed.	cow	-s
Both the <u>babies</u> are crying.	baby	y/i + -es
They have finished building six <u>houses</u>.	house	-s
The sky is filled with little white <u>clouds</u>.	cloud	-s
All her <u>dresses</u> need ironing.	dress	-es
I don't like <u>tomatoes</u>.	tomato	-es
I need some new coloured <u>pencils</u>.	pencil	-s
<u>Knives</u> and forks are in the top drawer.	knife	fe/v + -es
There are no <u>buses</u> running today.	bus	-es
The tree has lost all of its <u>leaves</u>.	leaf	f/v + -es
Seaweed is collected from the <u>beaches</u>.	beach	-es
Henry VIII had six <u>wives</u>.	wife	fe/v + -es
Please could you wash up the <u>dishes</u>?	dish	-es

Therefore, we can see that the root word endings which use the suffix -es to create a plural, include:

words ending -sh eg 'wi<u>sh</u>' > 'wishes'	words ending -ch eg 'coa<u>ch</u>' > 'coaches'	words ending -fe eg 'li<u>fe</u>' > 'lives' (change -fe to -v then add -es)
words ending – s eg 'bu<u>s</u>' > 'buses'	**-es endings**	words ending -f eg 'loa<u>f</u>' > 'loaves' (change -f to -v then add -es)
words ending -ss eg 'cla<u>ss</u>' > 'classes'	words ending -y eg 'fair<u>y</u>' > 'fairies' (change -y to -i then add -es)	words ending -o eg 'potat<u>o</u>' > 'potatoes'

Learning all these endings can be very difficult.

Therefore, having completed this activity which draws attention to the use of -s for some plurals and -es for others, the best way of learning these spellings is to use them. Use them in games. Award points for correct usage in mainstream writing. Create memory prompts for specific words if required.

Chapter four (creativity and ownership): page 79

Talking About Spellings

The four sentences should be:

1. I wouldn't like to <u>walk</u> ... to school in bare feet.
2. A flower is usually found ... at the top of a <u>stalk</u>.
3. The picture drawn with <u>chalk</u> ... got washed away in the rain.
4. Can you <u>talk</u> ... without moving your lips?

The underlined words all share an -alk spelling pattern.

These -alk letters usually sound like 'ork' (but different accents may change the sound of the 'al' pattern).

Chapter four (creativity and ownership): page 84

What is a Syllable?

It can also be useful to define a syllable in a more precise way using the incidence of vowel-sounds within a word:

A syllable contains a single vowel-sound

Exploring this rule provides an additional angle of focus and stimulates attention to both the audio and visual details present within different spellings.

'Li-on' exhibits two vowel-sounds whereas 'moon', although it also displays two vowels, they are combined to make just one sound.

Breaking 'lit-tle' between the consonants helps to emphasise them both, an approach which can also be useful with words such as 'cam-per' where the 'm' may be lost in everyday speech.

The words 'life' and 'boat' each contain two vowels in their spellings, but these are each expressed as one sound.

When spelling a word, using a 'spelling voice' can help to emphasise the presence of syllables which have got lost, or distorted, over time:

'Wed-nes-day'   'sep-a-rate'   'six-ty sec-onds make one min-ute'

Practise breaking spellings down into syllables to increase awareness of letters and sounds. Also build syllables into words to support reading.

Chapter four (creativity and ownership): page 86

One L or two?

although   careful   already   armful   awful   always   grateful

Question: What spelling error do the words above often share?

Answer: It is easy to spell these words with two 'L's not one.

The extra 'L' error could be due to the similar sounds we find in 'al-' and 'all' / '-ful' and 'full' leading us into mimicking those spellings by mistake.

The spellings of 'also' and 'almost' originated from Old English words of 'eallswa' and 'eallmaest'. Over time, al- replaced the 'eall-' (and eal-). See spelling history page 88.

Whilst it is easy to see how 'always' could be formed from the words 'all ways' (losing the second 'l' when the words were merged together), the <u>meaning</u> of 'all ways' (this way, that way and the other way) is not the same as 'always' (forever).

'Already' and 'all ready' also have different meanings.

The word 'alright' probably arises from its similarity with 'already', 'although' and 'also'. The word 'alright' is becoming more popular, although writing out the words 'all right' is still preferred by many.

The word 'careful' means 'full of care'.

If it was spelled 'carefull', when the suffix -ly was added, its spelling would become 'carefullly' with three 'L's.

English spellings do not have more than two of the same letter side by side ... with the exception of words such as 'aaaaargh!'

Exploring the history of words and their spellings offers more information to enhance spelling memories.

Look up 'etymology' online, then chose a dictionary to search out a word's history and origins.

Knowledge Empowers Thought

Once learners *understand* why '-ful' has lost the 'l' of 'full' in spellings such as 'careful' and 'wonderful', even though the meaning of 'full of care' or 'full of wonder' is where the suffix originated from, they have a much stronger memory trace.

They can also spell words through the application of reasoned thought. Whilst they might initially wonder how many 'l's to use for the spelling of 'carefully', by breaking it down into the suffixes involved, they know they need two.

Chapter five (brief history of spellings): page 97

American or British?

The challenge was to identify if the following spellings were American English or British English, and also identify any key features of their etymological journey.

Some words are used in both American and British English (rooted in Middle English).

colour British English: Latin origin (color) with 'u' inserted by influence of Norman-French.	**nappy** Middle English: 'nap' = fluffy cloth -y (suffix meaning 'has that character')	**autumn** British English: Latin origin
skillful American English: compound nouns tend to display double 'L' in American unlike (most) English spellings which only use one 'L' as in 'skilful'.	**meter** Old English: from Latin and Greek roots. A measuring device. American English: – word spells unit of length; tempo; and measurement device.	**travelling** British English spellings tend to use a double 'L' whereas American spellings have dropped one of them (e.g. 'woolen', 'marvelous', 'canceled', 'traveling', 'traveler' and 'traveled').
diaper Middle English: Latin / Greek / French origin but became obsolete in England.	**honour** British English: the original Latin suffix of -or changed to -our (Norman-French). The Americans reinstated -or to 'tidy-up' English spellings.	**defense** American English along with 'license', 'pretense' and 'offense'. However, they do not use the spelling 'practise' at all, but use 'practice' as both a noun and verb.
connexion Was the British English version but now 'connection' is the accepted form on both sides of the Atlantic.	**color** This American English spelling reverted to the original Latin suffix of -or (removing the 'u' inserted by Old French influences).	**fall** (fall-of-the-leaves) Middle English: (from Old Norse) term retained by Lowland Scots until it became obsolete in England.
honor American English: reverted to original Latin suffix of -or (removing the 'u' inserted by Old French influences).	**organize** American English: although the -ize endings are gaining more popularity in England in recent years.	**defence** British English: The -ce ending has been changed to -se in many American spellings, and often appears in global texts.
advertise British and American English: 'Surprise' and 'exercise' also retain their -ise endings.	**dialog** American English: The British English spellings favour the -gue ending. (Also 'catalog' / 'catalogue')	**metre** British English: from Latin and Greek roots with French -re ending. A unit of length.

Chapter six (spelling riddles): page 101

Misleading Ed

washed   jumped   hopped   tried   called   dropped
smiled   prodded   hoped   played   added   wished

In the list above, the words whose spellings end with the letters -shed or -ped are words which *sound* as if they end with a letter 't'.

Words ending with -ied, -led, -ded and -yed sound as if they end with a letter 'd'.

If you make your mouth say the word 'wash – d' you can feel that it is having to work harder than when it says 'wash – t'.

When the mouth finds it easier to express a -t rather than a 'd' then it often does.

The -ed pattern usually represents the past tense of a verb (fill / filled; push / pushed; wait / waited). When spelling words, it is important to think about their meaning (rather than just relying on their sound) as this will help you avoid spelling 'jumped' as 'jumpt' and 'hopped' as 'hopt'.

What other letters can you find which make -ed sound like -t?

See also the rules of -ed (page 52).

Many games and activities offer opportunities to practise the addition of -ed.

These include:

- Spelling Danger game   page 40
- Spelling Piles game   page 46
- Stepping Out game   page 82
- Suffering Suffixes game   page 71
- Switch Off Your Ears   page 47
- Syl-lab-i-fi-ca-tion game   page 84
- Three-in-a-row game   page 44
- Treasure Map activity   page 114
- Word-catcher Cobweb activity   page 53
- What's the Point? (adding suffixes)   page 144

Vary the word-spelling banks to keep games fresh, and repeat activities to build familiarity, confidence and positive outcomes.

Chapter six (spelling riddles): page 107

Identifying letters which affect vowels.

Most of the words in this activity contain the short-vowel sound of the vowel identified at the start of each row.

However, in the first, second and fourth rows, there are words whose pronunciation is changed from the short-vowel sound ...

by the presence of the letter 'r'.

These are often called r-controlled vowels and appear in words such as:

'c<u>ar</u>d' – 'f<u>er</u>n' – 'b<u>ir</u>d' – 'm<u>or</u>ning' – 'b<u>ur</u>n' – 'm<u>ar</u>k' – 't<u>ur</u>n' – 'f<u>ar</u>m<u>er</u>' – 'butt<u>er</u>'

'f<u>or</u>' – 'f<u>ore</u>' (the addition of a useless 'e' after 'or' is quite common) 'store' – 'wore'

The addition of an 'e' after 'ar' changes its sound again: 'car' / 'care' – 'far' / 'fare'
'E' also changes 'ir' in words such as 'fir' / 'fire' – 'sir' / 'sire'

In the third row, the short-vowel sound is changed in spellings ...

when 'a' is followed by the letter 'l'.

This phoneme appears in many spellings such as: '<u>tal</u>k' – '<u>wal</u>l' – '<u>al</u>together' – 'capit<u>al</u>'

In the fifth row, again, the vowel-sound is influenced by the presence of the letter 'r'.

'NEAR' – 'SPEAR' – 'CLEAR' – 'APPEAR' – 'DEAR' – 'EARWIG'

The influence of 'r' can also be heard in 'chain' / 'chair' – 'pail' / 'pair'

Accents can affect the way words are pronounced too.

> the 'i' vowel-sound: 'twig' – **'dirt'** – 'dip' – 'rim' – 'distant' – **'bird'**
>
> the 'e' vowel-sound: 'egg' – 'spend' – 'best' – **'verb'** – 'netting'
>
> the 'a' vowel-sound: 'cat' – '<u>walk</u>' – 'pattern' – 'flat' – '<u>called</u>'
>
> the 'o' vowel-sound: 'pond' – **'storm'** – 'w<u>orn</u>' – 'pot' – 'odd'
>
> the 'ea' vowel-sound: **'HEAR'** – 'seat' – 'east' – 'cream' – 'beak'

Play 'Phonetical Allsorts' (page 109) to explore and apply these spelling patterns.

Examine different words and their spellings and their sounds. There is often a lot of difference between how we think we say or hear a word, and how we actually speak or hear it. The brain often makes incorrect assumptions about the sounds of words.

Chapter six (spelling riddles): page 108

Sentences of Sound

Having read the passages together, learners are then invited to identify the presence of different key sounds using their ears.

The presence of the key sound is then identified within the words and matched to a variety of spelling patterns.

Variations of accent may alter some key sounds.

1. Key sound of /er/

Yesterday, I heard my mynah bird utter his first words: "Murderer under the sofa!" I turned and saw a purple-coloured jumper slither under the sofa ... it was an anaconda undertaking under-cover surveillance of my mynah bird!

2. Key sound of /or/

This morning I walked to the corner shop and bought pork from Cornwall, prawns caught off Dorset, apple-sauce from North Yorkshire, organic strawberries from Portugal and walnuts from California. As we live in Bournemouth, all this food has been brought 4,000km to the store, then forty steps more, before being gorged (eaten greedily).

3. Key sound of /ar/

Farmer Charles harnessed Ma and Pa (2 large cart-horses) to the cart ready for market. The cart was full of jars of marmalade, raspberry tarts and baskets of barn-eggs harvested from the farm. They hadn't gone far when a partridge darted in front of the cart and startled Ma. Farmer Charles spoke softly to calm her, then out of the grass barged a barking Chihuahua, a llama and an aardvark. "We are going to have to start charging the safari park for letting their bizarre animals on our* farm," Charles said to Ma, as an enchanting party of marmosets (type of monkey) danced in some branches ahead.

* 'our' is often pronounced 'are'.

As noted above, variations in accents can alter key sounds. When this happens discuss alternatives but recognise the importance of respecting alternative pronunciations.

Now play 'Phonetical Allsorts' (page 109).

Collecting spelling patterns into family-link story lines (see page 19) helps to identify between different options. Identify one of the spellings which is already established (or use Dicey Spellings, page 31 until one spelling of the group is secure), then use that to focus the story (or sentence) around.

Chapter seven (structured delivery): page 128

Spelling Riddles – Accurate or Accidental?

This activity could be used by a spelling tutor to inform them of a learner's level of understanding, memory or deduction powers, whilst also providing the learner with a challenge to rehearse and consolidate their learning.

All the spellings contain a double 'c'. Having read them through and discussed their meaning and spelling, the learner is asked to describe aspects of the double 'c'.

success	occupied	accurate	accuse
accident	accommodation	moccasin	accept
account	occur	occasion	accelerate

'success', 'accident', 'accept' and 'accelerate':

The double 'c' allows the sounds of /k/ and /s/ to be sounded in words such as 'success', 'accident', 'accept' and 'accelerate'.

These words could have been spelled: 'sucksess', 'acksident', 'acksept' and 'ackselerate' but spelling convention allows the double 'c' to work instead.

These four words all have Latin roots (such as 'accept' which stems from the Latin 'acceptare' meaning 'to receive'). Latin was considered an elite language and one that was favoured by scholars and scribes, printers and priests. Whilst the Romans adopted the letter 'k' they did not use it much, preferring the letter 'c' to make the 'k' sound.

In the four spellings, the second letter 'c' is followed by an 'e' or an 'i' making it into a soft c (pronounced 's').

'accurate', 'accuse', 'account' and 'accommodation':

These words are not usually expressed with a 'c' + 'c' sound which can lead the speller into the trap of only writing one 'c'. There is no 'i', 'e' or 'y' following the second 'c' so it does not make a soft 'c' sound.

The ac- beginning is actually a prefix (such as un- and dis-) which is added to the beginning of a root word. It derives from the prefix ad- (meaning at, to or near) as found in 'admire', 'advertise' and 'adventure'. Instead of ad- being added to a root word, when its spelling begins with the letter 'c', the letters ac- are used.

'occupied', 'occasion' and 'occur'
(and 'moccasin' from Algonquian Native Americans, which brings its own spelling rules)

These match the explanation above (oc- is a variation of the Latin prefix -ob meaning toward, on, or against). No soft 'c' created so both letter 'c's sound the same.

The pattern of 'occ-' sometimes makes an 'erk' sound in some words.

- For a number of spellings (e.g. 'success') the double consonant is keeping two vowels apart, ensuring the first one retains its short vowel sound.

Discuss ideas and thoughts. Promote enquiry and investigative activities.

Index of Words and Spelling Patterns

Index of Spelling Activities and Games

Index of Topics

AAT

Management Accounting:
Decision and Control

Level 4

West Herts College

Service

book

For assessments from
1 September 2016

First edition June 2016

ISBN 9781 4727 4819 5
ISBN (for internal use only) 9781 4727 4875 1

British Library Cataloguing-in-Publication Data
A catalogue record for this book is available from the British Library

Published by

BPP Learning Media Ltd
BPP House, Aldine Place
142-144 Uxbridge Road
London W12 8AA

www.bpp.com/learningmedia

Printed in the United Kingdom by Wheatons Exeter Ltd
Hennock Road
Marsh Barton
Exeter
EX2 8RP

Contents

Introduction To The Course

Syllabus Overview

Purpose

This paper recognises the importance of calculating and measuring financial performance in every organisation. This builds on the basic costing concepts and techniques required at level three. However, an understanding and application of performance indicators and cost management extends costing into management accounting.

Learning outcomes

On successful completion of this paper, learners should be able to:

1. Analyse a range of costing techniques to support the management accounting function of an organisation

2. Calculate and use standard costing to improve performance

3. Demonstrate a range of statistical techniques to analyse business information

4. Use appropriate financial and non-financial performance techniques to aid decision making

5. Evaluate a range of cost management techniques to enhance value and aid decision making

Computer-based test format

The *Management Accounting: Decision and Control* assessment is a 2½ hour computer based test, which comprises of 10 tasks. Learners must demonstrate competence across these tasks by scoring at least 70%.

This unit is about monitoring and managing financial performance. Learners will have the skills and knowledge to be able to analyse information on income and expenditure. They will then be able to use this to make reasoned judgements to support the decision making process.

The examiner has stated that it is important **not** to memorise tasks from the sample assessments and that they can and will vary the content and layout of tasks. However, the AAT have provided information about what the various tasks may contain. You should use this table to ensure you are happy with all of the material, putting a tick in the final column when you have completed the work.

*Note that this is only a guideline as to what might come up. The format and content of each task may vary from what we have listed below.

Results will normally be available approximately 6 weeks after the assessment.

Task	Expected Content	Max marks	Chapter Ref	Study complete
Task 1	**Identification of costing information** Preparation of a standard cost card or extract of information from a standard cost card or budgetary control report. Information can be given in a variety of forms for this task and students may be required to apply basic costing knowledge in order to arrive at the correct cost or quantity.	12	Cost classification and behaviour Methods of costing – Activity Based Costing (ABC)	
Task 2	**Direct materials, labour and variable overhead variances** Calculation of direct material and direct labour standard cost variances. Students may be given a budgetary control report and asked to calculate the four material and labour variances, alternatively this task may consist of several shorter tasks,	16	Variance analysis	

Task	Expected Content	Max marks	Chapter Ref	Study complete
	asking for the variances in turn. Tasks may also give a variance and require students to calculate one of the other variables (so called "backward" variances). The variances required for this task are: Direct material price Direct material usage Direct labour rate Direct labour efficiency Variable overhead rate Variable overhead efficiency			
Task 3	**Fixed Overhead variances** Same format as task 2, except here students will be required to calculate the following four variances: Fixed overhead expenditure Fixed overhead volume Fixed overhead capacity Fixed overhead efficiency	16	Variance analysis	
Task 4	**Standard cost reporting using an operating statement.** This task provides a budgetary control report and variances and requires the completion of an operating statement reconciling the standard cost of actual production with the actual costs. Only some variances will have a sign given, identification of the rest will be required.	12	Variance analysis	

Task	Expected Content	Max marks	Chapter Ref	Study complete
Task 5	**Statistical techniques** The following techniques could be tested in this task: Seasonal variations Moving averages Trend identification Forecasting using the identified trend and seasonal variation Index number calculations Using the regression equation	12	Forecasting data	
Task 6	**Drafting reports on variance analysis (written)** The requirement here can involve: Identifying signs for variances Explaining what they mean Suggesting reasons for each variance Explaining any links between the variances	22	Further aspects of variance analysis	
Task 7	**Calculation of Performance indicators** Calculations are required here from budgeted financial statements, for example: sales price per unit material/labour/fixed production cost per unit Gross and net profit margins Return on net assets Gearing Inventory holding period It is imperative that students learn the formulae for the ratios	20	Performance indicators	

Task	Expected Content	Max marks	Chapter Ref	Study complete
Task 8	**Decision making** This task requires students to use one or more of the key decision making topics: Breakeven analysis Margin of safety Limiting factor decisions Make or buy decisions Assessment of special orders It is essential that contribution theory and cost behaviour are understood for this task.	12	Decision making techniques	
Task 9	**Cost management techniques** This tasks covers the following topics: Lifecycle costing Target costing Cost Management Techniques (including NPV) Activity Based Costing (ABC)	12	Cost management	
Task 10	**Drafting reports on key performance indicators and scenario planning (written)** This task requires students to write a report analysing information including the gross profit margin, profit margin and key changes in the business. Students may also be asked to consider the stages of the product lifecycle and comment on the cost behaviour for different stages of the cycle and how the organisation may change as the product progresses through the cycle. Usually students will be	22	Performance indicators	

Task	Expected Content	Max marks	Chapter Ref	Study complete
	provided with two scenarios where there is a difference in the two gross profit margins and asked to analyse the differences by considering the variables of sales price, sales volume, direct material, direct labour and fixed overheads. The ability to understand the relationships between the variables is crucial here.			
	Remember to book your CBT! For UK centres call 0845 2262422			

You should ensure with all tasks that you follow any formatting guidelines provided, such as the display of decimals and adverse variances as ignoring this advice will cost you credit for responses.

Skills bank

Our experience of preparing students for this type of assessment suggests that to obtain competency, you will need to develop a number of key skills.

What do I need to know to do well in the assessment?

Management Accounting: Decision and Control is designed to build on your knowledge of costing systems, decision making techniques and the other topics introduced in the unit *Management Accounting: Costing* at Level 3, whilst also complimenting the topics covered in the Level 4 unit *Management Accounting: Budgeting*.

To be successful in the assessment you need to:

- Demonstrate your theoretical knowledge of the different management accounting techniques.

- Apply your knowledge to practical scenarios

Your knowledge will not only be tested in numerical tasks. At least two tasks in the assessment will require a written response. These usually revolve around variance analysis and performance analysis. Examples of written tasks include:

- Explaining the calculation of variances

- Interpreting the outcome of a variance – why has that variance been incurred?

- Assessing the performance of an organisation by explaining the calculation of and interpreting its performance indicators

- Explaining the ethical consequences of actions taken

Assumed knowledge

The following topics were covered in the Level 3 unit *Management Accounting: Costing* and as such form the foundation of *Management Accounting: Decision and Control*:

- Cost classification and behaviour

- Short-term decision making techniques – in particular breakeven analysis, margin of safety and required profit

- Long-term decision making techniques – in particular net present value

Cost classification, cost behaviour and statistical techniques are also covered in *Management Accounting: Budgeting*. However, the focus in *Management Accounting: Decision and Control* is how these techniques can enhance control and decision making within the business rather than help the business plan its resources.

Assessment style

In the assessment you will complete tasks by:

1. Entering narrative by selecting from drop down menus of narrative options known as **picklists**

2. Using **drag and drop** menus to enter narrative

3. Typing in numbers, known as **gapfill** entry

4. Entering **ticks**

5. **Free text** boxes for answering written tasks

You must familiarise yourself with the style of the online questions and the AAT software before taking the assessment. As part of your revision, login to the **AAT website** and attempt their **online practice assessments**.

Introduction to the assessment

The question practice you do will prepare you for the format of tasks you will see in the *Management Accounting: Decision and Control* assessment. It is also useful to familiarise yourself with the introductory information you **may** be given at the start of the assessment. For example:

You have 2 hours and 30 minutes to complete this assessment.

Each task is independent. You will not need to refer to your answers to previous tasks.

Read every task carefully to make sure you understand what is required.

Where the date is relevant, it is given in the task data.

Both minus signs and brackets can be used to indicate negative numbers UNLESS task instructions say otherwise.

You must use a full stop to indicate a decimal point. For example, write 100.57 NOT 100, 57 OR 100 57.

You may use a comma to indicate a number in the thousands, but you don't have to. For example, 10000 and 10,000 are both OK.

Complete all 10 tasks

Skills practice

1. As you revise, use the **BPP Passcards** to consolidate your knowledge. They are a pocket-sized revision tool, perfect for packing in that last-minute revision.

2. Attempt as many tasks as possible in the **Question Bank**. There are plenty of assessment-style tasks which are excellent preparation for the real assessment.

3. Always **check** through your own answers as you will in the real assessment, before looking at the solutions in the back of the Question Bank.

Key to icons

 Key term

A key definition which is important to be aware of for the assessment

 Formula to learn

A formula you will need to learn as it will not be provided in the assessment

 Formula provided

A formula which is provided within the assessment and generally available as a pop-up on screen

 Activity

An example which allows you to apply your knowledge to the technique covered in the Course Book. The solution is provided at the end of the chapter

 Illustration

A worked example which can be used to review and see how an assessment question could be answered

 Assessment focus point

A high priority point for the assessment

 Open book reference

Where use of an open book will be allowed for the assessment

 Real life examples

A practical real life scenario

AAT qualifications

The material in this book may support the following AAT qualifications:

AAT Professional Diploma in Accounting Level 4, AAT Professional Diploma in Accounting at SCQF Level 8 and Certificate: Accounting (Level 5 AATSA).

Supplements

From time to time we may need to publish supplementary materials to one of our titles. This can be for a variety of reasons, from a small change in the AAT unit guidance to new legislation coming into effect between editions.

You should check our supplements page regularly for anything that may affect your learning materials. All supplements are available free of charge on our supplements page on our website at:

www.bpp.com/learning-media/about/students

Improving material and removing errors

There is a constant need to update and enhance our study materials in line with both regulatory changes and new insights into the assessments.

From our team of authors BPP appoints a subject expert to update and improve these materials for each new edition.

Their updated draft is subsequently technically checked by another author and from time to time non-technically checked by a proof reader.

We are very keen to remove as many numerical errors and narrative typos as we can but given the volume of detailed information being changed in a short space of time we know that a few errors will sometimes get through our net.

We apologise in advance for any inconvenience that an error might cause. We continue to look for new ways to improve these study materials and would welcome your suggestions. Please feel free to contact our AAT Head of Programme at nisarahmed@bpp.com if you have any suggestions for us.

Costing techniques

1

Learning outcomes

1.1	Distinguish between different cost classifications and evaluate their use in a management accounting function.
	On completion of this chapter you should be able to:
	• Calculate direct and indirect costs
	• Calculate variable, fixed and stepped fixed costs
	• Use the high-low technique to calculate elements of a semi-variable cost
	• Calculate the prime cost of a product
	• Understand the differences between cost centres, profit centres and investment centres
1.2	Discriminate between and use marginal costing and absorption costing techniques.
	On completion of this chapter you should be able to:
	• Explain the difference between marginal costing and absorption costing
	• Reconcile a marginal costing profit with an absorption costing profit for changes in inventory

Assessment context

Cost classification and behaviour is essential knowledge used in many of the management accounting techniques.

Qualification context

Cost classification and behaviour is tested in *Management Accounting: Budgeting* and *Management Accounting: Decision & Control* at Level 4.

Business context

Grouping costs together is essential for a business to be able to analyse costs, budget and plan effectively.

Chapter overview

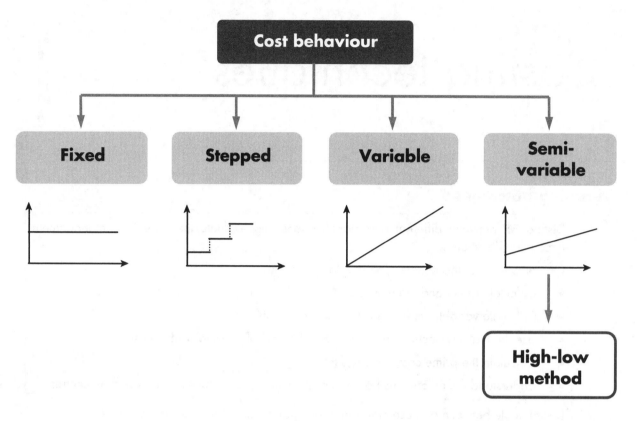

Cost behaviour

- Fixed
- Stepped
- Variable
- Semi-variable

High-low method

- Used to split fixed and variable elements
- Find highest and lowest activity levels
- Subtract Low from High
- Use remainder to calculate variable cost
- Substitute VC back into High or Low total cost formula to calculate fixed cost

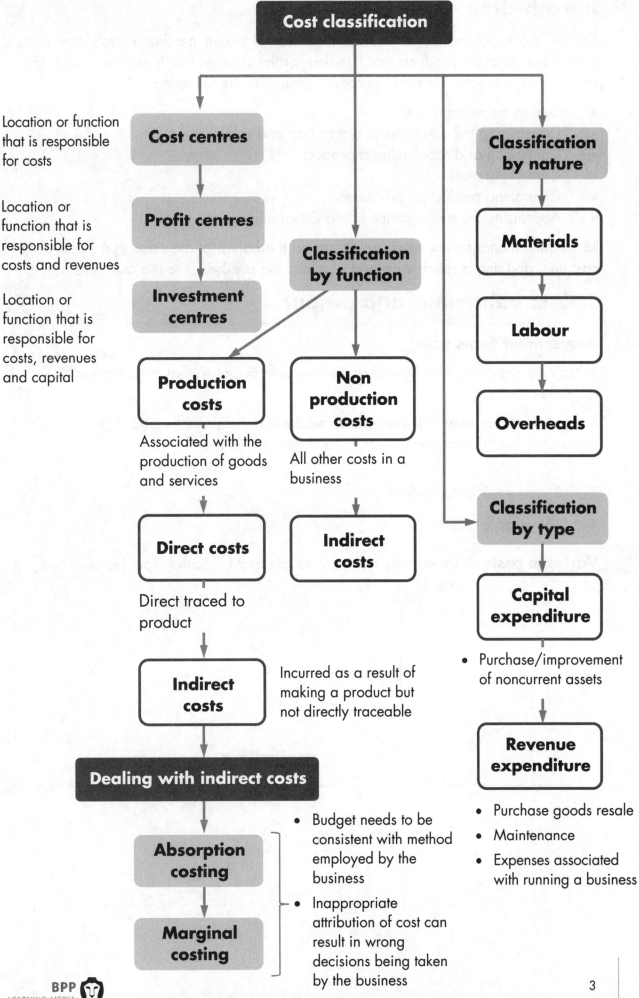

Cost classification

Location or function that is responsible for costs

Cost centres

Location or function that is responsible for costs and revenues

Profit centres

Location or function that is responsible for costs, revenues and capital

Investment centres

Classification by function

Production costs

Associated with the production of goods and services

Non production costs

All other costs in a business

Direct costs

Direct traced to product

Indirect costs

Indirect costs

Incurred as a result of making a product but not directly traceable

Dealing with indirect costs

Absorption costing

Marginal costing

- Budget needs to be consistent with method employed by the business
- Inappropriate attribution of cost can result in wrong decisions being taken by the business

Classification by nature

Materials

Labour

Overheads

Classification by type

Capital expenditure

- Purchase/improvement of noncurrent assets

Revenue expenditure

- Purchase goods resale
- Maintenance
- Expenses associated with running a business

BPP
LEARNING MEDIA

Introduction

One of the key concerns for the management of a commercial organisation is to know how much the products that it makes, or the services that it provides, cost. This information is needed for many purposes, including the following:

- Setting the selling price
- Determining the quantities of production and sales
- Continuing or discontinuing a product
- Controlling costs
- Controlling production processes
- Appraising the performance of individual managers

To do this, management need to understand the nature of the costs that make up a cost unit, and find a suitable method of allocating overheads to the cost units.

1 Cost behaviour and output

Assessment focus point

A business needs to know how costs behave with output so that costs can be forecasted.

It is expected that costs will increase as production increases (ie as output increases), but the exact way costs behave with output may vary.

1.1 Types of cost behaviour

1.1.1 Variable costs

Key term

| **Variable costs** | Those costs that vary, ie rise and fall with output (eg all direct costs). |

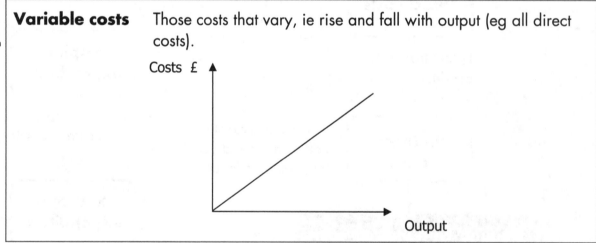

1.1.2 Fixed costs

Fixed costs   Those costs that will not vary with output, ie fixed overheads (eg rent and rates).

Costs £

Output

1.1.3 Stepped fixed costs

Stepped fixed costs   A stepped cost is a fixed cost in nature within certain levels of activity. These costs remain fixed for a certain level of output and then increase until a further level of output is reached (eg supervisors' costs and rent).

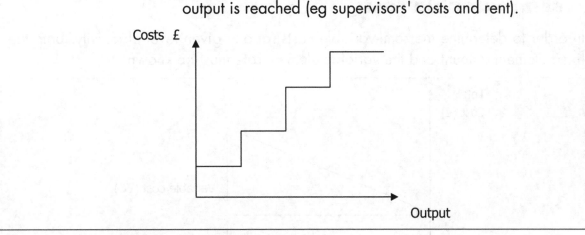

Costs £

Output

1.1.4 Semi-variable (mixed) costs

Semi-variable (mixed) costs   Those costs which are part fixed and part variable and are therefore partly affected by changes in the level of activity (eg telephone).

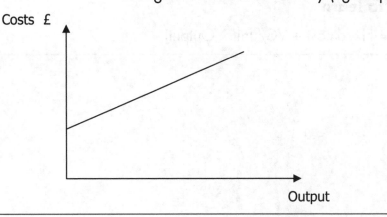

Costs £

Output

2 Behaviour of manufacturing costs

We assume all costs can be categorised as either fixed or variable. This fits together with previous definitions:

2.1 Direct costs

By their nature, direct costs will be variable costs.

2.2 Indirect costs/overheads

Overheads can be fixed (eg rent) or variable (eg tool hire).

	Fixed	Variable
Direct costs	X	✓
Production overheads	✓	✓
Non-manufacturing costs	✓	✓

3 Determining the fixed and variable elements of semi-variable costs

In order to determine the semi-variable costs, at any given level of activity, both the fixed element amount and the variable element rate must be known.

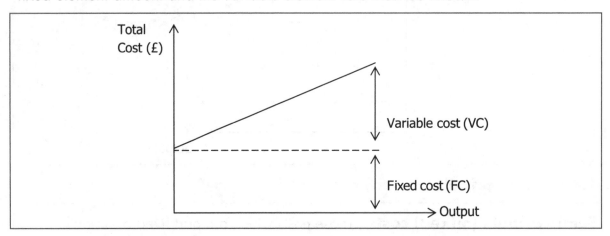

Formula to learn

Total cost = Fixed cost + VC/unit × Output)

Illustration 1: Classification of costs by behaviour

Here is a comprehensive example of the use of all the cost behaviour principles described above to forecast production costs.

Cameron Ltd will produce one product, which requires the following inputs, in the forthcoming quarter:

Direct materials	1 kg @ £3.50 per kg
Direct labour	1 hour @ £6.00 per hour
Rent	£4,000 per quarter
Leased machines	£1,500 for every 4,000 units of production
Maintenance costs	£1,000 per quarter plus £1.00 per unit

Calculate the budgeted total cost of production and the budgeted cost per unit for each of the following production levels for the coming quarter:

(a)   4,000 units
(b)   10,000 units
(c)   16,000 units

Direct materials – this is a variable cost with a constant amount per unit (1 kg × £3.50 = £3.50). Therefore, the total cost is found by multiplying the number of units by the unit cost:

£3.50 × 4,000 units	=	£14,000
£3.50 × 10,000 units	=	£35,000
£3.50 × 16,000 units	=	£56,000

Direct labour – another variable cost, with a unit cost of 1hr × £6 = £6:

£6.00 × 4,000 units	=	£24,000
£6.00 × 10,000 units	=	£60,000
£6.00 × 16,000 units	=	£96,000

Rent – this is a fixed cost and therefore, provided we are still operating within the relevant range, it will remain at £4,000, whatever the production level.

Leased machines – this is a stepped cost and the number of machines leased will depend upon the quantity of production:

4,000 units	=	1 machine	=	£1,500
10,000 units	=	3 machines	=	£4,500
16,000 units	=	4 machines	=	£6,000

Maintenance costs – this is a semi-variable cost with a fixed element of £1,000 and a variable cost of £1 per unit. The total cost for each activity level is:

4,000 units	=	£1,000 + (4,000 × £1.00)	=	£5,000
10,000 units	=	£1,000 + (10,000 × £1.00)	=	£11,000
16,000 units	=	£1,000 + (16,000 × £1.00)	=	£17,000

Thus, the total costs of production are:

	Production level – units		
	4,000	**10,000**	**16,000**
	£	£	£
Direct materials (variable)	14,000	35,000	56,000
Direct labour (variable)	24,000	60,000	96,000
Rent (fixed)	4,000	4,000	4,000
Leased machines (stepped)	1,500	4,500	6,000
Maintenance costs	5,000	11,000	17,000
Total cost	48,500	114,500	179,000
Number of units	4,000	10,000	16,000
Cost per unit	£12.13	£11.45	£11.19

The cost per unit will decrease if the production quantity increases. This is because the fixed cost and the fixed element of the semi-variable cost will then be spread over a larger number of units.

Variable costs with a discount

Suppose now that the supplier of the materials offers a bulk purchasing discount of 6% for all purchases if an order is placed for more than 8,000 kg.

What is the direct materials cost in total and per unit at each level of production?

4,000 units

| Total cost | 4,000 × £3.50 | = | £14,000 |
| Cost per unit | £14,000/4,000 | = | £3.50 |

10,000 units

| Total cost | 10,000 × (£3.50 × 94%) | = | £32,900 |
| Cost per unit | £32,900/10,000 | = | £3.29 |

16,000 units

Total cost	16,000 × (£3.50 × 94%)	=	£52,640
Cost per unit	£52,640/16,000	=	£3.29

The direct materials are now not a true variable cost, as the cost per unit falls once production is in excess of 8,000 units.

Note. Sometimes the term prime cost is used for the total direct costs, whereas the full production cost includes the overheads or indirect costs of production of the product. The prime cost for production of 4,000 units above would therefore be £14,000 + £24,000 = £38,000 with a full production cost of £48,500.

3.1 High-low method for semi-variable costs

Assessment focus point

This is a four-step method:

1 Select the highest and lowest activity level and their costs.
2 Find the difference in the output and costs.
3 Calculate the variable cost per unit.
4 Calculate the fixed cost.

Illustration 2: High-low calculation 1

The total costs of a business for differing levels of output are as follows.

Output (units)	Total Costs
10,000	27,000
12,000	31,000
14,000	35,000

The variable cost/unit and the fixed cost are calculated as follows.

	Output	Cost
Highest	14,000	35,000
Lowest	10,000	27,000
	4,000	8,000

∴ VC/unit = £8,000/4,000 = £2

Total costs	35,000
Variable cost	(28,000)
∴ Fixed cost	7,000

Illustration 3: High Low method 2

The following data has been collected from a business:

Units produced	5,000	7,500	10,000
Total costs (£)	54,500	76,500	90,000

Total costs are made up of two elements, a fixed cost (that changes when the units exceed 7,000) and some variable costs, which remain constant per unit.

Here we calculate the total fixed costs at production levels below and above 7,000 units and the variable cost per unit.

High/low method above volume of 7,000 units.

	Output	Cost
Highest	10,000	90,000
Lowest	7,500	76,500
	2,500	13,500

∴ VC/unit =   £13,500/2,500 = £5.40

NB. This is constant at all volumes of output

TC = FC + VC/unit × output

Substitute at lowest (or highest) level:

£76,500 = FC + £5.40 × 7,500

FC = £36,000 above output of 7,000 units.

So at 5,000 units:

TC = FC + VC/unit x output

£54,500 = FC + £5.40 × 5,000

FC = £27,500 below output of 7,000 units.

Remember, not all costs follow the textbook profiles. For example, direct labour is often described as a variable cost. In reality, basic wages are often fixed and overtime is then paid at a higher rate, should it be required.

4 Cost classification

Cost classification is the arrangement of cost items into logical groups, for example, by their **type** (capital and revenue expenditure), their **function** (administration, production etc) or by their **nature** (materials, wages etc).

The eventual aim of costing is to determine the cost of producing a product/service.

4.1 Capital expenditure vs. revenue expenditure

Capital expenditure includes:

- The purchase of non-current assets
- The improvement of the earning capability of non-current assets

Revenue expenditure includes:

- The purchase of goods for resale
- The maintenance of the existing earning capacity of non-current assets
- Expenditure incurred in conducting the business

Capital expenditure is shown as a non-current asset in the statement of financial position, while revenue expenditure is charged as a cost in the income statement.

4.2 Direct and indirect costs

Production costs can be split into direct costs and indirect costs.

4.2.1 Direct costs

Direct costs are those costs which can be **specifically identified** with, and allocated to, a single cost unit.

Key term

Total direct costs	Prime costs.

4.2.2 Indirect production costs

Key term

Indirect production costs	Those costs which are incurred in the course of making a product/service but which **cannot be identified with a particular cost unit**.

Indirect production costs are often referred to as production **overheads**.

Illustration 4: Identifying direct and indirect costs

Here are some of the costs involved in making chocolate bars, grouped by direct and indirect costs.

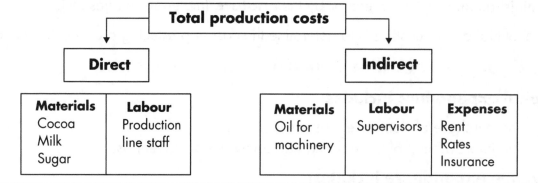

4.3 Classification by function

A company may first arrange cost items into groups by function. At the highest level, there could be groups of production costs and groups of non production costs.

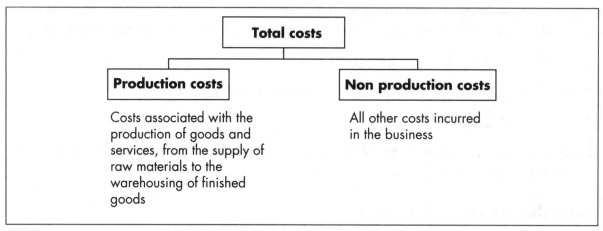

4.4 Classification by nature

Production costs can then be broken down further **by their nature**.

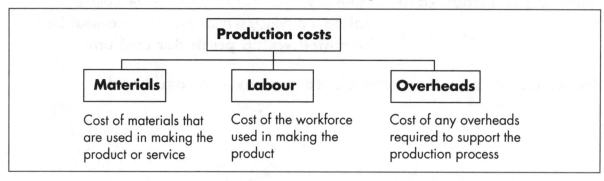

Non production costs can also be broken down further by their nature to aid analysis.

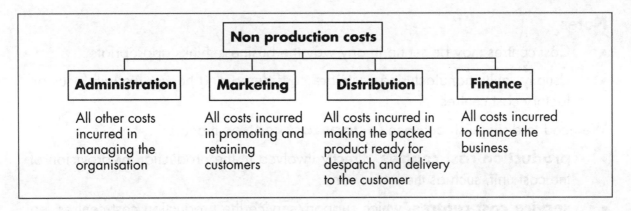

 Illustration 5: Classifying costs

The following items of expenditure can be classified by the headings below.

Administration	Marketing and distribution	Capital Expenditure	Cash flow
Depreciation charge of office equipment	Sales staff salaries	Factory extension	Payments to suppliers
Finance director's salary	Advertising	Van purchase	
Accounts staff salaries	Drivers' salaries		
Office staff salaries	Packing materials		
	Lorry repairs		

5 Responsibility centres

To structure an overall budget, the various department and functions within an organisation can be classified, in terms of their purpose and responsibilities, into responsibility centres. These can be cost centres, profit centres or investment centres.

This means that each centre has responsibility for the costs or revenues in its budget, and actual results will then be compared to budgets for each centre, to monitor and control performance.

5.1 Cost centres

Key term

Cost centre	An area of a business, maybe a department such as the factory or canteen, for which costs are incurred.

Each cost centre acts as a 'collecting place' for certain costs before they are analysed further.

Notes

- Cost centres may be set up in any way the business thinks appropriate.

- Usually, only manufacturing costs are considered and hence, we will focus on factory cost centres.

We need to distinguish between **factory cost centres** that are:

- **production cost centres**, directly involved in the production or provision of the cost unit, such as the factory and;

- **service cost centres**, which support/service the production cost centres, eg the canteen.

Activity 1: Classifying factory cost centres

Required

Identify from the following examples which cost centres are production cost centres and service cost centres within a clothes manufacturing factory.

Cost Centre	Type
Canteen	
Stores	
Stitching	
Maintenance	
Packing	
Finishing	

Picklist:

Production cost centre
Service cost centre

Key term

Profit centres	These are similar to cost centres but are accountable for costs and revenues; for example, a sales department in an organisation that earns revenue from sales but incurs costs such as a salesperson's salary and commission.
Revenue centres	These are similar to cost centres and profit centres but are accountable for revenues only.
Investment centres	These are profit centres with additional responsibilities for capital investment. An example might be a separate division of the organisation which has a factory from which it produces goods, sells and despatches them.

Using an example of a solicitors' firm, departments based on their activities (eg corporate law, private client and litigation departments) would be considered profit centres. This is because they incur costs, such as the salaries of the solicitors employed in each centre, but also generate income from charging work to clients.

The firm will also have service departments such as IT, HR (Personnel), Finance teams etc. These would be considered cost centres (or, more specifically, service cost centres) incurring their own costs such as staff salaries but not raising income for the firm.

If the firm had two different offices – one in the north and one in the south of the country, incurring the above costs and generating income, but each office was responsible for the costs of its own **building** – then the separate offices would each be considered investment centres.

Activity 2: Classifying centres

Suggest what types of centres are appropriate for the following list:

Factory canteen
An independent restaurant
Shop in chain
Car dealer

Options

Cost centre	Revenue centre	Profit centre	Investment centre

Activity 3: Classifying responsibility centres

Allocate the following costs and revenues to the responsibility centres in a business (as listed below):

- Client entertaining at horse racing
- Repair of security alarm system in offices
- Sick pay for production manager
- Bonus for sales managers
- Depreciation of production equipment

Select from:

- Production department
- Marketing department
- Administration department
- Sales team
- HR (Personnel) department

6 Methods of costing

There are three main methods of calculating a cost per unit which allocate overheads in different ways:

- **Absorption costing** – where **all production costs** are included in the costing of a cost unit

- **Marginal costing** – where only the **variable costs of production** are included in the cost per unit

The fixed overheads are treated as period costs and not as part of the cost unit. Instead, the fixed overheads are charged to the statement of profit or loss as an expense for the period.

- **Activity based costing** – this is a method of absorption costing which uses more sophisticated methods of allocating overheads to cost units. This is covered later in this Course Book.

> **Assessment focus point**
>
> In the assessment you will be required to calculate statements under both absorption and marginal costing principles. You therefore need to be comfortable with the differences between the two costing approaches, and how profit differs between them.

7 Absorption costing

Absorption costing is a method of costing whereby **all production costs** are included in the costing of a cost unit, ie direct materials, direct labour, variable production overheads and fixed production overheads.

Note that even when applying absorption costing, it is usually only the **production overheads of the production and service cost centres** that are absorbed. Administrative overheads (eg the salaries of the finance team, the depreciation of the office building) or selling overheads (eg the cost of an advertising campaign) will remain outside the cost units.

Absorption costing calculates an overhead absorption rate that can be used to absorb the production overheads into each cost unit. To calculate this, the following method is used:

(1) Allocate and apportion overheads to each production and service cost centre.

(2) Re-apportion service cost centres to production cost centres to find total production cost.

(3) Absorb into production using an overhead absorption rate. This can be calculated as follows:

$$\frac{\text{Total production overheads}}{\text{Total activity level}}$$

The activity level is usually one of the following:

- Budgeted machine hours (if the production process is more machine intensive)
- Budgeted labour hours (if the production process is more labour intensive)
- Budgeted cost units (if the difference between machine and labour hours is negligible)

Assessment focus point

You will not be asked to perform the entire absorption costing exercise in the assessment. Instead, you will be asked to calculate an overhead absorption rate in order to find over or under absorption of overheads. This is illustrated below.

Illustration 6: Absorption costing

Fenton Partners produce one product, the Fenton. The factory has two production departments, assembly and packing.

The expected costs of producing 100,000 units in the next quarter are as follows:

Direct materials	£24.00 per unit
Direct labour	2 hours assembly @ £7.00 per hour
	1 hour packing @ £6.00 per hour
Total assembly production overheads	£470,000
Total packing production overheads	£290,000

Overheads are absorbed on the basis of labour hours.

Production overheads

	Assembly	Packing
	£	£
	470,000	290,000
Absorption rate	200,000	100,000
=	£2.35 per labour hour	£2.90 per labour hour

Interpretation:

For every one hour that the product is worked on in the assembly department, it is charged with a £2.35 share of the overheads incurred.

For every one hour that the product is worked on in the packing department, it is charged with a £2.90 share of the overheads incurred.

Unit cost

		£
Direct materials		24.00
Direct labour	– assembly 2 hours × £7.00	14.00
Direct labour	– packing 1 hour × £6.00	6.00
Overheads	– assembly 2 hours × £2.35	4.70
	– packing 1 hour × £2.90	2.90
Unit cost (total absorption costing)		51.60

Activity 4: JK32

The following information has been calculated for the product JK32:

		Budget		Actual
Production JK32 (units)		36,000		38,000
		£		£
Direct materials	3,600 kg	32,400	3,700 kg	32,190
Direct labour	1,440 hours	11,520	1,560 hours	14,040
Fixed overheads	1,440 hours	14,400		10,400
Total		58,320		56,630

Required

Complete the standard cost card for the production of one unit of JK32:

1 unit of JK32	Quantity	Cost per kg/hr £	Total £
Direct materials			
Direct labour			
Fixed overheads			
Total			

The standard quantity of material for the production of 38,000 JK32s is [   ] kg.

The standard cost for the production of 38,000 JK32s is £ [   ].

7.1 Over- and under-absorption of overheads

Overhead absorption rates are usually decided in advance from budgeted overhead costs and activity levels.

However the problem is that actual overhead costs and activity levels may be different from the overhead costs and activity levels in the budget.

The difference between the budgeted and actual costs and activity levels will give rise to over or under absorption of overheads:

(1)   If more overheads are absorbed than have actually been incurred, this is known as **over-absorption**.

(2)   If fewer overheads are absorbed than have actually been incurred, this is known as **under-absorption**.

Over- or under-absorption is calculated as follows:

	£
Overhead absorbed (Budgeted OAR × actual activity level)	X
Actual overhead incurred	(X)
Over/under-absorbed overhead	X

The profit for the period must be adjusted for the amount of under-absorption or over-absorption as follows:

(1)   If there is over-absorption, too many overhead costs have been added to the cost of production, and **profit must be adjusted by adding the over-absorbed overhead to profit**.

(2)   If there is under-absorption, not enough overhead costs have been added to the cost of production, and **profit must be adjusted by subtracting the under-absorbed overhead from profit**.

Illustration 7: Over- and under-absorption

Cowslip Limited incurred the following actual overheads and machine hours worked in February and March:

	Units made	Machine hours	£
February	10,000	30,000	140,000
March	9,000	28,000	160,000

The budgeted absorption rate is £5 per machine hour.

In **February**, the actual overheads are £140,000, but 30,000 machine hours were worked. Absorbed overheads are more than actual overhead costs, so we have over-absorption.

	£
Actual overheads	140,000
Absorbed overheads (30,000 hours × £5)	150,000
Over-absorption	10,000

This over-absorption of £10,000 is credited to the statement of profit or loss (income statement), ie it is added back to profit as an adjustment.

In **March** actual overheads are £160,000 and machine hours are only 28,000. This time, there is under-absorbed overhead.

	£
Actual overheads	160,000
Absorbed overheads (28,000 hours × £5)	140,000
Under-absorption	20,000

Under-absorption means that not enough overheads have been charged against the cost of production and profits, so we deduct the under-absorption from profit to make up for this. Profit should therefore be adjusted down by £20,000.

Activity 5: Galaxy

The Galaxy production department produces two types of units. The overheads for the department are as follows:

	£
Supervisors' salaries	10,000
Machine running costs	15,000
Machine maintenance	8,000
Depreciation of machines	5,000
	38,000

The department produces 2,000 units of Pluto. Production uses 5,000 machine hours.

The actual overheads incurred were £40,000, and actual machine hours used was 4,000 hours.

Required

Complete the following statement.

(a) **The overhead recovery rate will be £** [   ] **per**
[   ] .

Picklist:

Labour hour
Machine hour

(b) **Overheads are** [＿＿＿＿＿＿＿＿＿＿] **by £** [＿＿＿＿＿] .

Picklist:

over-absorbed
under-absorbed

8 Marginal costing

Marginal costing (also known as variable costing) is a costing system that measures only the variable (or marginal) cost of cost units – ie direct material, direct labour and variable overheads. This differs from absorption costing which considers both the variable and fixed costs of production.

In marginal costing, fixed costs are treated as a charge against profit in each time period and are therefore subtracted off in full from profit.

Activity 6: Absorption vs. marginal costing

A business expects to produce 5,000 units of its single product in the next month, with the following costs being incurred:

	£
Direct materials	12,000
Direct labour	15,000
Variable overheads	23,000
Fixed overheads	25,000

Complete the following table to show the cost per unit under both absorption costing and marginal costing methods.

Costing method	Cost per unit £
Absorption costing	
Marginal costing	

8.1 Contribution

A key term in marginal costing is **contribution**.

Key term

Contribution	Total contribution is the difference between sales revenue and total variable costs.
	The contribution per unit is the difference between the sales price and the variable cost per unit.
	Contribution can be thought of as standing for 'contribution towards covering fixed costs and making a profit'.

Contribution is an important concept, and we will look at the use of contribution for decision making later in the Course Book.

Assessment focus point

In the assessment you may be required to compare unit costs and profits under both absorption and marginal costing principles. You therefore need to ensure you fully understand the difference in calculating costs and why profits differ under each method.

9 Marginal and absorption costing, inventory levels and profit

Under **absorption costing**, inventory is valued at full production cost, which includes the absorbed fixed overhead.

Under **marginal costing**, the cost per unit only includes variable costs, therefore the value of inventory is lower. Fixed overheads are charged to the statement of profit or loss as an expense for the period.

Due to the differences in the treatment of fixed overhead and the valuation of inventory, absorption costing and marginal costing will not produce the same profit figure.

Illustration 8: Inventory levels and profit

Spa Ltd makes a single product and produces management accounts, including a costing statement of profit or loss each month. In both May and June, 100,000 units of the product were produced.

The production costs in both May and June were:

	£
Direct materials	200,000
Direct labour	300,000
Fixed overheads	300,000
Total production costs	800,000

There were no opening inventories at the start of May and all of the production for May was sold. However, in June only 75,000 units of production were sold, leaving 25,000 units in inventory. Each unit is sold for £10.

(a) Unit cost

    (i)   Absorption costing:

        £800,000/100,000 = £8 per unit

    (ii)   Marginal costing:

        £500,000/100,000 = £5 per unit

(b) Statements of profit or loss

(i) Absorption costing (AC):

	May		June	
	£	£	£	£
Sales		1,000,000		750,000
Less cost of sales				
Opening inventory	–		–	
Cost of production				
100,000 units × £8	800,000		800,000	
	800,000		800,000	
Less closing inventory				
25,000 units × £8	–		(200,000)	
Cost of sales		800,000		600,000
Profit (AC)		200,000		150,000

(ii) Marginal costing (MC):

	May		June	
	£	£	£	£
Sales		1,000,000		750,000
Less cost of sales				
Opening inventory	–			
Cost of production				
100,000 units × £5	500,000		500,000	
	500,000		500,000	
Less closing inventory				
25,000 units × £5	–	–	(125,000)	
Marginal cost of sales		500,000		375,000
Contribution		500,000		375,000
Less fixed costs		300,000		300,000
Profit (MC)		200,000		75,000

In May, the profit is the same under both costing methods – £200,000. This is because there is no movement in inventory during the period, since all of the production is sold.

In June, however, profit under absorption costing is £150,000, whereas it is only £75,000 under the marginal costing method. The reason for the £75,000 difference in profit is that the closing inventory, under absorption costing, includes £75,000 (£300,000/100,000 × 25,000 units) of fixed costs that are being carried forward to the next accounting period, whereas under marginal costing, they were all written off in June.

The difference in the two profit figures can be reconciled using the overhead absorption rate per unit, and the increase or decrease in inventory levels. Using the above example, the profit under the two methods can be reconciled as follows:

	May £	June £
Absorption cost profit	200,000	150,000
Increase in inventory × OAR per unit (25,000 units × £3 per unit)	0	(75,000)
Marginal cost profit	200,000	75,000

The rules are that:

(1) **If inventory levels are rising, then absorption costing will give higher profits** (as the fixed overheads are being carried forward into the next accounting period).

(2) **If inventory levels are falling, then absorption costing will give a lower profit figure** (as more fixed overheads from the previous period are charged to the statement of profit or loss in this period).

(3) **Where inventory levels are constant (provided that unit costs are constant), then absorption costing and marginal costing will give the same level of profit.**

Activity 7: Marginal vs. absorption costing profit

Given below are the budgeted figures for a factory producing a single product. Overheads are absorbed on a production unit basis:

	Month 1	Month 2
Opening inventory (units)	0	
Selling price (£)	100	110
Production (units)	15,000	15,000
Sales (units)	11,000	12,000
Direct materials (£ per unit)	10	10
Direct labour (£ per unit)	8	8
Other variable production costs (£ per unit)	180,000	180,000
Fixed production costs (£)	300,000	300,000

Required

(a) Complete the table below

| | Absorption costing | | Marginal costing | |
	Month 1	Month 2	Month 1	Month 2
	£	£	£	£
Sales				
Opening inventory				
Production costs				
Closing inventory				
Cost of sales				
Fixed overheads				
Profit/Loss				

(b) Reconcile the absorption costing profit to the marginal costing profit by completing the table below:

	Month 1	Month 2
	£	£
Absorption costing profit		
Change in inventory		
Marginal costing profit		

10 Comparison of absorption and marginal costing

Advantages of absorption costing:

(a) Fixed overheads have to be incurred to produce output so it is fair to charge each unit of product with a share of the fixed costs.

(b) Using full absorption cost to value inventory is consistent with the closing inventory value that is required for financial reporting, as it incorporates fixed production cost to inventory valuation.

(c) In the long run a business needs to cover its fixed costs to be profitable so when setting selling prices, an organisation needs to be aware of the full cost of the product.

Advantages of marginal costing:

(a) Fixed costs are the same regardless of output and therefore it makes sense to charge them in full as a period cost.

(b) Marginal costing does not require apportionment of fixed costs which can be arbitrary methods of apportionment and choice of activity for absorption.

(c) By charging fixed costs as a period cost there is no under- or over-absorption of fixed overheads.

(d) Marginal costing focuses on variable costs and contribution which can be more useful for decision making (see Chapter 10).

Chapter summary

- The structure of an organisation depends on its activities.

- Different departments or functions can be classified, according to responsibility, as profit centres, investment centres or cost centres.

- These responsibility centres each have a budget associated with them which are combined to form the organisation's budget.

- Costs must be allocated and attributed to the relevant responsibility centre.

- The nature of costs must be determined before budgets can be constructed.

- Costs are either capital or revenue in nature. Revenue expenditure is included in the cost of a product, but capital expenditure is not. Capital expenditure is converted to revenue expenditure in the form of depreciation.

- Direct costs are costs that can be related directly to a cost unit, whereas indirect costs (or overheads) cannot be attributed directly to a cost unit and instead are initially allocated or apportioned to a cost centre.

- Costs are often classified according to their behaviour as activity levels change – the main classifications are variable costs, fixed costs, stepped costs and semi-variable costs.

- There are three main methods of attributing indirect costs to production units – absorption costing, marginal costing and activity based costing (ABC).

- Absorption costing is where the production overheads are included in the cost of each cost unit.

- Under marginal costing, only variable overheads are included in the cost of cost units, with the fixed overheads being charged to the statement of profit or loss as period cost.

- **Absorption costing**: a costing method which includes all production overheads within the cost of the cost units

- **Capital expenditure**: purchases of non-current assets or the improvement of the earning capability of non-current assets

- **Cost centre**: an area of the business for which costs are incurred

- **Cost unit**: in a manufacturing business, each unit of production; in service industries such as hospitality, it may be for example, each meal served

- **Direct cost**: cost that can be directly attributed to a cost unit

- **Fixed cost**: cost that remains constant as activity levels change

- **Full production cost**: prime cost plus indirect costs of production

- **Indirect cost** (overhead): cost that cannot be attributed directly to a cost unit but is initially attributed to a cost centre

- **Investment centre**: an area which incurs costs, generates income but also accounts for its own capital employed

- **Marginal costing**: a costing method which includes only variable costs within the cost of the cost units with fixed costs written off as period costs

- **Prime cost**: the total of all direct costs

- **Profit centre**: an area of the business which incurs costs, but also generates income

- **Relevant range**: the range of activity levels over which a fixed cost will not change

- **Revenue expenditure:**

  - Purchase of goods for resale
  - Maintenance of the existing earning capacity of non-current assets
  - Expenditure incurred in conducting the business

- **Semi-variable cost**: cost which has both a fixed element and variable element

- **Stepped cost**: cost which is fixed over a relatively short range and then increases in steps

- **Variable cost**: cost that increases/decreases directly in line with any change in activity level

Activity answers

Activity 1: Classifying factory cost centres

Cost Centre	Type
Canteen	Service cost centre
Stores	Service cost centre
Stitching	Production cost centre
Maintenance	Service cost centre
Packing	Production cost centre
Finishing	Production cost centre

Activity 2: Classifying centres

Canteen in a factory – Cost centre
Car dealer – Revenue centre
Shop in chain – Profit centre
An independent restaurant – Investment centre

Activity 3: Classifying responsibility centres

Cost/revenue	Responsibility centre
Client entertaining at horse racing	Marketing department
Repair of security alarm system in offices	Administration department
Sick pay for production manager	Production department
Bonus for sales managers	Sales team
Depreciation of production equipment	Production department

Activity 4: JK32

1 unit of JK32	Quantity	Cost per unit	Total
		£	£
Direct materials	0.1	9	0.9
Direct labour	0.04	8	0.32
Fixed overheads	0.04	10	0.40
Total			1.62

Standard quantity of materials for 38,000 is 3,800 kg.

(0.1 kg × 38,000 units)

Standard cost is £61,560

(£1.62 × 38,000 units)

Activity 5: Galaxy

The overhead recovery rate will be **£7.60** per **machine hour**.

(£38,000/5,000 machine hours)

Overheads were under-absorbed by £9,600:

	£
Actual overheads	40,000
Absorbed overheads (£7.60 x 4,000 hours)	30,400
Under-absorption	9,600

Activity 6: Absorption vs. marginal costing

Cost per unit – absorption costing

	£
Direct materials	12,000
Direct labour	15,000
Variable overheads	23,000
Fixed overheads	25,000
Total cost	75,000
Cost per unit =	£75,000/5,000
=	£15 per unit

Cost per unit – marginal costing

	£
Direct materials	12,000
Direct labour	15,000
Variable overheads	23,000
Total cost	50,000
Cost per unit =	£50,000/5,000
=	£10 per unit

Activity 7: Marginal vs. absorption costing profit

	Absorption Costing		Marginal costing	
	Month 1	Month 2	Month 1	Month 2
	£	£	£	£
Sales	1,100,000	1,320,000	1,100,000	1,320,000
Opening inventory	0	200,000	0	120,000
Production costs	750,000	750,000	450,000	450,000
Closing inventory	200,000	350,000	120,000	210,000
Cost of sales	550,000	600,000	330,000	360,000
Fixed overheads	0	0	300,000	300,000
Profit/Loss	550,000	720,000	470,000	660,000

Workings

Sales:

Month 1: £100 × 11,000 = £1,100,000

Month 2: £110 × 12,000 = £1,320,000

Production costs

	£
Direct material	10
Direct labour	8
Variable production overhead (£180,000 / 15,000 units)	12
Marginal cost per unit	30
Fixed production overhead (£300,000 / 15,000 units)	20
Absorption cost per unit	50

Absorption production cost: £50 × 15,000 = £750,000

Marginal production cost: £30 × 15,000 = £450,000

Closing inventory

	Month 1	Month 2
	Units	
Opening inventory	0	4,000
Production	15,000	15,000
Sales	11,000	12,000
Closing inventory	4,000	7,000

Month 1

Absorption costing: £50 × 4000 = £200,000

Marginal costing: £30 × 4,000 = £120,000

Month 2

Absorption costing: £50 × 7,000 = £350,000

Marginal costing: £30 × 7,000 = £210,000

(b)

	Month 1	Month 2
	£	£
Absorption costing profit	550,000	720,000
Change in inventory	(80,000)	(60,000)
Marginal costing profit	470,000	660,000

Workings

Month 1: 4,000 units × £20 per unit = £80,000

Month 2: 3,000 units × £20 per unit = £60,000

Test your learning

1   The direct materials cost for 10,000 units is estimated to be £43,600 and for 12,000 it is estimated to be £52,320. This is a variable cost.

   True or false? Tick the correct answer.

   True   ☐

   False ☐

2   A business expects to incur fixed costs of £64,000 in the following month.

   Complete the table below to show the total fixed cost and the fixed cost per unit at each of the following activity levels.

Activity level	Total fixed cost £	Fixed cost per unit £
3,000 units		
10,000 units		
16,000 units		

3   A business makes 3,500 units per month with the following costs:

   Direct materials   £5 per unit

   Direct labour   £10 per unit

   Rent   £10,000 per month

   Supervisor costs   £7,500 per month for every 5,000 units of production

   The marginal cost per month is

   The full production cost per month is

4   Given below are the activity levels and production costs for the latest six months for a factory:

	Activity level Units	Production cost £
July	103,000	469,000
August	110,000	502,000
September	126,000	547,000
October	113,000	517,000
November	101,000	472,000
December	118,000	533,000

(a) **The variable element of the production cost is**

[   ]

The fixed element of the production cost is

[   ]

(b) **Complete the following table to show the estimated production costs at each of the following levels of production.**

Level of production	Production cost £
120,000 units	
150,000 units	

5   A manufacturing business has two production departments P1 and P2. P1 is a labour intensive department, while P2 is highly mechanised with relatively few machine operatives. Budgeted figures are as follows:

	P1	P2
Overheads apportioned	£50,000	£60,000
Machine hours	800	4,000
Labour hours	2,500	600

(a) **The overhead absorption rate for department P1 is:**

£62.50   ☐
£20.00   ☐
£15.00   ☐
£100.00 ☐

(b) **The overhead absorption rate for department P2 is:**

£62.50   ☐
£20.00   ☐
£15.00   ☐
£100.00 ☐

6 **Complete the following table to show the amount of under- or over-absorption of overheads in each of the three cases below. State in each case whether there is an under- or over-absorption and indicate what adjustment is required in the statement of profit or loss.**

	Amount of under-/over-absorption £	Under- or over-absorption	Add or subtract in statement of profit or loss
An overhead absorption rate of £3 per unit, based on expected production levels of 500 units. Actual overheads turn out to be £1,600, and actual production is 650 units.			
The budget is set at 1,000 units, with £9,000 overheads recovered on the basis of 600 direct labour hours. At the end of the period, overheads amounted to £8,600, production achieved was only 950 units and 590 direct labour hours had been worked.			

7 The budgeted overheads apportioned to two production cost centres, X and Y, together with the budgeted labour hours and machine hours, are given below:

	X	Y
Overheads	£260,000	£380,000
Direct labour hours	20,000	120,000
Machine hours	100,000	10,000

Production cost centre X involves a highly mechanised process, with only a few machine workers. Production Y involves a highly labour intensive process.

(a) **Complete the table to calculate separate departmental overhead absorption rates for each production cost centre using an appropriate basis.**

Department	Overhead absorption rate
X	
Y	

(b) **Each unit of Product A utilises the following hours in each production department.**

	X	Y
Direct labour hours	1	4
Machine hours	5	2

The overhead to be included in the cost of each unit of product A is £ _____ .

8 **Explain how fixed production overheads are treated in an absorption costing system and in a marginal costing system.**

9 Given below is the budgeted information about the production of 60,000 units of a single product in a factory for the next quarter:

Direct materials	£12.50 per unit
Direct labour – assembly	4 hours @ £8.40 per hour
– finishing	1 hour @ £6.60 per hour
Assembly production overheads	£336,000
Finishing production overheads	£84,000

It is estimated that 60% of the assembly overhead is variable cost and that 75% of the finishing overhead is variable cost.

Complete the table below to show the budgeted cost of the product using each method of costing.

Method of costing	Budgeted cost £
Absorption costing	
Marginal costing	

10 Given below are the budgeted figures for production and sales of a factory's single product for the months of November and December:

	November	December
Production	15,000 units	15,000 units
Sales	12,500 units	18,000 units
Direct materials	£12.00 per unit	£12.00 per unit
Direct labour	£8.00 per unit	£8.00 per unit
Variable production cost	£237,000	£237,000
Fixed production cost	£390,000	£390,000

Overheads are absorbed on the basis of budgeted production and the selling price of the product is £75.

There were 2,000 units of the product in inventory at the start of November.

(a) **Prepare the budgeted statements of profit or loss for each of the two months using:**

(i) **Absorption costing**

(ii) **Marginal costing**

Absorption costing – statement of profit or loss

	November		December	
	£	£	£	£
Sales				
Less cost of sales				
Opening inventory				
Production costs				
	———		———	
Less closing inventory				
	———		———	
		———		———
Profit		———		———

Marginal costing – statement of profit or loss

	November		December	
	£	£	£	£
Sales				
Less cost of sales				
Opening inventory				
Production costs				
	———		———	
Less closing inventory				

	November		December	
	————		————	
		————		————
Contribution		————		————
Less fixed overheads		————		————
Profit		————		————

(b) Complete the table below to reconcile the absorption costing profit and the marginal costing profit for each of the two months.

	November £	December £
Absorption costing profit		
Inventory changes		
Marginal costing profit		

Statistical techniques

2

Learning outcomes

3.1	**Calculate key statistical indicators.**
	On completion of this chapter you should be able to:
	• Calculate index numbers, moving averages, seasonal variations and trend information
	Use the regression equation
3.2	**Use and appraise key statistical indicators.**
	On completion of this chapter you should be able to:
	• Use statistical indicators to forecast income and costs
	Give recommendations around cost forecasting, providing reasons for your recommendations

Assessment context

Using statistical techniques in order to forecast costs and revenues is likely to form the basis of one task in the assessment.

Qualification context

Forecasting techniques are tested in *Management Accounting: Budgeting* and *Management Accounting: Decision and Control* at Level 4.

Business context

Business will use a variety of models and techniques to help them forecast the performance of their business.

Chapter overview

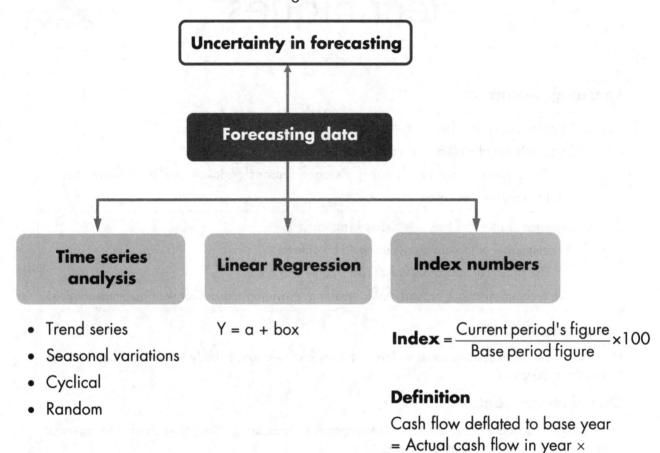

Reduce by:
- Planning models
- Regular re-forecasting
- Flexible budgets

Uncertainty in forecasting

Forecasting data

Time series analysis

- Trend series
- Seasonal variations
- Cyclical
- Random

TS = T + SV

Linear Regression

Y = a + box

Index numbers

$$\text{Index} = \frac{\text{Current period's figure}}{\text{Base period figure}} \times 100$$

Definition

Cash flow deflated to base year
= Actual cash flow in year ×
$$\frac{\text{RPI of base year}}{\text{RPI of year underconsideration}}$$

Introduction

A business may collect data about its previous activities, costs and sales revenues and use it to estimate future levels of activity, costs or sales. This chapter considers a number of statistical techniques that can be used in this way to produce forecasts from historical data.

1 Time series analysis

> **Time series**   A series of figures or values recorded over time.

- Output at a factory each day for the last month
- Total costs per annum for the last ten years
- Monthly sales over the last five years

Time series analysis is an analysis of past patterns of demand or sales which will be used to construct expected patterns in the future. .

1.1 Components of a time series (TS)

Trend (T)

(a)   General movement of a time series over a long period of time (ie growth, inflation)

(b)   Generally expected to be a smooth line/curve

(c)   Find by method of moving averages

For example, a steady decline in the average sales of a national daily newspaper or a steady increase in sales of the Xbox 360.

Seasonal variations (SV)

A predicted movement away from the trend due to repetitive events over a short but fixed period of time (weekly, quarterly).

For example, sales of tabloid newspapers being higher on Mondays and Saturdays than other days due to the extra sports coverage, or sales of ice cream being higher in summer than in winter.

Cyclical variations (C)

Recurring patterns over a longer period of time, not generally of a fixed nature (ie recession/depression/economic growth).

For example, changes in unemployment, movement from recession to economic growth.

Random variations (R)

Irregular/unpredictable variations, due to rare/chance occurrences (hurricanes, floods, nuclear war).

For example, high sales of a tabloid newspaper due to exclusive photographs of a member of the royals in a compromising position.

1.2 The additive model

This is where the components are assumed to add together to give the forecast sales.

Formula to learn

TS = T + SV + R + C

Where:

TS = Time series forecast

T = Trend

SV = Seasonal variations

R = Random variations

C = Cyclical variations

In the assessment, students will only be required to deal with the trend and seasonal variations in calculations. So the formula becomes:

Formula to learn

TS = T + SV

The seasonal variations in time series analysis can be expressed as additions to, or subtractions from, the trend.

1.3 Moving averages

The main method for calculating a trend from a time series is the technique of moving averages, which is an average of the results of a fixed number of periods and relates to the mid-point of the overall period.

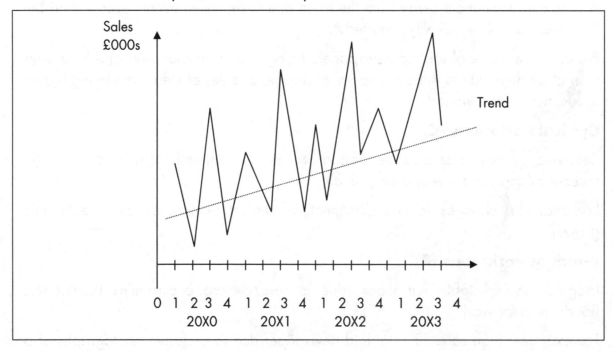

In the above example, there would appear to be a large seasonal variation in demand, but there is also a basic upward trend.

Illustration 1: Moving averages

Suppose that the sales figures for a business for the first six months of the year are as follows:

	£
January	35,500
February	37,500
March	34,500
April	40,000
May	42,000
June	39,000

It is felt that the sales cycle is on a quarterly basis – ie the seasonal variations repeat themselves every three months. What is required, therefore, is a three month moving average. This is done by first totalling the figures for January, February and March and then finding the average:

$$\frac{35,500+37,500+34,500}{3} = £35,833$$

Then we move on by one month, and the average for February, March and April sales is calculated:

$$\frac{37,500+34,500+40,000}{3} = £37,333$$

Then, the average for March, April and May would be calculated as follows:

$$\frac{34,500+40,000+42,000}{3} = £38,833$$

Finally the average for April, May and June can be determined:

$$\frac{40,000+42,000+39,000}{3} = £40,333$$

Now we can show these moving averages, together with the original figures – the convention is to show the moving average next to the middle month of those used in the average.

	Actual data	Moving average – Trend	Seasonal variation
	£	£	£
January	35,500		
February	37,500	35,833	+1,667
March	34,500	37,333	–2,833
April	40,000	38,833	+1,167
May	42,000	40,333	+1,667
June	39,000		

1.4 Calculating forecast sales using the additive model

Once the trend has been established, the forecast sales can be determined.

Formula to learn

Additive model: TS = T + SV

Activity 1: The additive model – YSP Games Ltd

You are employed as an accounting technician at YSP Games Ltd.

The market research department has gathered information about the typical trend and seasonal variation for sales volume for the year ended November 20X7. This information is produced below.

Month	Dec	Jan	Feb	Mar	Apr	May	Jun	Jul	Aug	Sept	Oct	Nov
(000's) Trend	250	255	260	265	270	275	280	285	290	295	300	305
SV												
Actual volume of sales	600	55	50	115	140	175	220	285	290	445	475	480

Required

(a) Explain the terms 'trend' and 'seasonal variation'.

(b) **Complete the table above, by calculating the seasonal variation for 20X7.**

(c) **Using the information in the table above, calculate the forecast sales volume per month for the period August 20X8 to December 20X8.**

Month	Aug X8	Sept X8	Oct X8	Nov X8	Dec X8
Trend (000s)					
SV (000s)					
Forecast (000s)					

Activity 2: The additive model 2

This year, sales are £400,000. Analysis of recent years' sales shows a growth trend of 6% per year.

The seasonal variation has been:

Quarter 1	−£8,000
Quarter 2	−£1,000
Quarter 3	−£2,000
Quarter 4	+£11,000

Required

Forecast the sales revenue for each quarter of next year.

Quarter	£
1	
2	
3	
4	
Year	

1.5 The multiplicative model

The seasonal variations in time series analysis can also be shown as percentages of the trend in the multiplicative model:

Illustration 2: Multiplicative model

The trend figures for sales in units for Earthware Design for the four quarters of 20X0 are given below:

Quarter 1   158,400

Quarter 2   159,900

Quarter 3   161,500

Quarter 4   163,100

The seasonal variations are expressed as follows:

Quarter 1   +8%

Quarter 2   –5%

Quarter 3   –17%

Quarter 4   +14%

What are the forecast sales for each of the quarters of 20X0?

Quarter 1	$158,400 \times 1.08$	=	171,072
Quarter 2	$159,900 \times 0.95$	=	151,905
Quarter 3	$161,500 \times 0.83$	=	134,045
Quarter 4	$163,100 \times 1.14$	=	185,934

1.6 Forecasting problems

Whilst time series analysis has the advantage of being simple to calculate and is useful for identifying an underlying pattern to be developed, it suffers from forecasting problems.

- The further into the future, the more unreliable
- Pattern of trend and seasonal variations may not continue
- Random variations may upset trends
- Environmental changes
- Technological changes

2 Linear regression

Linear regression analysis involves the prediction of the value of one variable, for example total cost, given the value of another variable, such as the volume of output. It assumes that there is a linear relationship (straight line on a graph) between the two variables.

2.1 The equation of a straight line

To find the straight line on a graph the following equation is used:

y = a + bx

Both a and b are constants and represent specific figures:

* a is the point on the graph where the line intersects the y axis.
* b represents the gradient of the line (how steep it is).

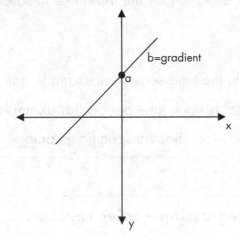

2.2 Using the equation to forecast costs

To **forecast the amount of a semi-variable cost** at a given production level. In the linear equation y = a + bx:

a = Fixed costs

b = Variable cost per unit

y = Total costs

x = Number of units of activity or output

Illustration 3: Linear regression – costs

The linear regression equation for the canteen costs (y) of a business for a month is as follows:

y = 20,000 + 45x

The variable x represents the number of employees using the canteen.

It is anticipated that the number of employees using the canteen in the next three months will be as follows:

	Number of employees
January	840
February	900
March	875

What are the forecast canteen costs for each period?

		£
January	20,000 + (45 × 840)	57,800
February	20,000 + (45 × 900)	60,500
March	20,000 + (45 × 875)	59,375

To **forecast future sales volumes or sales revenue** using the linear regression equation as the equation for the trend line in sales. In the linear equation $y = a + bx$:

> y = Total sales
>
> x = The time period in the time series (for example, the year number)
>
> b = The increase in sales each time period (for example, each year)
>
> a = A constant value, which has no specific meaning

Illustration 4: Linear regression – sales revenue

The trend for sales volume for one of Trinket Ltd's products is given:

> $y = 16.5 + 0.78x$

where y is the volume of sales in thousands in any given time period and x is the time period.

Step 1 Find the values of x for the four quarters in 20X4.

Q1	20X1	$x = 1$
Q2	20X1	$x = 2$
Q3	20X1	$x = 3$
Q4	20X1	$x = 4$
Q1	20X2	$x = 5$

and so on until

Q1	20X4	$x = 13$

Step 2 Calculate the trend for each quarter using the linear regression equation.

20X4	**x value**	**$y = 16.5 + 0.78 x$** '000 units
Q1	13	26.64
Q2	14	27.42
Q3	15	28.20
Q4	16	28.98

Assessment focus point

In assessments you will not be required to derive the linear regression equation for a straight line. Either you will be given this equation and asked to find values of x and y, or you will be given values of x and y and asked to determine the values of a and b.

Activity 3: Linear regression – costs

The linear regression equation for production costs (y) for a business is:

$$y = 63{,}000 + 3.20x$$

Where x = the number of production units.

Required

Calculate the production costs if production is expected to be 44,000 units in the next quarter.

The production costs will be £ [＿＿＿＿＿＿＿]

Activity 4: Linear regression – sales

The linear regression equation for the trend of sales in thousands of units based upon time series analysis of the monthly figures for the last two years is:

$$y = 4.8 + 1.2x$$

Required

Calculate estimated sales trend for each of the first three months of next year.

Month 1 [＿＿＿＿＿＿＿＿＿＿＿＿＿＿＿]

Month 2 [＿＿＿＿＿＿＿＿＿＿＿＿＿＿＿]

Month 3 [＿＿＿＿＿＿＿＿＿＿＿＿＿＿＿]

2.3 Determining a & b

Assessment focus point

If you are asked to calculate the values for a & b in the assessment, you are usually given a range of values for x & y. The a & b variables can then be found by using the high/low method. This is covered in an earlier chapter.

2.4 Extrapolation and interpolation

To forecast a range of figures both extrapolation and interpolation are used:

Interpolation is forecasting a data set within the historical data range.

Extrapolation is forecasting a data set outside of the historical data range.

3 Index numbers

Index Measures over time the average changes in the values, prices or quantities of a group of items.

An index can either be a price or a quantity index for an item or a group of items.

3.1 Characteristics

- Base year – a point in time with which current prices/quantities are compared.
- Weightings are used and they give the relative importance of each item.
- Index numbers may be used to deflate costs for comparison.

3.2 Retail price index (RPI) or cost of living index

The RPI measures the changes in the costs of items of expenditure of the average household.

It can also be used to deflate time-related data (covered later in this chapter).

3.3 Limitations of index numbers

Decisions need to be made regarding the following.

- What items to select for a 'basket'

- What weightings to use to reflect performance

- How to determine a 'typical' base year

- New products or items may appear; old ones might get discontinued. Hence, the index needs to be regularly revised.

- How to source the data and determine its accuracy

We can get a feel for how data is moving over time by converting the actual figures into a series of index numbers.

This is done by, firstly, determining a base period, which is the period for which the actual figure is equated to an index of 100.

Formula to learn

Each subsequent periodic figure is converted to the equivalent index using the following formula:

$$\text{Index} = \frac{\text{Current period figure}}{\text{Base period figure}} \times 100$$

3.4 Interpreting an index

If the index for a period is greater than 100, this means that the current period figure is larger than the base period figure. If it is less than 100, the figure is lower than the base period figure. If the index is generally rising then the figures are increasing over the base period but if the index is decreasing, the figures are decreasing in comparison to the base period.

Remember when interpreting an index that it represents the current period figure compared to the base period, not compared to the previous period.

3.5 Usefulness of indexation in forecasting

Like time series analysis, indexing is another technique for analysing figures for income (or cost) collected over a period of time. From this, management have a greater awareness of the trend of this income, and by extrapolating this trend, sales forecasts can be produced.

As with time series analysis, however, the trend will not continue indefinitely into the future, and external factors regarding the product's market and also its life cycle, should also be taken into account.

Activity 5: Index numbers 1

The cost per kg for the materials used in production has been as follows for the last four months.

January X8	February X8	March X8	April X8
£26.20	£26.80	£26.90	£25.80

Required

(a) Convert the costs per kg for January to April into index numbers using January 20X7 as the base period. The price per kg at January 20X7 was £24.95.

(b) It is expected that the index number in January 20X9 will be 108.26. Calculate the expected cost per kg for January 20X9.

(c) Calculate the percentage increase in the price of materials from January 20X7 to January 20X9.

Note. Round answers to 2dp.

Activity 6: Index numbers 2 – JB Ltd

JB Ltd is planning ahead and wishes to forecast the cost of its main ingredient used in the manufacture of product X.

Required

(a) **Complete the table to show the underlying cost and the forecast cost for each of the months April to June.**

Month	Jan	Feb	Mar	Apr	May	Jun
Underlying cost per kg (£)	180	210	240			
Seasonal variation (£)	40	12	–18	–8	15	–4
Actual cost/forecast cost (£)	220	222	222			

(b) The cost per unit of its other key material – BR3 was £50 per kilogram on 1 January X1 and is £80 per kilogram on 1 January X8.

Using January X1 as the base year, the cost index for material BR3 as at 1 January X8 is ☐

The cost per unit has increased by ☐ **% between January X1 and X8.**

3.6 Time related data and indices

An index can be used to deflate or inflate time-related data, such as wages, to see whether the data in question is rising faster or slower than prices.

3.6.1 Deflation

Formula to learn

$$\text{Cash flow deflated to base year} = \text{Actual cash flow in year under consideration} \times \frac{\text{RPI of base year}}{\text{RPI of year under consideration}}$$

3.6.2 Inflation

> **Formula to learn**
>
> | Cash flow inflated to the current year | = | Actual cash flow in year under consideration | × | $\dfrac{\text{RPI in current year}}{\text{RPI of year under consideration}}$ |
> |---|---|---|---|---|

Activity 7: Index numbers 3 – Tees R Us

Tees R Us Ltd makes and packs tea bags. The tea is imported from India and the historical cost per kilogram is shown below.

June X7	July X7	Aug X7	Sept X7	Oct X7	Nov X7
£4.95	£4.97	£4.99	£5.05	£5.08	£5.10

Required

(a) **Convert the costs per kg for June and November into index numbers using January 20X7 as the base period. The price per kg at January 20X7 was £4.80.**

(b) **It is expected that the index number for tea in January 20X8 will be 108.25. Calculate the expected cost per kg for January 20X8.**

(c) **Calculate the percentage increase in the price of tea from January 20X7 to January 20X8.**

Activity 8: Ashby Ltd

Ashby Ltd uses a raw material, ZZ20, in its production. The industry maintains a price index for ZZ20. The index for May 20X9 was 107 and the actual price per tonne was £800. The forecast index for the three months ending November 20X9 is shown below.

Month	September	October	November
Underlying trend in index	110	115	120
Seasonal variation in index	+12	−9	+5
Seasonally adjusted Index	122	106	125

Required

(a) **Calculate the expected cost of one tonne of ZZ20 for each of the three months.**

(b) **The company is able to secure a contract price for 80 tonnes of ZZ20 per month for the three months at a price of £900 per tonne. Calculate whether the contract would result in a lower price.**

4 Uncertainties in forecasting

All forecasts are likely to include errors, but be aware of some of the following general limitations in the use of forecasting:

- The more data that is used, the better the results of the forecast will be, so a forecast based on limited data will inevitably be of limited use.

- The further into the future that the forecast considers, the more unreliable it will become.

- Forecast figures will often be based upon the assumption that current conditions will continue in the future, eg extrapolation of a trend based upon historical data, which may not be a valid assumption.

- If the forecast is based upon a trend, there are always random elements or variations which cause the trend to change.

- The forecast produced from the historical data may be quite accurate but the actual future results may be very different from the forecast figures due to changes in the political, economic or technological environment within which the business operates.

Uncertainties in forecasting can be addressed by using techniques such as planning models, regular re-forecasting, re-budgeting, rolling budgets and budget flexing.

Assessment focus point

In assessments, the limitations of any income or expenditure forecasts will depend upon each scenario and the task set. Therefore, try to use the information given and consider these general limitations within that context.

Chapter summary

- The creation of budgets requires information or data.

- Both internal and external sources of data must be used in forecasting and budgeting.

- Internal information can be found from the historical financial accounting records, files of documents such as invoices, payroll details and inventory records, and many other sources in an organisation.

- External information can be found from government statistics, trade journals, newspapers and the internet.

- To prepare budgets, forecasts must be constructed.

- Forecasts of activity will be required, in particular for the key budget factor (limiting factor), but also for other elements of income and expense.

- The key budget factor may not necessarily be sales demand but may instead be related to a shortage of materials, a shortage of suitable labour or a lack of production capacity.

- The natural starting point for a sales forecast would be information from the sales experts within the business.

- Market research might be an appropriate method of forecasting sales for a new or substantially improved product.

- Time series analysis can be used to estimate the trend for future periods and then apply seasonal variations to find the forecast sales figures.

- The position of a product within its life cycle needs to be taken into account when forecasting future demand.

- Indexing can also be used to look at trends over time. Index numbers measure the change in value of a figure over time, by reference to its value at a fixed point.

- Linear regression analysis can be used to estimate either semi-variable costs at a particular activity level or future sales volumes at a particular point in time, based on the assumption of a linear trend in sales.

- The linear regression line, y = a + bx, will always be given to you in an assessment and you will not need to derive it. However, care should be taken with the variables x and y; x is always the independent variable and y is the dependent variable.

- You may also need to calculate y given values for a, b and x, or a value for x given values for a, b and y. You may also be required to apply the high low method to calculate values for a and b given two pairs of values for x and y.

Keywords

- **Base period:** the period for which the index is expressed as 100 and against which all other period figures are compared

- **Centred moving average:** the average of two consecutive moving averages when the period for the moving average is an even number

- **Forecast**: an estimate of what may happen in the future based upon historical data and knowledge of future changes

- **Index number:** conversion of actual figures compared to a base year where the base year index is expressed as 100

- **Key budget factor:** the element or resource of the business that places limitations on the activities of the business

- **Linear regression:** a technique for forecasting semi-variable costs or future sales using the equation for a straight line

- **Linear regression equation** $y = a + bx$

  where:　　a is the point on the graph where the line intersects the y axis
  　　　　　b is the gradient of the line

- **Moving average:** the calculation of an average figure for the results of consecutive periods of time

- **Population:** all of the items of data we are interested in for a particular data collecting purpose

- **Quota sampling:** the number of items required from each group is determined and then a non-random sample is taken to provide the required numbers

- **Random sampling:** all items in the population are known and are picked using random numbers

- **Retail Price Index:** a measure of the increase or decrease in general prices in the UK

- **Sampling:** a method of finding out information about a population by only testing a sample of the items in the population

- **Seasonal variations:** the regular short-term pattern of increases or decreases in figures in a time series

- **Time series:** a series of income or expense figures recorded for a number of consecutive periods

- **Time series analysis:** a method of calculating the trend and other relevant figures from a time series

- **Trend:** the underlying movements of the time series over the period

Activity 1: The additive model – YSP Games Ltd

(a) The **trend** refers to the general direction in which a time series changes over time. This could be a steady increase, decrease or static level.

The **seasonal variation** is a predicted movement away from the trend for segments of the time series. These segments could be hours, days or months.

(b)

Month	Dec	Jan	Feb	Mar	Apr	May	Jun	Jul	Aug	Sept	Oct	Nov
(000's) Trend	250	255	260	265	270	275	280	285	290	295	300	305
SV	**350**	**(200)**	**(210)**	**(150)**	**(130)**	**(100)**	**(60)**	**0**	**0**	**150**	**175**	**175**
Actual volume of sales	600	55	50	115	140	175	220	285	290	445	475	480

(c) Forecast sales volumes for August X8 to December X8

The trend rises by 5 each month, therefore:

Month	Aug	Sept	Oct	Nov	Dec
(000's) Trend	350	355	360	365	370
SV	0	150	175	175	350
Forecast sales volume	350	505	535	540	720

Activity 2: The additive model 2

Quarter	Underlying trend (W1) £	Seasonal Variation £	Forecast £
1	106,000	–8,000	**98,000**
2	106,000	–1,000	**105,000**
3	106,000	–2,000	**104,000**
4	106,000	+11,000	**117,000**
Year	106,000	0	**424,000**

(W1) The sales for the year are forecast to increase by 6%

£400,000 × 1.06 = £424,000.

This equates to an underlying trend of £106,000 per quarter.

Activity 3: Linear regression – costs

The total production costs will be **£203,800**.

63,000 + 3.2 × 44,000

Activity 4: Linear regression – sales

y = 4.8 + 1.2x

The first two years account for x = 1 to x = 24

Therefore the x values in which we are interested are x = 25, 26, 27

Month 1   x = 25:   y = 4.8 + 1.2(25)   = 34.8   ie £34,800

Month 2   x = 26:   y = 4.8 + 1.2(26)   = 36.0   ie £36,000

Month 3   x = 27:   y = 4.8 + 1.2(27)   = 37.2   ie £37,200

Activity 5: Index numbers 1

(a)   Jan X8 = $\dfrac{26.20}{24.95}$ × 100 = 105

Feb X8 = $\dfrac{26.80}{24.95}$ × 100 = 107.41

Mar X8 = $\dfrac{26.90}{24.95}$ × 100 = 107.82

Apr X8 = $\dfrac{25.80}{24.95}$ × 100 = 103.41

(b)   £24.95 × $\dfrac{108.26}{100}$ = £27.01 per kg

(c) $\dfrac{£27.01 - £24.95}{£24.95}$ = 8.26%

Activity 6: Index numbers 2 – JB Ltd

JB Ltd is planning ahead and wishes to forecast the cost of its main ingredient used in the manufacture of product X.

(a)

Month	Jan	Feb	Mar	Apr	May	Jun
Underlying cost per kg (£)	180	210	240	**270**	**300**	**330**
Seasonal variation (£)	40	12	−18	−8	15	−4
Actual cost/forecast cost (£)	220	222	222	**262**	**315**	**326**

(b) Index = $\dfrac{£80}{£50} \times 100 = \boxed{160}$

The percentage increase during this period is $\boxed{60\%}$

$\dfrac{80-50}{50} \times 100\% = 60\%$

Activity 7: Index numbers 3 – Tees R Us

(a) June X7 = $\dfrac{4.95}{4.8} \times 100 = 103.125$

Nov X7 = $\dfrac{5.1}{4.8} \times 100 = 106.25$

(b) $£4.80 \times \dfrac{108.25}{100} = £5.196$ or $£5.20$

(c) $\dfrac{£5.20-£4.80}{£4.80} = 8.33$ per kg

Or $\dfrac{£5.196-£4.80}{£4.80} = 8.25\%$

Activity 8: Ashby Ltd

(a)

September	= £800 × 122/107	£912.15
October	= £800 × 106/107	£792.52
November	= £800 × 125/107	£934.58

(b)

Total cost for the 3 months is:

		£
912.15 × 80	=	72,972.00
792.52 × 80	=	63,401.60
934.58 × 80	=	74,766.40
		211,140.00

Forward contract cost = £900 × 80 = £72,000 × 3 months = £216,000

The contract does not result in a lower price.

Test your learning

1   Given below are the production cost figures for a business for the last year.

    Complete the table to calculate a three-month moving average for these figures.

	Actual £	Three-month moving average £
July	397,500	
August	403,800	
September	399,600	
October	405,300	
November	406,100	
December	408,500	
January	407,900	
February	410,400	
March	416,000	
April	413,100	
May	417,500	
June	421,800	

2   Given below are the quarterly sales figures for a business for the last three and a half years.

Complete the table to calculate a four-quarter moving average, the trend using a centred moving average and the seasonal variations.

		Actual £	Four-quarter moving average £	Centred moving average = TREND £	Seasonal variations £
20X5	Quarter 1	383,600			
	Quarter 2	387,600			
	Quarter 3	361,800			
	Quarter 4	328,600			
20X6	Quarter 1	385,900			
	Quarter 2	392,400			
	Quarter 3	352,500			
	Quarter 4	338,800			
20X7	Quarter 1	392,500			
	Quarter 2	410,300			
	Quarter 3	368,900			
	Quarter 4	344,400			
20X8	Quarter 1	398,300			
	Quarter 2	425,600			

3   Given below are the direct materials costs of business operations for the last six months.

Complete the table to calculate the index for each month's costs using January as the base month. Give your answers to one decimal place.

	Cost £	Index
January	59,700	
February	62,300	
March	56,900	
April	60,400	
May	62,400	
June	66,700	

4   Given below are the wages costs of a business for the last six months together with the Retail Prices Index for those months.

(a) **Complete the table to calculate the RPI adjusted wages cost figures for each of the six months, with all costs expressed in terms of June prices.**

	Wages cost £	RPI	Adjusted cost £
January	126,700	171.1	
February	129,700	172.0	
March	130,400	172.2	
April	131,600	173.0	
May	130,500	172.1	
June	131,600	171.3	

(b) **Using the adjusted RPI wages costs, complete the table to calculate an index for the wages costs for each month with January as the base year.**

	Adjusted cost £	Index
January		
February		
March		
April		
May		
June		

5   The total production costs of a business are £15,000 if 1,000 units are produced, and £25,000 if 2,000 units are produced. The linear regression equation

$y = a + bx$

can be used to forecast the production costs where y is the total production cost and x is volume of production.

Calculate a and b, and then the production costs if 1,400 units are produced.

6   The linear regression equation for costs of the stores department of a business is given as follows:

$y = 13,000 + 0.8x$

where x is the number of units produced in a period.

The anticipated production levels for the next six months are given below.

Complete the table to calculate the forecast stores department costs for the next six months.

	Production Units	Costs £
January	5,400	
February	5,600	
March	5,700	
April	6,000	
May	5,500	
June	6,100	

7   A time series analysis of sales volumes each quarter for the last three years, 20X6 to 20X8, has revealed that the trend can be estimated by the equation:

$y = 2,200 + 45x$

where y is the sales volume and x is the time period.

The seasonal variations for each quarter have been calculated as:

Quarter 1   −200
Quarter 2   +500
Quarter 3   +350
Quarter 4   −650

Use the table below to estimate the sales volume for each quarter of 20X9.

	Value of x	Trend	Seasonal variation	Forecast sales
Quarter 1 20X9				
Quarter 2 20X9				
Quarter 3 20X9				
Quarter 4 20X9				

Standard costing

3

Learning outcomes

2.1	**Discuss how standard costing can aid the planning and control of an organisation**
	On completion of this chapter you should be able to:
	• Explain how standard costs can be established, and the different types of standard that can be set (ideal, target, normal and basic)
	• Explain how the type of standard chosen can affect behaviour of staff within an organisation
	• Explain how standard costs aid the flexible budgeting process, and how the standard cost is affected by changes in output
2.2	**Calculate standard costing information.**
	On completion of this chapter you should be able to:
	• Prepare a standard cost card from given information
	• Extract information contained in a budgetary control report

Assessment context

Standard costing forms the basis of variance analysis (covered later in the course). It is therefore important that you are able to accurately calculate standard costs. Standard costing is therefore likely to form the basis of the first task in the assessment.

Business context

Many manufacturing organisations and some service industries make use of standard costing systems. Standard costs provide management with information to aid planning, decision making and controlling the business operations.

Chapter overview

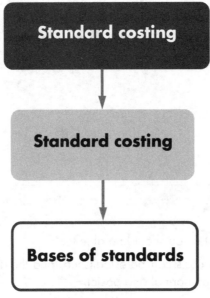

Standard costing

Standard costing

Bases of standards

- Ideal
- Attainable
- Current
- Basic

1 Introduction

A **standard costing system** is one in which a business produces a number of standard products. Every unit of a standard product is expected to use the same quantity of direct materials and requires the same amount of time to make.

The standard cost is the planned unit cost of a standard product or service, and is therefore expected cost of producing one unit of that product or service.

2 Standard cost card

The standard cost of each unit is set out in a **standard cost card**, which is then used for budgeting and control within an organisation.

Illustration 1: Standard cost card

The below details a standard cost card for Product A:

	£	£
Direct materials		
Material X – 3 kg at £4 per kg	12.00	
Material Y – 9 litres at £2 per litre	18.00	
		30.00
Direct labour		
Grade A – 6 hours at £7 per hour	42.00	
Grade B – 8 hours at £8 per hour	64.00	
		106.00
Prime cost		136.00
Variable production overhead – 14 hours at £0.50 per hour		7.00
Fixed production overhead – 14 hours at £4.50 per hour		63.00
Standard full production cost		206.00

This cost card can then be used when setting budgets and controlling production of Product A.

Activity 1: Latt

Latt expects to make 5,000 units of production in the coming year.

The following has been estimated:

Each unit will require 3 kg of material with a total cost of £15.

Each unit will require 2 hours of labour paid at £7 per hour.

Fixed overheads are expected to be £50,000.

Required

Complete the standard cost card below:

Unit	Quantity	Cost per unit	Total unit cost
Material			
Labour			
Fixed overheads			
Total			

3 Setting standard costs

A standard cost is calculated from management expectations of:

- Usage and efficiency levels on the use of materials and labour
- Prices of materials, labour and overheads
- Budgeted overhead costs and budgeted levels of activity

To aid budgeting and control, it is important that the standard cost is accurate and reviewed regularly.

3.1 Information used to set the standard

In order to set an accurate standard cost, the following information can be used:

- **Materials price per unit** can be obtained from supplier invoices and quotations. This needs to be reviewed regularly for inflation and general increases in the market price.

- **Materials usage per unit** can be obtained from initial product specifications. If the specification changes this may in turn change the material used per unit.

- **Labour rate per unit** can be obtained from employee payroll records. This needs to be reviewed regularly for anticipated pay increases and any overtime that is regularly worked.

- **Labour time per unit** can be obtained from employee timesheets and clock cards. Consideration also needs to be given to the skill level of employees used on the product, as more skilled workers will produce the product in less time.

70

- **Variable production overhead** is usually assumed to vary with direct labour hours worked.

- **Fixed production overhead** is the Overhead Absorption Rate per unit.

Assessment focus point

The methods of setting standards may form part of a written assessment question. It is important that you are able to describe the different ways a standard can be set, and explain why a standard may need to be regularly reviewed.

3.2 Bases of standard

Target/attainable standards

- A standard that contains achievable improvements to the current standard.
- Allows for wastage and inefficiency.
- Employees should be motivated to improve performance as the target set is within their reach.
- The improvement is reliant on the target being realistic and achievable.

Ideal standards

- A standard that is set assuming perfect operating conditions apply
- No allowance for wastage, inefficiencies and idle time
- This base usually demotivates employees as they see the standard as being unrealistic and unachievable.
- Budgets set using ideal standards can be inaccurate as it doesn't reflect realistic working conditions.

Bases

Normal standards

- A standard based on current working conditions
- Any inefficiencies in the current conditions will be taken forward in the standard.
- This base can to stagnation and underperformance, as managers have little incentive to improve further.

Basic standards

- An historical standard that is unaltered over a long period
- This is easy to set, but becomes out of date quickly.
- This base encourages slack in budgets, so managers are demotivated to find improvements.
- Basic standards are not usually used in practice.

Assessment focus point

A written question may involve you explaining the behavioural implications of setting a standard using a certain base. This is demonstrated in the activity below.

Activity 2: GreenGrass Ltd

GreenGrass Ltd have always used ideal standards when setting standard costs. Recently, the managers at GreenGrass have been complaining that the standards that they are monitored against are unrealistic and unachievable. This has led to increased demotivation throughout GreenGrass.

The Finance Director is now considering using attainable standards in order address this demotivation.

Required

Explain how setting attainable standards can improve motivation within GreenGrass Ltd.

4 Purposes of standards

The uses of standard costing are:

- Prediction of costs and times for **decision making**, eg for allocating resources.

- In setting **budgets** for **planning** purposes – an accurate standard will increase the accuracy of the budget.

- Variance analysis is a **control** technique which compares actual with standard costs and revenues. This is covered in a later chapter.

- **Performance evaluation** systems make use of standards as motivators and also as a basis for assessment.

- **Inventory valuation** – this is often less time consuming than alternative valuations methods such as LIFO, FIFO and weighted average.

Assessment focus point

Some assessment questions will ask you to extract information from standard cost cards and budget control reports. This can be either a written or numerical task. The following activity demonstrates an example of this type of question.

Activity 3: Press Co

The budgeted and actual results for Press Co for the month of February 20X1 are as follows:

	Budget		Actual	
Production (units of C06)		12,000		15,000
Direct materials	21,000 kg	£63,000	26,000 kg	£79,000
Direct labour	2,400 hours	£36,000	3,100 hours	£47,000
Fixed overheads (absorbed on a unit basis)		£54,000		£60,000
Total		£153,000		£186,000

Required

Complete the following sentences:

(a) The standard quantity of labour per unit is [   ] minutes.

(b) The budgeted quantity of materials needed to produce 15,000 units of C06 is [   ] kg.

(c) The budgeted labour hours to produce 11,500 units of C06 is [   ] hours.

(d) The budgeted labour cost to produce 15,000 units of C06 is £ [   ].

(e) The budgeted overhead absorption rate per unit is £ [   ].

(f) The fixed production overheads were [   ] by £ [   ].

Chapter Summary

- In a standard costing system, all output is valued at a standard cost per unit.

- The direct materials standard cost is set by determining the estimated quantity of material to be used per unit and the estimated price of that material.

- The direct labour standard cost is set by determining the estimated labour time per unit and the estimated rate per hour.

- The fixed overhead standard cost is determined by finding a realistic estimate of each of the elements of the fixed overhead.

- The standards that can be set are an ideal standard, attainable standard, current standard and basic standard.

Keywords

- **Standard costing system:** a costing system where costs of production are recorded at a standard cost as set out in a standard cost card. Actual costs are compared in detail with this standard cost card and variances (differences) are recorded and reported

- **Standard cost card:** document detailing the standard cost of a unit of a product

- **Ideal standards:** standards based on perfect working conditions

- **Target/attainable standards:** realistically achievable standards into which are built elements of normal wastage and inefficiency

- **Normal standards:** standards based on current working conditions

- **Basic standards:** historical standards that are normally set when the product is initially produced

Activity 1 – Latt

Unit	Quantity	Cost per unit	Total unit cost
Material	3 kg	5.00	15.00
Labour	2 hours	7.00	14.00
Fixed overheads	2 hours	5.00	10.00
Total			39.00

Activity 2: GreenGrass Ltd

Attainable standards are **more realistic** as they reflect current operating conditions within GreenGrass Ltd. This is because allowances are made for idle time, wastage and other inefficiencies in the production process. This will improve motivation as managers are appraised against realistic conditions.

Although attainable standards include some improvements to the current standard, they do not encourage excessive improvement such as an ideal standard does. This makes the attainable standard **more achievable** than ideal standards. Managers are therefore more motivated as the target set is within their reach.

Managers are likely to be **less tightly controlled** using an attainable standard. This is because the budget set will be more accurate as it reflects realistic operating conditions. Whilst there will still be an element of control it will be less strict than under ideal standards, which motivates managers in turn.

Activity 3: Press Co

(a) The standard quantity of labour per unit is [12] minutes.

(b) The budgeted quantity of materials needed to produce 15,000 units of C06 is [26,250] kg.

(c) The budgeted labour hours to produce 11,500 units of C06 is [2,300] hours.

(d) The budgeted labour cost to produce 15,000 units of C06 is £ [45,000].

(e) The budgeted overhead absorption rate per unit is £ [4.50].

(f) The fixed production overheads were [over] by £ [7,500].

Test your learning

1 **Explain where the information for setting the standard direct labour cost would be found and what factors should be taken into consideration when setting it.**

2 **Explain where the information for setting the standard direct material cost would be found and what factors should be taken into consideration when setting it.**

3 **Explain the difference between ideal standards, target standards and basic standards.**

4 **Explain the motivational impact of setting an ideal standard.**

Variance analysis

4

Learning outcomes

2.3	**Calculate the following standard costing variances:**
	• Raw materials variances (total raw material, price and usage)
	• Labour variances (total, rate, and efficiency)
	• Variable overhead variances (total, rate and efficiency)
	• Fixed production variances (total, expenditure, volume, capacity and efficiency)

Assessment context

Variance analysis will be frequently examined in the assessment, and is split between two tasks – one on variable cost variances and one on fixed costs variances.

Business context

Variance calculations are universally performed to enable management to understand which areas of the business are/are not performing well.

Chapter overview

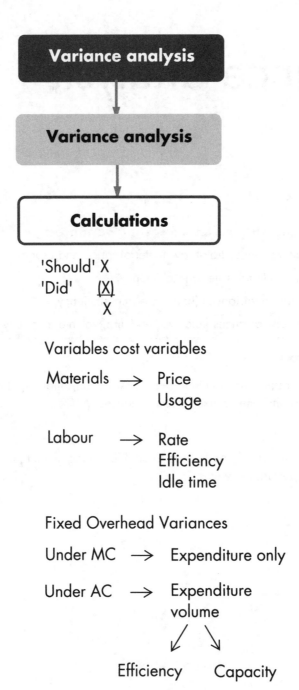

Variance analysis

Variance analysis

Calculations

'Should'   X
'Did'   (X)
           X

Variables cost variables

Materials → Price
              Usage

Labour   → Rate
              Efficiency
              Idle time

Fixed Overhead Variances

Under MC → Expenditure only

Under AC → Expenditure
             volume

         Efficiency   Capacity

1 Introduction

Variances explain the difference between actual results and expected results.

They can either be **favourable** (F), ie better than expected, or **adverse** (A), ie worse than expected.

Each standard cost is made up of a quantity element and an expenditure element. Differences in quantities are known as efficiency, usage or volume variances. Differences in expenditure are known as rate, price or expenditure variances.

The variances are performed in order to flex the budget to actual levels, so that a like-for-like comparison can be made.

> **Assessment focus point**
>
> You will be asked to calculate all of the variances detailed below, so make sure you learn each proforma set out below.

2 Direct cost variances

The direct cost variances cover direct materials, direct labour and variable overheads. Each of the total variances can be broken down as follows:

Summary of variances: standard absorption costing

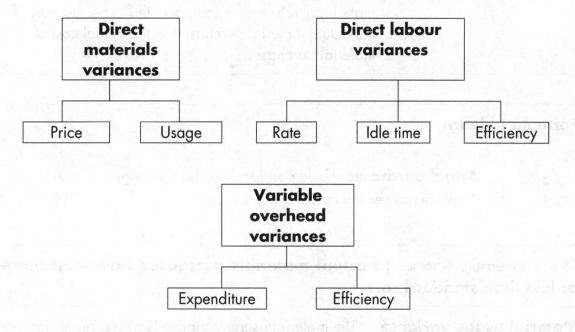

2.1 Materials variances

Total material variance   The total material variance is based on actual production. It compares the expected total cost of materials for actual production to the total actual cost of materials.

Formula to learn

			£
'Should'	**Actual units** should cost (Act units × std kg per unit × std £ per kg)		X
'Did'	Actual material used did cost		(X)
			X

This will measure whether the **materials cost more or less than standard cost**.

The total material variance can then be split into the material price and material usage variances as follows:

Material price variance   The material price variance is based on the actual material purchased. It compares the expected cost of the actual material purchased to the actual cost of material purchased.

Formula to learn

		£
'Should'	**Actual purchases** should cost (Act kg × std £ per kg)	X
'Did'	Actual purchases did cost	(X)
		X

This will measure whether the **actual materials purchased have cost more or less than standard cost**.

Material usage variance   The material usage variance is based on actual production units. It compares the expected usage of material for actual production to the actual usage of material for actual production. This kg variance is then valued at standard cost per kg to calculate a monetary variance.

Formula to learn

			Kg
'Should'	**Actual production** should use (Act units × std kg per unit)		X
'Did'	Actual production did use		(X)
			X
	Difference valued at standard cost		£X

This will measure the **cost of using more or less material than the standard allows.**

Illustration 1: Direct materials variances

The standard cost card for one of Lawson Ltd's products, the George, is shown below:

	£
Direct materials 4 kg @ £2.00 per kg	8.00
Direct labour 2 hours @ £7.00 per hour	14.00
Fixed overheads 2 hours @ £3.00 per hour	6.00
Total standard absorption cost	28.00

The budgeted level of production for July was 20,000 units but in fact only 18,000 units were produced.

The actual quantity of materials used in July was 68,000 kg. The total cost of the materials was £142,800.

Calculate the following variances:

(a) Direct materials total variance
(b) Direct materials price variance
(c) Direct materials usage variance

(a) Direct materials total variance

	£
18,000 units should have cost (18000 units × 4 kg × £2.00)	144,000
But did cost	142,800
Total materials cost variance	1,200 (F)

The actual price is less than the standard, so the price variance is favourable.

(b) Direct materials price variance

	£
68,000 kg of materials should have cost	136,000
(68000 kg × £2.00)	
But did cost	142,800
Materials price variance	6,800 (A)

The actual price paid for the materials is more than the standard price, so the price variance is adverse.

(c) Direct materials usage variance

	Kg
18,000 units should have used (× 4 kg)	72,000
But did use	68,000
Materials usage variance in kg	4,000 (F)
× Standard price per kg of materials	×£2
Material usage variance in £	£8,000 (F)

The actual quantity of materials used is less than the expected or standard quantity, so the usage variance is favourable.

The materials variances can be reconciled as follows:

	£
Materials price variance	6,800 (A)
Materials usage variance	8,000 (F)
Total materials cost variance	1,200 (F)

Activity 1: News Co

News Co operates a standard costing system. It purchases and uses 53,000 kg of material at a cost of £2.38 per kg.

The budgeted production was 25,000 units which requires 50,000 kg of material at a total standard cost of £125,000. The actual production was 27,000 units.

Required

Calculate:

(a) **the total materials variance**
(b) **the material price variance**
(c) **the material usage variance**

(a)   The total materials variance is   £ [_____]   [_____ ▼]

(b)   The material price variance is   £ [_____]   [_____ ▼]

(c)   The material usage variance is   £ [_____]   [_____ ▼]

Picklist:

Adverse
Favourable

2.2 Labour variances

Key term

Total labour variance	The total labour variance is based on actual production units. It compares the expected labour cost of actual production to the actual cost of actual production.

Formula to learn		£
'Should'	**Actual units** should cost (Act units × std hrs per unit × std £ per hour)	X
'Did'	Actual labour used did cost	<u>(X)</u>
		<u>X</u>

This will measure whether the **labour cost more or less than standard cost.**

This total labour cost variance is then split into labour rate and labour efficiency variances as follows:

Key term

Labour rate variance	The labour rate variance is based on actual hours paid. It compares the expected cost of actual hours paid to the actual cost of actual hours paid.

Formula to learn		£
'Should'	**Actual hours paid** should cost (Act hrs paid × std £ per hour)	X
'Did'	Actual hours paid did cost	<u>(X)</u>
		<u>X</u>

This will measure whether the **actual hours paid for cost more or less than standard**.

Key term

Labour efficiency variance   The labour efficiency variance is based on actual production. It compares the expected hours of actual production to the actual hours of actual production. The hour variance is then multiplied by the standard cost per labour hour to calculate a monetary variance.

Formula to learn

		Hrs
'Should'	**Actual production** should take (Act units × std hrs per unit)	X
'Did'	Actual production did take	(X)
		X
	Difference valued at standard rate per hour	£X

This will measure the **cost of production taking more or less time than the standard allows.**

This will measure the cost of employees being unproductive in the period.

Illustration 2: Direct Labour Variances

The standard direct labour cost of product X is as follows.

   2 hours of labour at £5 per hour = £10 per unit

During the period, 1,500 units of product X were made. The cost of labour was £17,500. 2,980 hours were worked.

Calculate the following variances.

(a) **The direct labour total variance**
(b) **The direct labour rate variance**
(c) **The direct labour efficiency variance**

(a) **The direct labour total variance**

	£
1,500 units of product X should have cost £10 per unit	15,000
But did cost	17,500
Direct labour total variance	2,500 (A)

   Actual cost is greater than standard cost. The variance is therefore adverse.

(b) Direct labour rate variance

	£
2,980 hours should have cost (2,980 hours × £5 per hour)	14,900
But did cost	17,500
Direct labour rate variance	2,600 (A)

Actual cost is greater than standard cost. The rate variance is therefore adverse.

(c) Direct labour efficiency variance

	Hrs
1,500 units should take (1,500 units × 2 hours)	3,000
But did take	2,980
Direct labour efficiency variance in hours	20 (F)
× Standard rate per hour	× £5
Direct labour efficiency variance in £	£100 (F)

20 fewer hours were worked to produce 1,500 units, so the variance is favourable

The variances can be reconciled as follows:

	£
Direct labour rate variance	2,100 (A)
Direct labour efficiency variance	100 (F)
Direct labour total cost variance	2,500 (A)

Activity 2: Yard Co

Yard Co, operating a standard costing system, expects to produce 3,000 units of Y using 12,000 hours of labour. The standard cost of labour is £12.50 per hour.

Last month the company actually made 2,195 units. The actual labour cost was £110,750 for the 9,200 hours worked.

Required

Calculate:

(a) the total labour variance

(b) the labour rate variance

(c) the labour efficiency variance

(a) The total labour variance is   £ [   ] [▼]

(b) The labour rate variance is   £ [   ] [▼]

(c) The labour efficiency variance is £ [   ] [▼]

2.3 Variable overheads variances

Key term

Total variable overhead variance	The total variable overhead variance is based on actual production units. It compares the expected variable overhead cost for actual production to the actual variable overhead cost for actual production.

Formula to learn

		£
'Should'	**Actual units** should cost	X
'Did'	Actual variable overheads did cost	(X)
		X

This will measure whether the **overheads cost more or less than standard cost**.

The total variable overhead variance is then split into variable overhead expenditure and variable overhead efficiency variances as follows:

Key term

Variable overhead expenditure variance	The variable overhead expenditure variance is based on actual hours worked. It compares the expected variable overhead cost of actual hours worked to the actual variable overhead cost of actual hours worked.

Formula to learn

		£
'Should'	**Actual hours paid** should cost (Act hrs paid × std £ per hour)	X
'Did'	Actual hours paid did cost	(X)
		X

This will measure whether the **actual hours worked have cost more or less in overhead than expected.**

Key term

Variable overhead efficiency variance	The variable overhead efficiency variance is based on actual production. It compares the expected hours for actual production to the actual hours for actual production. The hour variance is then multiplied by the standard variable overhead per hour to calculate a monetary variance.

Formula to learn

		Hrs
'Should'	**Actual production** should take	X
'Did'	Actual production did take	(X)
		X
	Difference valued at standard variable overhead rate per hour	£X

This will measure whether **actual production took more or less time than the standard allowed, therefore using more overhead.**

Activity 3: Bee Co

Bee Co uses the following standard cost card for product H:

2 hours of labour at £15 per hour = £30 per unit

During the period, 1,000 units of product Z were made in 1,960 hours. The cost of variable production overhead was £30,750.

Required

Calculate:

(a) the total variable overhead variance

(b) the variable overhead expenditure variance

(c) the variable overhead efficiency variance

(a)   The total variable overhead variance is £ ⬚ ⬚ ▼

(b)   The variable overhead expenditure variance is £ ⬚ ⬚ ▼

(c)   The variable overhead efficiency variance is £ ⬚ ⬚ ▼

Picklist:

Adverse

Favourable

3 Fixed overhead variances (under absorption costing)

Under **absorption costing**, the total fixed overhead variance is known as over or under absorption. Overheads can be over- or under-absorbed because:

(1) The overhead incurred cost more or less than expected or;

(2) Greater or fewer units were produced than expected.

The over/under-absorbed overhead can therefore be broken down as follows:

Total variance (over/under absorption)

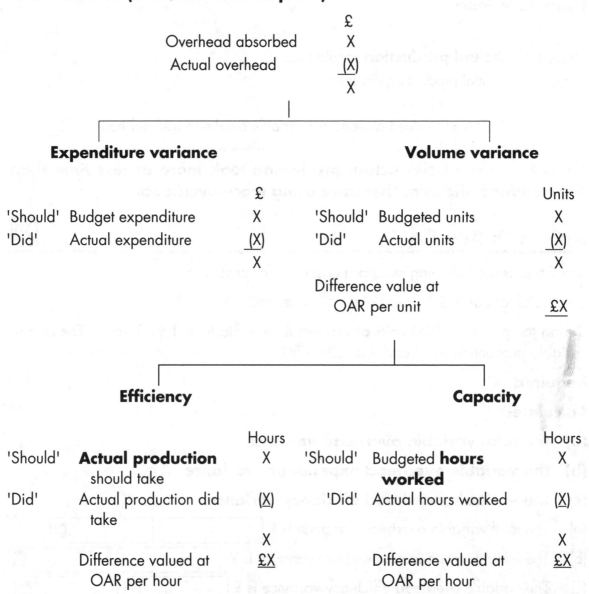

		£
	Overhead absorbed	X
	Actual overhead	(X)
		X

Expenditure variance

		£
'Should'	Budget expenditure	X
'Did'	Actual expenditure	(X)
		X

Volume variance

		Units
'Should'	Budgeted units	X
'Did'	Actual units	(X)
		X
	Difference value at OAR per unit	£X

Efficiency

		Hours
'Should'	**Actual production** should take	X
'Did'	Actual production did take	(X)
		X
	Difference valued at OAR per hour	£X

Capacity

		Hours
'Should'	Budgeted **hours worked**	X
'Did'	Actual hours worked	(X)
		X
	Difference valued at OAR per hour	£X

The **fixed overhead expenditure variance** measures the difference between the budgeted and actual fixed production overhead incurred. It should be apparent

BPP
LEARNING MEDIA

that if actual fixed overhead is higher than budgeted fixed over head, then under absorption has occurred.

The **fixed overhead volume variance** looks at the level of production that was achieved and the related cost of that production. This is the second reason for over- or under-absorption:

- If actual units produced was higher than budgeted units, then there are more units to spread the fixed cost over. This can therefore lead to **over-absorption of overheads** and a favourable volume variance.

- If actual units produced was lower than budgeted units, then there are fewer units to spread the fixed cost over. This can therefore lead to **under-absorption of overheads** and an adverse volume variance.

The volume variance is then broken down into efficiency and capacity variances as follows:

The **fixed overhead efficiency variance** considers whether the volume variance was due to the workforce working more or less efficiently than expected. This variance is therefore calculated in the same way as the direct labour efficiency variance, but uses standard **overhead absorption rate (OAR) per hour** to convert it into a monetary variance.

The **fixed overhead capacity variance** considers whether the volume variance was due to the workforce working for more or fewer hours than budgeted. This variance is calculated in the same way as labour idle time, but uses standard **OAR per hour** to convert in into a monetary variance.

It is important to remember with the capacity variance that if **more hours are achieved** out of our workforce than forecast in the budget, that's good use of capacity – and so a **favourable** variance.

Illustration 3: Fixed Overhead Variances

Below is the standard cost card for one of Kettle Ltd's products, T:

	£
Fixed overheads 2 hours @ £3.00 per hour	6.00

Actual production was 18,000 units rather than the budgeted figure of 20,000 and the production work took a total of 38,000 labour hours.

The actual fixed overhead incurred in the period was £115,000.

Calculate:

(a) **The total fixed overhead cost variance**
(b) **The fixed overhead expenditure variance**
(c) **The fixed overhead volume variance**
(d) **The fixed overhead efficiency variance**
(e) **The fixed overhead capacity variance**

(a) Fixed overhead cost variance

	£
Fixed overhead expenditure incurred	115,000
Fixed overhead absorbed (18,000 units × £6.00 per unit)	108,000
Total cost variance = Fixed overhead under-absorbed	7,000 (A)

There is under-absorption of overhead and under-absorption is an adverse variance.

(b) Fixed overhead expenditure variance

	£
Budgeted fixed overhead	120,000
Actual fixed overhead	115,000
Fixed overhead expenditure variance	5,000 (F)

As the actual fixed overhead expenditure is less than the budgeted amount, this is a favourable variance.

(c) Fixed overhead volume variance

	Units
Actual production in units	18,000
Budgeted production in units	20,000
Fixed overhead volume variance in units	2,000 (A)

	£
Standard fixed overhead cost **per unit**	£6
Fixed overhead volume variance in £	12,000 (A)

The variance is adverse, as actual production is less than budgeted production.

(d) Fixed overhead efficiency variance

	Hours
18,000 units should take (18,000 units × 2 hours)	36,000
But did take	38,000
Fixed overhead efficiency variance in hours	2,000 (A)
× Standard fixed overhead absorption rate **per hour**	×£3
Fixed overhead efficiency variance in £	6,000 (A)

As the actual production of 18,000 units took more hours than the standard hours for 18,000 units, this is an adverse efficiency variance.

(e) **Fixed overhead capacity variance**

	Hours
Budgeted hours of work	40,000
Actual hours of work	38,000
Fixed overhead capacity variance	2,000 (A)
× Standard fixed overhead absorption rate **per hour**	×£3
Fixed overhead capacity variance in £	6,000 (A)

Only 38,000 hours were worked, although 40,000 hours were budgeted for. This is therefore an adverse capacity variance, since actual hours worked were less than budget and not all the productive capacity has been used.

The variances can be reconciled as follows:

	£	£
Fixed overhead expenditure		5,000 (F)
Fixed overhead efficiency	6,000 (A)	
Fixed overhead capacity	6,000 (A)	
Fixed overhead volume		12,000 (A)
Total fixed overhead variance		7,000 (A)

Activity 4: Armour

Armour Ltd has budgeted to make 1,100 units of a product called Soul during the month of April 20X3. The budgeted fixed overhead cost is £33,000 and the standard time to make a unit of Soul is 3 hours.

The actual fixed overhead cost during the month turns out to be £33,980. 1,000 units of Soul were produced and the labour force worked for 3,500 hours.

Required

Calculate the following variances:

(a) Fixed overhead total variance

(b) Fixed overhead expenditure variance

(c) Fixed overhead volume variance

(d) Fixed overhead efficiency variance

(e) Fixed overhead capacity variance

Select the appropriate answer from the following:

£3,980 A	£3,980 F	£980 F
£980 A	£3,000 A	£3,000 F
£2,000 F	£5,000 F	£1,000 A
£2,000 A	£5,000 A	£1,000 F

4 Fixed overheads variances (under marginal costing)

Under **marginal costing**, the fixed overhead variance is just the difference between budgeted and actual fixed overhead costs, ie **fixed overhead expenditure variance**.

Chapter summary

- For this unit materials, labour, variable overhead and fixed overhead variances must be calculated.

- The total direct materials cost variance can be split into a materials price variance and a materials usage variance.

- The total direct labour cost variance can be split into the labour rate variance and the labour efficiency variance.

- The total variable overhead variance can be split into an expenditure and an efficiency variance.

- The total fixed overhead cost variance in an absorption costing system is the amount of fixed overhead that has been under- or over-absorbed in the period.

- The total fixed overhead variance can then be analysed into the fixed overhead expenditure variance and fixed overhead volume variance.

- The fixed overhead volume variance can be split into a fixed overhead efficiency variance and a fixed overhead capacity variance.

- In a standard marginal costing system there is only one fixed overhead variance, the fixed overhead expenditure variance.

Keywords

- **Adverse variance:** where the actual cost is higher than the standard cost, or where actual performance is worse than expected

- **Favourable variance:** where the actual cost is less than the standard cost, or where actual performance is better than expected

- **Fixed overhead capacity variance:** the difference between the actual hours worked and the hours budgeted to be worked, valued at the standard fixed overhead absorption rate per hour

- **Fixed overhead efficiency variance:** the difference between the standard hours for the actual production and the actual hours, valued at the standard fixed overhead absorption rate per hour

- **Fixed overhead expenditure variance:** the difference between the budgeted fixed overhead and the actual fixed overhead expenditure

- **Fixed overhead volume variance:** the difference between actual production level and budgeted production level in units, valued at the standard absorption rate per unit

- **Labour efficiency variance:** the difference between the standard hours for the actual production and the actual hours worked, valued at the standard labour rate per hour

- **Labour rate variance:** the difference between the standard rate of pay for the actual hours paid for and the actual cost of those hours

- **Materials price variance:** the difference between the standard price of the materials purchased and their actual purchase cost

- **Materials usage variance:** the difference between the standard quantity of material for the actual production and the actual quantity used, valued at the standard price of the material

- **Total fixed overhead variance:** the total under- or over-absorbed fixed overhead for the period

- **Total labour variance:** the difference between the standard labour cost for the actual production and the actual cost of the labour

- **Total material variance:** the difference between the standard materials cost for the actual production and the actual cost of the materials

- **Under-absorption of overheads:** where the amount of fixed overhead absorbed into cost units for the period is less than the overhead incurred. In standard costing under-absorption creates an adverse variance

- **Variances:** the difference between the standard costs and the actual costs for a period

Activity answers

Activity 1: News Co

(a)   Total material variance

		£
Actual units should cost (27,000 × 2 kg × £2.50)		135,000
Actual material used did cost (53,000 kg × £2.38)		(126,140)
		8,860 (F)

(b)   Material price variance

Price variance

		£
Actual purchases should cost (53,000 × £2.50)		132,500
Actual purchases did cost (53,000 kg × £2.38)		(126,140)
		6,360 (F)

(c)   Material usage variance

Usage variance

		Kg
Actual production should use (27,000 × 2 kg)		54,000
Actual production did use		(53,000)
		1,000 F
@ std cost £2.50		£2,500 F

Activity 2: Yard

(a)   Total labour variance

		£
Actual units should cost (2,195 × 4 hrs × £12.50)		109,750
Actual labour used did cost		(110,750)
		(1,000) A

(b)   Labour rate variance

		£
Actual hours paid should cost (9,200 × £12.50)		115,500
Actual hours paid did cost		(110,750)
		4,250 F

(c)   Labour efficiency variance

		Hrs
Actual production should use (2,195 × 4 hrs)		8,780
Actual production did use		(9,200)
		(420) A
@ std cost £12.50		£5,250 A

Activity 3: Bee Co

(a) Total variable overhead variance

	£
Actual units should cost (1,000 units × £30)	30,000
Actual units did cost	(30,750)
	750 (A)

(b) Variable overhead expenditure

	£
Actual hours worked should cost (1,960 hrs × £15)	29,400
Actual hours worked did cost	(30,750)
	1,350 (A)

(c) Variable overhead efficiency

	Hrs
Actual units should take (1,000 units × 2 hrs)	2,000
Actual units did take	(1,960)
	40 F
@ std cost £15	£600 F

Activity 4: Armour

The standard fixed overhead cost of a Soul is 3 hours at £10 per hour = £30 per unit

(a) **The fixed overhead total variance**

	£
Amount of overhead absorbed (1,000 units × £30 per unit)	30,000
Fixed overhead incurred	(33,980)
Fixed overhead total variance (under absorbed)	(3,980) (A)

(b) **The fixed overhead expenditure variance**

	£
Budgeted fixed overhead expenditure	33,000
Actual fixed overhead expenditure	33,980
Fixed overhead expenditure variance	980 (A)

(c) **The fixed overhead volume variance**

Budgeted production	1,100 units
Actual production	1,000 units
	(100) units (A)
× standard absorption rate per unit	× £30
Fixed overhead volume variance	(£3,000) (A)

Or

Budgeted labour hours (3 hrs × 1,100 units)	3,300 hrs
Standard hours produced (3 hrs × 1,000 units)	3,000 hrs
	300 hrs (A)
× standard OAR per hour	× £10
Fixed overhead volume variance	£3,000 A

(d) The fixed overhead efficiency variance

1,000 units of Soul should take (× 3 hrs)	3,000 hours
But did take	3,500 hours
	500 hours (A)
× standard absorption rate per hour (× £10)	× £10
Fixed overhead volume efficiency variance	£5,000 (A)

(e) The fixed overhead capacity variance

Budgeted hours of work (3 hrs × 1,100 units)	3,300 hours
Actual hours of work	3,500 hours
	200 hours (F)
× standard absorption rate per hours (× £10)	× £10
Fixed overhead volume capacity variance	£2,000 (F)

The following budgeted and actual information is provided by Crispy PLC for their product YG:

	Budget	Actual
Production	1,600	1,800
Materials – kg	11,200	12,000
Materials – £	67,200	70,800
Direct labour – hrs	4,000	5,000
Direct labour – £	27,200	25,000
Total hours paid	4,000	5,500

1 **Using the information in the table above, calculate the following variances:**

(a) The total materials cost variance

Total materials cost variance £ [   ]

(b) The materials price variance

Materials price variance £ [   ]

(c) The materials usage variance

Materials usage variance £ [   ]

2 **Using the information in the table above, calculate the following variances:**

(a) The total labour cost variance

Total labour cost variance £ [   ]

(b) The labour rate variance

Labour rate variance £ [   ]

(c) The labour efficiency variance

Labour efficiency variance £ [   ]

The table below shows management accounting information for a chocolate manufacturer:

	Budget		Actual	
Units		7,000		6,400
Machine hours		21,000		20,000
		£		£
Materials	5,500 kg	16,500	4,750	13,300
Labour	10,000 hrs	70,000	12,800	76,800
Fixed overheads		52,500		56,000

Fixed overheads are absorbed on the basis of machine hours

3 **Using the information in the above table, calculate the following:**

(a) Standard materials for 6,400 units

(b) Standard labour hours for 6,400 units

(c) Standard machine hours for 6,400 units

4 **Using the information in the above table, calculate the following variances:**

(a) Total fixed overhead variance

(b) Fixed overhead volume variance

(c) Fixed overhead efficiency variance

(d) Fixed overhead capacity variance

Operating statements

5

Learning outcomes

2.4	**Prepare and reconcile standard costing operating statements**
	On completion of this chapter you should be able to:
	• Prepare a standard costing operating statement reconciling budgeted cost with actual cost of actual production
	• Explain the differences between marginal costing and absorption costing operating statements
	• Reconcile the difference between the operating statement under marginal costing and absorption costing

Assessment context

Operating statements will form one question within the assessment.

Business context

As part of the control process, managers frequently use operating statements to show the link between budgeted and actual performance. These are regularly referred to as a 'profit bridge' or a 'profit reconciliation statement'. Managers use these statements to make decisions to ensure the organisation remains on track to its profit target.

Chapter overview

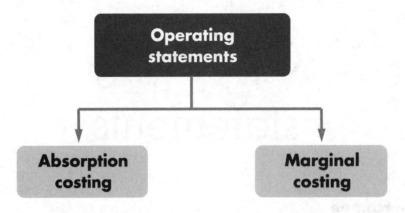

Operating statements

Absorption costing

- Preparation of operating statements under an absorption costing system

Marginal costing

- Preparation of operating statements under a marginal costing system

1 Introduction

All the cost variances together explain the difference between actual costs of production and the standard cost of production.

A reconciliation between the standard cost and actual cost of production can be presented in a management report known as an **operating statement**.

2 Reconciling total standard cost to total actual cost under absorption costing

It is usual practice to start with the total standard cost for the actual production, then adjust this for the variances calculated in order to finish with the total actual cost of production. This can be illustrated as follows:

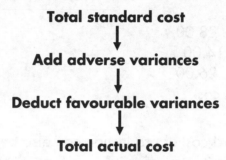

Total standard cost

↓

Add adverse variances

↓

Deduct favourable variances

↓

Total actual cost

Under absorption costing variances for both variable and fixed costs will be included.

Illustration 1: Operating statement under absorption costing

The standard cost card for Product X is given below:

	£
Direct materials 4 kg @ £2.00 per kg	8.00
Direct labour 2 hours @ £7.00 per hour	14.00
Fixed overheads 2 hours @ £3.00 per hour	6.00
Total standard absorption cost	28.00

The actual production costs and units during March were as follows:

Production units	18,000 units
	£
Direct materials	142,800
Direct labour	254,600
Fixed overhead	115,000
Total actual production cost	512,400

The following variances were generated:

	£
Materials price variance	6,800 (A)
Materials usage variance	8,000 (F)
Labour rate variance	11,400 (F)
Labour efficiency variance	14,000 (A)
Fixed overhead expenditure variance	5,000 (F)
Fixed overhead efficiency variance	6,000 (A)
Fixed overhead capacity variance	6,000 (A)
Fixed overhead volume variance	12,000 (A)

The standard cost of actual production is:

	£
Direct materials 18,000 × £8.00	144,000
Direct labour 18,000 × £14.00	252,000
Fixed overhead 18,000 × £6.00	108,000
Total standard production cost	504,000

(The figure for total standard cost of production can also be calculated as 18,000 × £28, ie standard cost per unit × actual units)

The standard cost of actual production can be reconciled with the actual cost of actual production as follows:

Operating statement under absorption costing – March

			£
Standard cost of actual production			504,000
Variances	**Favourable (Subtract)** £	**Adverse (Add)** £	
Materials price		6,800	
Materials usage	8,000		
Labour rate	11,400		
Labour efficiency		14,000	
Fixed overhead expenditure	5,000		
Fixed overhead efficiency		6,000	
Fixed overhead capacity		6,000	
Total variance	24,400	32,800	8,400 (A)
Actual cost of actual production			512,400

As the net total variance is adverse this is added onto the standard cost of actual production to arrive at actual cost of actual production.

Note. That the fixed overhead volume variance is not included in the operating statement. This is because it has been broken down into the efficiency and capacity variances, so the volume variance does not need to be included.

Activity 1: Tivvel

Tivvel plc manufactures plastic bottles at various locations in the UK. It has recently set up a plant in Tayside to provide plastic bottles to the local spring water distributors.

The standard cost card for each bottle is as follows:

	Units	Unit cost	Cost/bottle
Materials	4 kg	£4.50	£18.00
Labour	5 hrs	£5.00	£25.00
Fixed overheads	5 hrs	£3.00	£15.00
			£58.00

The new plant's actual results for the first four weeks of operations are shown below.

Production (bottles)		8,900
		£
Material	36,490 kg	156,907
Labour	51,620 hrs	252,938
Fixed overheads		134,074
Cost of production		543,919

Other information relating to the new factory:

- The plastic bottle is the only product made.
- Budgeted fixed overheads total £1,566,000 per year.
- Fixed overheads are charged to production on the basis of labour hours.
- There are 48 operating weeks in the year.
- Production is budgeted to take place evenly throughout the 48 operating weeks.

You are employed in the central accounts department of Tivvel plc. One of your responsibilities is to prepare and monitor standard costing variances at the new plant.

Required

(a) Calculate the following information relating to the new plant.

(i) Actual price of material per kg [ ]

(ii) Actual labour rate per hour [ ]

(iii) Actual labour hours per bottle [ ]

(iv) Budgeted production of bottles for the year [ ]

(v) Budgeted production of bottles for the first four weeks of operation [ ]

(vi) Budgeted fixed overheads for the first four weeks of operation [ ]

(b) Calculate the following variances for bottle production at the new plant.

(i) Material price variance [ ]

(ii) Material usage variance [ ]

(iii) Labour rate variance [ ]

(iv) Labour efficiency variance [ ]

(v) Fixed overhead expenditure variance [ ]

(vi) Fixed overhead volume variance [ ]

(vii) Fixed overhead capacity variance [ ]

(viii) Fixed overhead efficiency variance [ ]

(c) Prepare a statement reconciling the standard cost of actual production to the actual cost of actual production for the first four weeks of the year (under absorption costing).

			£
Standard cost of actual production			
	£(F)	£(A)	
Cost variances:			
Materials price			
Materials usage			
Labour rate			
Labour efficiency			
Fixed overhead expenditure			

			£
Fixed overhead capacity			
Fixed overhead efficiency	_____	_____	
			_____
Actual cost of actual production			_____

3 Reconciling total standard cost to total actual cost under marginal costing

If you are asked to prepare an operating statement under marginal costing, the standard cost for actual production is calculated differently, and the operating statement is presented differently as follows:

Illustration 2: Operating statement under marginal costing

Let's assume that Product X is now being produced under marginal costing principles.

The standard cost of actual production is now calculated by flexing the direct material and direct labour costs to actual levels, and adding on the fixed cost in full as follows:

	£
Direct materials 18,000 × £8.00	144,000
Direct labour 18,000 × £14.00	252,000
Marginal cost of production (18,000 × £22)	396,000

The total standard cost is the marginal cost of production plus budgeted fixed costs:

	£
Marginal cost of production	396,000
Budgeted fixed cost	108,000
Marginal cost of production (18,000 × £22)	504,000

The marginal costing operating statement includes all of the direct cost variances and the fixed overhead expenditure variance. The fixed overhead capacity and efficiency variances are not included.

Activity 2: Blast Co

Blast Co uses a standard marginal costing system. The following budgetary control report has been provided together with the variances calculated below:

	Budget	£	Actual	£
Production units		20,000		20,500
Direct material A1	50,000 kg	500,000	51,000 kg	616,000
Direct material A2	70,000 kg	490,000	72,000 kg	168,000
Direct labour	45,000 hrs	450,000	51,000 hrs	700,000
Fixed Overhead		720,000		680,000
Total cost		2,160,000		2,164,000

Variance	£	
A1 material price	−106,000	A
A1 material usage	2,500	
A2 material price	336,000	F
A2 material usage	−1,750	
Fixed overhead expenditure	40,000	
Direct labour rate	−190,000	
Direct labour efficiency	−48,750	A

Required

Drag and drop the correct variance into the correct column and enter the standard cost for actual production, the total variance and the actual cost for actual production in the appropriate boxes.

Enter minus signs where necessary.

Drag and drop options:

£106,000	£2,500	£336,000
£1,750	£40,000	£190,000
£96,000	£78,000	£48,750

Variance	Fav	Ad	£
Standard cost of actual production			
A1 material price			
A1 material usage			
A2 material price			
A2 material usage			
Direct labour rate			
Direct labour efficiency			
Fixed overhead expenditure			
Total variance			
Actual cost of actual production			

Chapter Summary

- The operating statement is sometimes referred to as a reconciliation statement.

- A reconciliation of the standard cost for the actual production to the actual cost of production can be performed by adding the adverse variances to the standard cost and deducting the favourable variances.

- In an absorption costing operating statement all variances except the fixed overhead volume variance are included.

- In a marginal costing operating statement the only fixed overhead variance that is included is the fixed overhead expenditure variance.

- The format for an operating statement is slightly different for standard marginal costing from an operating statement for standard absorption costing, to allow for the differing treatments of fixed costs.

Keywords

- **Operating statement or reconciliation statement:** a statement which uses the variances for the period to reconcile the standard cost for the actual production to the actual cost

Activity 1: Tivell

(a) (i) Actual cost of £156,907 for 36,490 kg

$$\therefore \text{ Actual cost per kg} = \frac{£156,907}{36,490} = £4.30$$

(ii) Actual cost of £252,938 for 51,620 hrs

$$\therefore \text{ Actual cost per hour} = \frac{£252,938}{51,620} = £4.90$$

(iii) 8,900 bottles took 51,620 hours

$$\therefore \text{ hours per bottle} = \frac{51,620}{8,900} = 5.80$$

(iv) Budgeted fixed overheads = £1,566,000 per year

Standard fixed overhead absorption rate per bottle = £15.00

$$\frac{£1,566,000}{15.00} = 104,400 \text{ bottles} = \text{budget production level}$$

(v) There are 48 operating weeks in the year and so budgeted production in a 4-week period represents 4/48 of the year's budgeted output.

$$\therefore \text{ 4 weeks' production} = 104,400 \times \frac{4}{48} = 8,700 \text{ bottles}$$

(vi) Standard fixed OAR = £15.00

Budgeted fixed overheads (4 weeks) = 8,700 × £15.00 = £130,500

$$\left(\text{or, } \frac{4}{48} \times £1,566,000 = £130,500\right)$$

(b) (i)

	£
36,490 kg should cost (× £4.50)	164,205
Did cost	156,907
Material price variance	7,298 (F)

(ii)

	Kg
8,900 units should use (× 4 kg)	35,600
Did use	36,490
	890 A
× std £/kg	4.50
Material usage variance	£4,005 (A)

(iii)

	£
51,620 hours should cost (× £5.00)	258,100
Did cost	252,938
Labour rate variance	5,162 (F)

(iv)

	Hrs
8,900 units should take (× 5 hrs)	44,500
Did take	51,620
	7,120 (A)
× std £/hr	5.00
Labour efficiency variance	35,600 (A)

(v)

	£
Budgeted fixed overheads	130,500
Actual fixed overheads	134,074
Fixed overhead expenditure variance	3,574 (A)

(vi)

	Bottles
Budget	8,700
Actual	8,900
	200 (F)
× std jar/bottle	15
Fixed overhead volume variance	£3,000 (F)

(vii)

	Hrs
Budged hours of work	43,500
(8,700 units × 5 hrs)	
Actual hours of work	51,620
Capacity variance in hrs	8,120 (F)
× std OAR/hr	3.00
Fixed overhead capacity, variance	£24,360 (F)

(viii)

	Hrs
Standard hours	44,500
(8,900 × 5 hrs)	
Actual hours	51,620
	7,120 (A)
× std OAR/hr	3
Fixed overhead efficiency variance	£21,360 (A)

(c) Statement of reconciliation

	£(F)	£(A)	£
Standard cost of production (8,900 units × £58.00)			516,200
	£(F)	£(A)	
Materials price	7,298		
Material usage		4,005	
Labour rate	5,162		
Labour efficiency		35,600	
Fixed overhead expenditure		3,574	
Fixed overhead capacity	24,360		
Fixed overhead efficiency	___	21,360	
	36,820	64,539	27,719 (A)
Actual cost of actual production			543,919

Activity 2: Blast Co

Variance	Fav	Ad	£
Standard cost of actual production (W1)			2,196,000
A1 material price (W2)		–106,000	
A1 material usage (W3)	2,500		
A2 material price (W4)	336,000		
A2 material usage (W5)		–1,750	
Direct labour rate (W6)		–190,000	
Direct labour efficiency (W7)		–48,750	
Fixed overhead expenditure (W8)	40,000		
Total variance	378,500	–346,500	32,000
Actual cost of actual production			2,164,000

(W1)

((£500,000 + 490,000 + 450,000) / 20,000 × 20,500) + 720,000 = £2,196,000

(W2)

	£
51,000 kg should cost (× £10)	510,000
Did cost	616,000
Material price variance	106,000 (A)

(W3)

	Kg
20,500 units should use (× 2.5 kg)	51,250
Did use	51,000
	250 F
× std £/kg	10
Material usage variance	£2,500 (F)

(W4)

	£
72,000 kg should cost (× £7)	504,000
Did cost	168,000
Material price variance	336,000 (F)

(W5)

	Kg
20,500 units should use (× 3.5 kg)	71,750
Did use	72,000
	250 A
× std £/kg	7
Material usage variance	£1,750 (A)

(W6)

	£
51,000 hours should cost (× £10.00)	510,000
Did cost	700,000
Labour rate variance	190,000 (A)

(W7)

	Hrs
20,500 units should take (× 2.25 hrs)	46,125
Did take	51,000
	4,875 (A)
× std £/hr	10.00
Labour efficiency variance	48,750 (A)

(W8)

	£
Budgeted fixed overheads	720,000
Actual fixed overheads	680,000
Fixed overhead expenditure variance	40,000 (F)

Test your learning

1 The standard cost card for a business's product, the MU, is shown below:

	£
Direct materials 4.2 kg at £3.60 per kg	15.12
Direct labour 1.5 hours at £7.80 per hour	11.70
Fixed overheads 1.5 hours at £2.80 per hour	4.20
	31.02

The budgeted production was for 1,800 units of MU. The actual costs during the month of June for the production of 1,750 units of the MU were as follows:

	£
Direct materials 7,500 kg	25,900
Direct labour 2,580 hours	20,600
Fixed overheads	8,100

Required:

(a) Calculate the materials price and usage variances.

Materials price variance £ [   ]

Materials usage variance £ [   ]

(b) Calculate the labour rate and efficiency variances.

Labour rate variance £ [   ]

Labour efficiency variance £ [   ]

(c) Calculate the fixed overhead expenditure, efficiency and capacity variances.

Fixed overhead expenditure variance £ [   ]

Fixed overhead efficiency variance £ [   ]

Fixed overhead capacity variance £ [   ]

(d) **Complete the table to prepare a reconciliation statement reconciling the standard cost of the production to the total cost.**

Operating statement – Absorption costing

			£
Standard cost of production			
Variances	**Favourable variances**	**Adverse variances**	
Materials price			
Materials usage			
Labour rate			
Labour efficiency			
Fixed overhead expenditure			
Fixed overhead efficiency			
Fixed overhead capacity			
Total variance			
Actual cost of production			

2 A business operates a marginal standard costing system and the cost card for its single product is given below:

	£
Direct materials 12 kg @ £4.80	57.60
Direct labour 3 hours @ £8.00	24.00
	81.60

The budgeted output for the period was 2,100 units and the budgeted fixed overhead was £95,000.

The actual production in the period was 2,400 units and the actual costs were as follows:

	£
Direct materials 29,600 kg	145,000
Direct labour 6,900 hours	56,200
Fixed overhead	92,000

You are to:

(a) Calculate the total direct materials cost variance and the materials price and usage variances.

Direct materials cost variance £ [　　　　　　　]

Materials price variance £ [　　　　　　　]

Materials usage variance £ [　　　　　　　]

(b) Calculate the total direct labour cost variance and the labour rate and efficiency variances.

Direct labour cost variance £ [　　　　　　　]

Labour rate variance £ [　　　　　　　]

Labour efficiency variance £ [　　　　　　　]

(c) Calculate any relevant fixed overhead variances.

Fixed overhead expenditure variance £ [　　　　　　　]

(d) Complete the table to produce an operating statement reconciling the standard cost of the production to the actual cost.

			£
Standard variable cost of actual production			
Budgeted fixed overhead			
Variances	**Favourable variances**	**Adverse variances**	
Materials price			
Materials usage			
Labour rate			
Labour efficiency			
Fixed overhead expenditure			
Total variances			
Total actual cost			

Interpreting variances

6

2.5	**Analyse and present effectively a report to management based on standard costing information**
	On completion of this chapter you should be able to:
	• Identify the nature of variances
	• Identify what causes standard costing variances and the possible action that can be taken to reduce adverse variances and increase favourable variances
	• Effectively communicate what the standard costing variance means in report format
	• Explain how variances may interrelate

Assessment context

Explaining why variances have arisen and the interrelationship of variances will form a written task in the assessment. It is important that you are able to describe how each variance has been generated, and explain what has caused each variance.

Business context

Once variances have been calculated businesses need to understand why those variances have arisen. This will help manages control the operations of the business. Variance reporting is therefore an important part of an organisation's control process – indeed many businesses still use variance reporting as their primary control tool.

Chapter overview

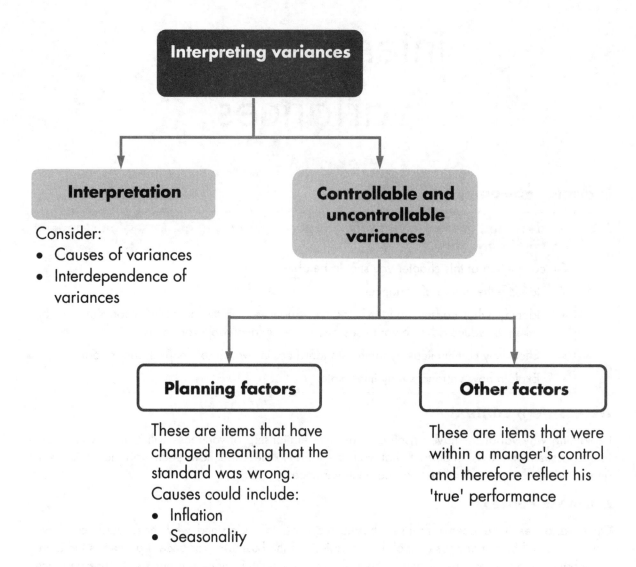

Interpreting variances

Interpretation

Consider:
- Causes of variances
- Interdependence of variances

Controllable and uncontrollable variances

Planning factors

These are items that have changed meaning that the standard was wrong.
Causes could include:
- Inflation
- Seasonality

Other factors

These are items that were within a manger's control and therefore reflect his 'true' performance

1 Introduction

Assessment focus point

Having calculated variances, the cause of the variance must then be determined before appropriate action can be taken. This will form the basis of a written task within the assessment.

2 Causes of variances

Causes of variances can fall into the following categories:

(a) **Controllable** expenditure, eg incorrect buying decisions

(b) **Uncontrollable** expenditure, eg market price rise of raw materials

(c) Inaccurate standard due to:

- Poor planning
- Use of unrealistic standard

The following table may help you to think about some of the operational causes of variances.

Variance	Favourable	Adverse
Material price	Unforeseen bulk/trade discounts received Negotiating better prices with suppliers Lower quality material purchased	Market price increase Using a more expensive supplier than expected Higher quality material purchased
Material usage	Material used of higher quality than standard More efficient use of material Errors in allocating material to jobs	Defective material Excessive waste or theft Stricter quality control Errors in allocating material to jobs
Labour rate	Use of lower paid workers than standard Less overtime worked	Use of higher paid workers than standard Wage rate increase More overtime worked
Idle time	The idle time variance is always adverse	Machine breakdown Illness or injury to worker Materials delivered late

Variance	Favourable	Adverse
Labour efficiency	Output produced more quickly than expected due to: • Increased worker motivation • Better quality materials used • Higher skilled staff used	Lower output than the standard set due to: • Lack of training • Less skilled staff used • Inefficient machinery used • Lower quality materials used
Fixed overhead expenditure	Savings in costs incurred More economical use of services	Increase in cost of services used Excessive use of services Change in type of service used
Fixed overhead volume	Production or level of activity greater than budgeted	Production or level of activity less than budgeted
Fixed overhead efficiency	Reasons for this tie in exactly to labour efficiency	
Fixed overhead capacity	Labour worked for more hours than budgeted. Maybe due to more production than expected	Maybe a result of lower production volumes or higher absenteeism, eg holidays/sickness

2.1 Interdependence of variances

In order to interpret variances effectively, any interdependence between variances must be identified. Items which impact one variance very often impact other variances too.

Illustration 1: Interdependence of variances

The following direct cost variances were generated in January for Armada Ltd:

	£
Materials price variance	6,300 (F)
Materials usage variance	6,000 (A)
Labour rate variance	5,040 (A)
Labour efficiency variance	2,400 (F)

Required

Explain why each variance has occurred.

The causes of these variances can be explained by referring to the **interdependence of the variances**.

The **materials price variance** is favourable, potentially due to a lower grade of material being purchased. This has caused the **materials usage variance** to be adverse as more material has been wasted and therefore more needed to be used in production.

The **labour rate variance** is adverse, potentially due to a higher grade of labour being used who were more skilled in production. This in turn has caused the **labour efficiency variance** to be favourable – because the higher skilled staff knew how to produce efficiently, they spent less time producing each unit as a result.

Assessment focus point

You will be given hints in a short scenario about what may have caused each variance. Make sure you read the scenario carefully, spotting any instances where the variances may interrelate.

Activity 1: Shoebox Ltd

Shoebox Ltd is a manufacturer of trainers. It operates a standard absorption costing system. It has provided the following operating statement and information relating to its operations during the previous month:

	£
Standard cost of actual production	588,000
Variances	
Material price variance	21,740
Material usage variance	(11,760)
Labour rate variance	27,930
Labour efficiency variance	13,230
Fixed overhead expenditure variance	(2,000)
Fixed overhead capacity	3,330
Fixed overhead efficiency	4,410
Actual cost of production	644,880

Recent Events

<u>Supplier</u>

One of our suppliers went out of business during the month. We had to unexpectedly change to a new supplier who was more expensive, but provided a higher quality material.

<u>Machinery</u>

A machine on the production line was upgraded during the month. Production was halted for 4 days whilst the machinery was installed. Overtime then had to be worked in order for us to meet our production target for the month.

<u>Warehouse</u>

During the month our warehouse rent contract was renewed. We unexpectedly managed to negotiate our rent down for the coming year. This was so unexpected that we even estimated a rental increase when we set the budget.

Required

Write a memo to a colleague explaining what impact each of the events described above has had on the variances in the operating statement.

To: Colleague	Subject: Variance explanations
From: Accounting Technician	Date: xx/xx/20xx

Supplier

Machinery

Warehouse

3 Backward variances

Sometimes an assessment question may be set that requires you to work back from a set of variances in order to derive budgeted or actual data.

Illustration 2: Backwards Variances

The direct labour cost data relating to last month was as follows.

Actual hours	28,000
Total direct labour cost	£117,600
Direct labour rate variance	£8,400 (A)
Direct labour efficiency variance	£3,900 (A)

Required

To the nearest thousand, what were the total standard hours last month?

To answer this question we need to take the following steps:

(1) Work the labour rate variance backwards to find actual hours paid at standard cost. We need this in order to work out the standard labour cost per hour. This is done as follows:

	£
Labour rate variance	
Actual hours paid (28,000) should cost (balancing figure)	109,200
Actual hours paid did cost	(117,600)
	(8,400) A

The standard labour cost per hour is therefore £109,200/28,000 = £3.90

(2) Use the standard labour cost per hour to work out the total standard labour hours.

The variance is currently £3,900 adverse. We can convert this to hours by taking £3,900/£3.90 = 1,000 hours.

(3) Work the labour efficiency variance backwards to find total standard hours. This is done as follows:

	Hrs
Efficiency variance	
Actual production should use (balancing figure)	27,000
Actual production did use	28,000
	(1,000) A

Activity 2: Grace

Grace manufactures product WT. Grace operates a standard cost system in which production overheads are fixed and absorbed on a unit basis.

The budgeted activity is for the production of 66,000 units at a total fixed production cost of £726,000.

The actual volume of production was 60,000 units and the fixed overhead expenditure variance was £70,000F.

Complete the following sentences:

(a) The fixed overhead volume variance is £ [   ].

(b) The actual fixed production overheads incurred were £ [   ].

4 Controllable and uncontrollable variances

The traditional variances we have seen so far can be investigated further to look at the elements that were controllable and those that were not.

An **uncontrollable variance** is driven by an error in the planning of the standard and is therefore deemed as uncontrollable by management decisions. This is sometimes referred to as a planning variance.

A **controllable variance** is the element that was within the manager's control. Their decisions will have direct impact on this part of the variance. This is sometimes referred to as a control variance.

For example, a materials price variance can therefore be broken down as follows:

	£
Actual kg should have cost	X
But did cost	X
Materials price variance	X

This can then be analysed into:

Price variance due to known price change (non-controllable variance)	£	Price variance due to other factors (controllable variance)	£
Standard price for actual quantity used	X	Price-adjusted cost for actual quantity used	X
Price-adjusted cost for actual quantity used	X	Actual cost	X
Non-controllable price variance	X	Controllable price variance	X

Illustration 3: Controllable and uncontrollable variances

The standard direct materials cost for Tiger Ltd's product is:

> 4 kg @ £5.00 per kg = £20.00

During the month, Tiger generated a materials price variance of £20,000 adverse. However, it was later recognised that the standard should have been set at a price per kg of £5.50.

Required

Calculate the non-controllable and controllable elements of the materials price variance.

The **non-controllable element** is calculated by comparing the original standard against the revised standard. Therefore we need to compare the original total cost for actual kg against the revised total cost for actual kg as follows:

	£
Standard price for actual quantity 45,600 kg × £5.00	228,000
Adjusted price for actual quantity 45,600 kg × £5.50	250,800
	22,800 (A)

The **controllable element** is calculated by comparing the revised standard against the actual cost that was incurred. Therefore we need to compare revised total cost for actual kg against the actual cost for actual kg as follows:

	£
Adjusted price for actual quantity 45,600 × £5.50	250,800
Actual quantity at actual price	248,000
	2,800 (F)

Activity 3: Tivvel

Tivvel plc manufactures plastic bottles at various locations in the UK. It has recently set up a plant in Tayside to provide plastic bottles to the local spring water distributors.

The material element of the standard cost card for each bottle is as follows:

	Units	Unit cost	Cost/bottle
Materials	4 kg	£4.50	£18.00

The new plant's actual results for the first four weeks of operations are shown below.

Production (bottles)	8,900
Material 36,490 kg	£156,907

You are informed by the production manager that the standard price for materials on the cost card was incorrect and should have been £5 per kg.

Required

Calculate the controllable and non-controllable elements of the materials price variance.

(a)   The controllable element of the materials price variance is

	.

(b)   The non-controllable element of the materials price variance is

£ | | .

5 Seasonality

Often material prices will fluctuate at different times of the year. It may therefore be useful to analyse the price variance into the element due to seasonality and the element due to other factors.

Activity 4: Patch

The material used in making Patch is subject to seasonal price variations.

The seasonal variations are:

Month 1–3 –10%

Month 4–6 +5%

Month 7–9 +15%

Month 10–12 –10%

The standard cost is £10/kg and each Patch uses 3 kg.

During month 8, 10,000 units were made. 34,000 kg were bought at a price of £355,000.

Required

(a) **Calculate the materials price variance.**

(b) **How much of the variance is due to planning, ie as a result of the season and how much is due to other factors?**

(a)

	£
Actual purchases should cost	
Actual purchases did cost	
Material price variance	

(b)

	£
Actual purchases should cost	
Actual purchases at revised standard cost	
Price variance due to difference in index value	

	£
Actual purchases at revised standard cost	
Actual purchases did cost	
Price variance due to other reasons	

Open book reference

If a company analyses its variances into controllable and non-controllable elements, some managers may try to suggest that any adverse variances that occur are not controllable but instead are due to planning reasons.

Activity 5: Blossom

Blossom Ltd manufactures and sells garden statues. You work as an Accounting Technician reporting to the Finance Director. The company uses a standard cost stock system.

The actual and budgeted results for the production department for November are as follows:

Production department: Extract of actual and budgeted results for November 20X4

	Actual		Budget
Production	6,500 units		7,500 units
	£		£
Materials 20,800 kg	91,520	22,500 kg	90,000
Labour 7,150 hours	44,330	7,500 hours	45,000

The following variances have been calculated for the period:

	£
Material price	8,320 A
Material usage	5,200 A
Labour rate	1,430 A

At a meeting of senior management, the validity of the November variance data was questioned. Particular comments were as follows:

Purchasing Manager

'I don't think it's fair to measure my performance against the standard materials cost. This was set in January 20X4 when the price index for materials was 110. In November, the same price index was 123.2.'

Personnel Manager

'We have had real difficulties recruiting production labour and we're seeing the result in overtime working.'

Required

(a) **Calculate the uncontrollable part of the material price variance.**

(b) **Calculate the controllable part of the material price variance.**

(c) **Respond to the comments made by the purchasing and personnel manager, explaining whether their comments fully account for the labour and material variances given.**

(a) The uncontrollable part of the materials price variance is [   ].

(b) The controllable part of the materials price variance is [   ].

(c) **Response to the purchasing manager**

Response to the personnel manager

Chapter summary

- Each type of variance can have a variety of causes. Often the variances are interdependent, meaning that a factor that caused one variance is also the factor that causes other variances.

- Information about standard costs and usage can be derived by working a variance backwards.

- Variances can be split into the non-controllable element caused by inaccurate standards (ie a planning variance) and the controllable variance caused by other variances (ie a control variance).

- A manager may be tempted to manipulate departmental results and variances. This will give rise to both ethical and goal congruence issues.

Keywords

- **Interdependence of variances:** this is where the reasons for two or more variances may be the same, so that the variances are interrelated: the factor which causes one variance can also be the cause of another variance

- **Non-controllable variances:** the part of a variance that is due to a cause outside the control of the manager responsible for the aspect of performance to which the variance relates

- **Controllable variances:** the part of a variance that is due to controllable operational factors or decisions

Activity 1: Shoebox Ltd

To: Colleague	Subject: Variance explanations
From: Accounting Technician	Date: xx/xx/20xx

Supplier

The new supplier being more expensive has meant that more was paid for materials per kg than was originally planned. This has led to more being spent overall on materials and an adverse materials price variance.

The materials from the new supplier was of better quality. This has led to less wastage of material when the trainers were produced, and consequently less material being used overall in production. This has helped to generate a favourable material usage variance.

Machinery

The installation of the new machine caused production to be stopped in the month. Overtime then had to be worked to recover the lost time. This has led to more time being taken in production that was originally planned, and staff being less efficient as a result. This has led to adverse labour and fixed overhead efficiency variances.

As production had to be halted, production operatives could not produce trainers for four days. This has led to increased idle time and an adverse fixed overhead capacity variance.

As overtime had to be worked to recover the lost time staff were paid overtime premiums. This has led to a higher labour cost per hour than was planned and an adverse labour rate variance.

Warehouse

The renegotiation of the warehouse rent downwards has meant that less was spent on rent than was budgeted. This has led to reduced fixed overhead expenditure and a favourable fixed overhead expenditure variance. The reduced rent needs to be reflected in future budgets to stop this variance occurring again.

Activity 2: Grace

(a) The fixed overhead volume variance is £ | 66,000 (A) | .

	Units
Budgeted production	66,000
Actual production	60,000
Difference	6,000

Valued at standard OAR per unit = $\dfrac{£726,000}{66,000}$ = £11.00   £66,000(A)

(b) The actual fixed production overheads incurred were £ | 656,000 | .

Actual fixed production overhead incurred.

	£
Budget	726,000
Actual (balancing figure)	656,000
Fixed overhead expenditure variance	70,000(F)

Activity 3: Tivvel

(a)

	£
36,490 kg at standard price (× £4.50)	164,205
36,490 kg at revised standard price (× £5.00)	182,450
Price variance due to difference in index value	18,245 (A)

(b)

	£
36,490 kg at revised standard price	182,450
But did cost	156,907
Price variance due to other reasons	£25,543 (F)
Total price variance	£7,298 (F)

Activity 4: Patch

(a)

	£
Actual purchases should cost	340,000
Actual purchases did cost	355,000
Material price variance	(15,000) A

(b)

	£
Actual purchases should cost	340,000
Actual purchases at revised standard cost 34,000 × (£10 × 115%)	391,000
Price variance due to difference in index value	(51,000) (A)

	£
Actual purchases at revised standard cost	391,000
Actual purchases did cost	355,000
Price variance due to other reasons	36,000 (F)

Activity 5: Blossom

(a)

	£
20,800 kg at standard price (× £90,000/22,500kg)	83,200
20,800 kg at revised standard price (× £90,000/22,500kg × 1.23/110)	93,184
Price variance due to difference in index value	9,984 (A)

(b)

	£
20,800 kg at revised standard price	93,184
20,800 kg at actual price	91,520
Price variance due to other factors	1,664 (F)

(c) **Response to the purchasing manager**

The incorrect standard for materials price makes up £9,984 of the total adverse materials price variance of £8,320. As this element is uncontrollable by the purchasing manager, it isn't fair to judge their performance on this part of the variance. Indeed the controllable variance is £1,664 favourable, implying that the purchasing manager has made good operational decisions to limit the total adverse variance suffered.

Response to personnel manager

The overtime working has had the effect of increasing the hourly rate paid to production staff. This would have had a negative effect on the labour rate variance and would be a key driver of the adverse variance reported. This can be substantiated as the actual hourly rate was £6.20; 20 pence more than the standard rate of £6.00.

Test your learning

1   Given below is the operating statement for one of the factories of a business for the month of November, reconciling the total standard cost to the total actual cost for the month.

Operating statement – November

	Variances		
	Adverse	Favourable	
	£	£	£
Total standard cost			634,200
Variances:			
Materials price	9,200		
Materials usage	14,600		
Labour rate		15,400	
Labour efficiency	13,200		
Fixed overhead expenditure	7,200		
Fixed overhead efficiency	11,500		
Fixed overhead capacity		6,000	
	55,700	21,400	
Add adverse variances			55,700
Less favourable variances			(21,400)
Total actual cost			668,500

You also discover the following information:

*   Due to staff shortages a more junior grade of labour than normal, from one of the other factories, had to be used in the production process, giving rise to inefficiencies and additional wastage.

*   The material price has been increased by all suppliers and it is doubtful that the materials can be purchased more cheaply than this in future.

*   Due to its inventory-holding policy the factory has had to rent some additional space but this has not been recognised in the standard fixed overhead cost.

*   Due to the inefficiencies of labour, more hours had to be worked than normal in the month.

Write a report to the Managing Director explaining

(a)   **Possible reasons for the variances**
(b)   **Future actions that could be taken**

2   **What possible effect will the following scenarios have on variances? (You will need to create a table on a separate sheet of paper.)**

Scenarios	Possible effects
A business replaces machinery with new equipment	
A company has supply issues with a raw material	

3   The following information has been given for Ballpoint Ltd:

	£	Hours
Favourable material price variance	268	
Standard cost per kg of material	22	
Actual cost of material	1,000	
Adverse labour rate variance	636	
Actual labour hours		768
Actual cost of labour	22,560	

Complete the following two sentences:

The actual quantity of material purchased is [   ] kg.

The standard labour rate is £ [   ] .

4   Mugshot Ltd absorbs its fixed production overheads on a labour hour base. It has provided the following information:

	£
Favourable fixed overhead expenditure variance	8,500
Adverse fixed overhead volume variance	12,900
Actual units produced	49,500
Standard OAR per labour hour	4.20
Budgeted fixed overheads	78,000

Complete the following sentence:

The standard labour hours for the period were [   ] hrs,

5   Eggcup has provided the following standard cost information:

	Budget	Actual
Production units	500	400
Actual hours worked		800
Labour cost per hour	£5.00	
Adverse labour rate variance		£900
Actual cost of labour		£4,900

The production manager has since informed you that, due to a general wage increase, the standard cost per labour hour should have been £6.50

Required

Calculate:

(a) The uncontrollable part of the labour rate variance

(b) The controllable part of the labour rate variance

(a) The uncontrollable variance is [   ]

(b) The controllable variance is [   ]

Performance indicators

7

Learning outcomes

4.1	**Identify and calculate key financial and non-financial performance indicators** On completion of this chapter you should be able to: • Identify and select key performance indicators • Calculate key performance indicators
4.2	**Evaluate key financial and non-financial performance indicators** On completion of this chapter you should be able to: • Explain what the performance indicator means • Explain how the various elements of the indicator affect its calculation • Explain how some performance indicators interrelate with each other • Explain how proposed actions may affect the indicator • Explain what actions could be taken to improve the indicator • Explain how lack of goal congruence can affect the overall business objectives when managers are attempting to maximise a given indicator • Explain how ethical and commercial considerations can affect the behaviour of managers aiming to achieve a target indicator
4.4	**Make recommendations and effectively communicate to management based on analysis** On completion of this chapter you should be able to: • Explain how analysis and calculations lead to recommendations • Use the analysis to make reasoned recommendations and communicate them effectively

Assessment context

Performance indicators are likely to form one question in the assessment. Be prepared not just to calculate the performance indicator, but explain what the indicator tells the organisation about their performance.

Business context

Performance measurement is an important control tool within organisations, and organisations produce regular reports about their performance. This will include calculated performance indicators alongside written analysis of them.

Organisations need a range of indictors to fully understand their performance. Therefore organisations produce a performance report containing both financial and key non-financial performance indicators that qualify the financial performance.

Chapter overview

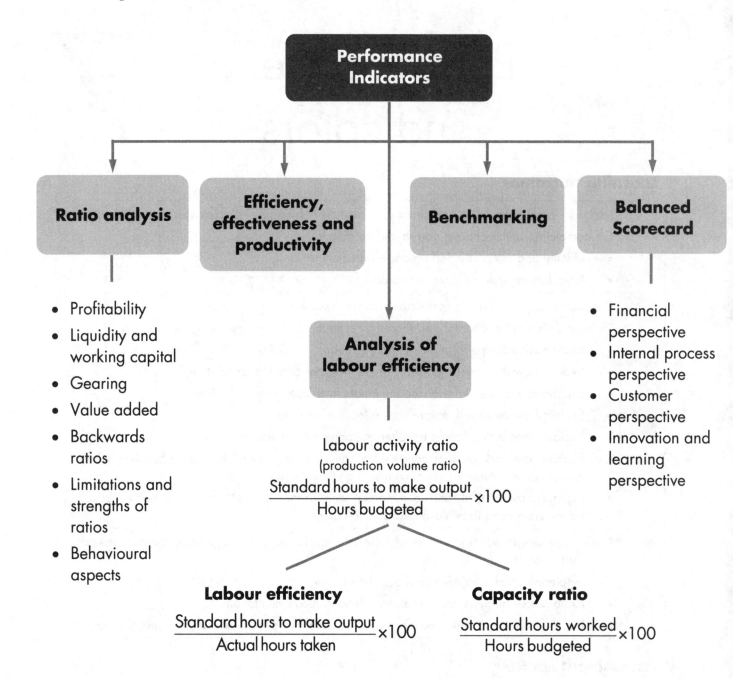

Performance Indicators

Ratio analysis

Efficiency, effectiveness and productivity

Benchmarking

Balanced Scorecard

- Profitability
- Liquidity and working capital
- Gearing
- Value added
- Backwards ratios
- Limitations and strengths of ratios
- Behavioural aspects

Analysis of labour efficiency

Labour activity ratio
(production volume ratio)

$$\frac{\text{Standard hours to make output}}{\text{Hours budgeted}} \times 100$$

- Financial perspective
- Internal process perspective
- Customer perspective
- Innovation and learning perspective

Labour efficiency

$$\frac{\text{Standard hours to make output}}{\text{Actual hours taken}} \times 100$$

Capacity ratio

$$\frac{\text{Standard hours worked}}{\text{Hours budgeted}} \times 100$$

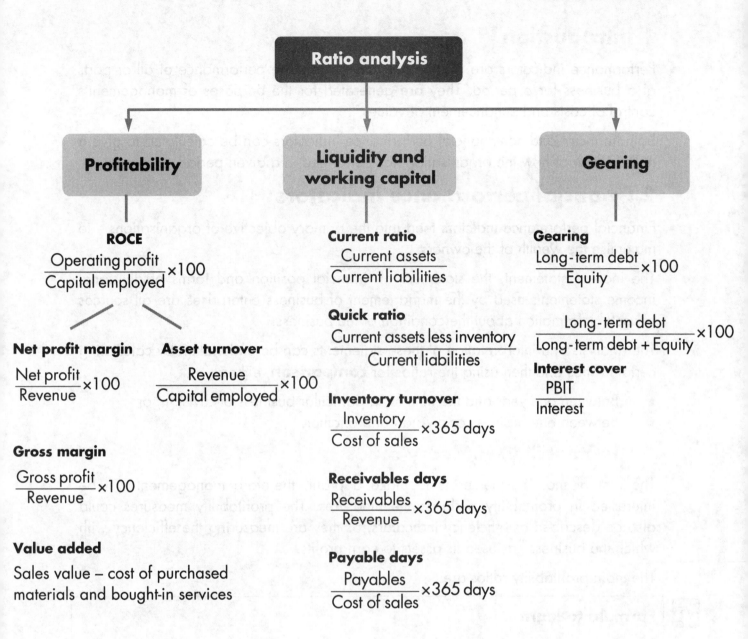

Ratio analysis

Profitability

ROCE

$$\frac{\text{Operating profit}}{\text{Capital employed}} \times 100$$

Net profit margin

$$\frac{\text{Net profit}}{\text{Revenue}} \times 100$$

Asset turnover

$$\frac{\text{Revenue}}{\text{Capital employed}} \times 100$$

Gross margin

$$\frac{\text{Gross profit}}{\text{Revenue}} \times 100$$

Value added

Sales value – cost of purchased materials and bought-in services

Liquidity and working capital

Current ratio

$$\frac{\text{Current assets}}{\text{Current liabilities}}$$

Quick ratio

$$\frac{\text{Current assets less inventory}}{\text{Current liabilities}}$$

Inventory turnover

$$\frac{\text{Inventory}}{\text{Cost of sales}} \times 365 \text{ days}$$

Receivables days

$$\frac{\text{Receivables}}{\text{Revenue}} \times 365 \text{ days}$$

Payable days

$$\frac{\text{Payables}}{\text{Cost of sales}} \times 365 \text{ days}$$

Gearing

Gearing

$$\frac{\text{Long-term debt}}{\text{Equity}} \times 100$$

$$\frac{\text{Long-term debt}}{\text{Long-term debt} + \text{Equity}} \times 100$$

Interest cover

$$\frac{\text{PBIT}}{\text{Interest}}$$

1 Introduction

Performance indicators are methods of summarising the performance of all or parts of a business for a period. They are generated for the purposes of management's control of costs and enhancement of value.

Both financial and non-financial performance indicators can be calculated to give a holistic view of how the organisation has performed in a given period.

2 Financial performance indicators

Financial performance indictors feed into the primary objective of organisations – to maximise the wealth of the owners.

The income statement, the statement of financial position and forms of divisional income statements used by the management of business enterprises are all sources of useful information about the condition of the business.

The analysis and interpretation of these statements can be undertaken by calculating certain ratios and then using the ratios for **comparison**, either:

- Between one year and the next for a particular business or division; or
- Between one business or division and another.

2.1 Profitability/efficiency ratios

The aim of most businesses is to make a profit, therefore management will be interested in profitability performance measures. The profitability measures could also be described as efficiency indicators, as they are measuring the efficiency with which the business has used its assets to earn profits.

The main profitability ratios are:

Formula to learn

(a) **Return on capital employed**

$$= \frac{\text{Profit from operations}}{\text{Capital employed}} \times 100$$

Note. Capital employed = Non-Current Assets + Current Assets – Current Liabilities = Total Assets Less Current Liabilities.

This shows the return that is being generated to the owners and is the profit that is generated from each £1 worth of assets employed – ie how well total capital employed has been utilised.

Formula to learn

(b) **Profit margins**

(i) Operating/Net = $\dfrac{\text{Profit from operations}}{\text{Revenue}} \times 100$ or $\dfrac{\text{Net profit}}{\text{Revenue}} \times 100$

(ii) **Gross profit margin** = $\dfrac{\text{Gross profit}}{\text{Revenue}} \times 100$

Both ratios show the % of profit generated by every £1 of sales revenue

A high profit margin indicates that either:

(i) Costs are being controlled; or
(ii) Sales prices are high compared to costs.

Formula to learn

(c) **Asset turnover** = $\dfrac{\text{Revenue}}{\text{Capital employed}}$

This shows the revenue that is generated from each £1 worth of assets employed. These ratios are related to each other as follows:

| ROCE | = | Asset turnover | × | Net profit margin |

If we look at how each of these ratios are calculated you will see how this works:

$$\frac{\text{Operating profit}}{\text{Capital employed}} = \frac{\text{Turnover}}{\text{Capital employed}} \times \frac{\text{Operating profit}}{\text{Turnover}}$$

The importance of this relationship is that we can explain any change in ROCE by changes in asset turnover and changes in the operating profit margin.

Formula to learn

(d) **Return on net assets** = $\dfrac{\text{Operating profit}}{\text{Net assets}} \times 100$

This is an alternative way of calculating the return to the owners as it uses the capital figures stated on the statement of financial position as net assets.

2.2 Liquidity ratios

Liquidity is a measure of how safe the business is in terms of the availability of cash. It can be measured using the following ratios:

Formula to learn

(a) **Current ratio** = $\dfrac{\text{Current assets}}{\text{Current liabilities}}$

The current ratio shows how many times the current liabilities of a business are covered by its current assets.

Formula to learn

(b) **Quick ratio** (or acid test) = $\dfrac{\text{Current assets less inventory}}{\text{Current liabilities}}$

This ratio recognises that stock takes time to convert to cash; it takes time to sell and receive payment. It is therefore a measure of immediate liquidity.

2.3 Working capital ratios

Working capital is the total of the current assets of a business less its current liabilities. They help to clarify the liquidity position of the business – the more cash that is tied up in working capital, the less liquid the organisation is overall.

Formula to learn

(c) **Inventory turnover in days** = $\dfrac{\text{Inventory}}{\text{Cost of sales}} \times 365$ days

This shows the average period that stock is stored.

(d) **Receivables collection period** = $\dfrac{\text{Receivables}}{\text{Turnover}} \times 365$ days

This shows the average credit period taken by customers.

(e) **Payables payment period** = $\dfrac{\text{Payables}}{\text{Cost of sales}} \times 365$ days

This shows the average credit period taken by the business.

Assessment focus point

In the assessment you may be asked to calculate inventory holding period, receivables' collection period or payables' payment period in months rather than in days. In these situations simply substitute 12 months for 365 days in the formulae and the answer will automatically be expressed in months.

2.4 Gearing

Formula to learn

(a) **Financial gearing** = $\dfrac{\text{Long-term debt}}{\text{Equity}}$ or $\dfrac{\text{Long-term debt}}{\text{Long-term debt} + \text{Equity}} \times 100$

Gearing measures the **financial risk** of a company. If the ratio is high then it means that the company is mostly financed by long-term debt, increasing risk of default on that debt.

Assessment focus point

In the assessment both calculations are valid. The marking for both computer- and human-marked tasks will accept answers based on either calculation.

Formula to learn

(b)   **Interest cover** $= \dfrac{\text{PBIT}}{\text{Interest}}$

This looks at how many times the interest payment is covered by profits, and therefore measures the company's ability to service its debt.

Activity 1: LNG Ltd

Extracts from the latest operating statements of LNG Ltd and certain performance indicators from its competitor Ads Ltd are shown below.

Statement of profit or loss extract for the year ended 30 November 20X5

LNG Ltd	
	£000
Advertising revenue	4,200
Less: Cost of sales:	
Materials	(1,900)
Direct labour	(430)
Fixed production overheads	(880)
Gross profit	990
Sales and distribution costs	(540)
Administration costs	(240)
Profit from operations	210
Finance charges	(60)
Profit for year	150

Statement of financial position

LNG Ltd	
	£000
Non-current assets	3,265
Receivables	1,050
Cash and cash equivalents	85
Payables	(600)
Net assets	3,800

Other operating data

	LNG Ltd
Newspapers produced	7,500,000
Number of employees	70
Advertising transactions	40,000

Performance indicators for Ads Ltd

Gross profit margin	33.2%
Operating profit margin	10.0%
Return on capital employed	15.4%
Administration costs as % of sales	4.0%
Receivables age (in months)	2.0
Payables age (in months)	1.5
Current ratio	2.0
Average advertising revenue per newspaper	£0.75
Advertising revenue per employee	£88,500.00
Advertising revenue per advertising transaction	£120.00
Interest cover	3.5 times

Required

(a) **Calculate the following performance indicators for LNG. Where rounding is required, give your answer to 1 decimal place:**

    (i)   **Gross profit margin**

    (ii) **Operating profit margin**

    (iii) **Administration costs as a percentage of sales**

    (iv) **Return on capital employed**

    (v) **Average advertising revenue per newspaper produced**

    (vi) **Advertising revenue per employee**

    (vii) **Average advertising revenue per advertising transaction**

    (viii) **Current ratio**

    (ix) **Average receivables age in months**

    (x) **Average payables age in months**

    (xi) **Gearing**

(b) **Write a memo to LNG's managing director which explains why the following indicators are different to those of Ads:**

    (i)   **Gross profit margin**

    (ii) **Operating profit margin**

    (iii) **Return on capital employed**

    (iv) **Current ratio**

    (v) **Interest cover**

(a)

Gross profit margin	
Operating profit margin	
Administration costs as a percentage of sales	
Return on capital employed	
Average advertising revenue per newspaper produced	
Advertising revenue per employee	
Average advertising revenue per advertising transaction	
Current ratio	
Average age of receivables in months	
Average age of payables in months	
Interest cover	

(b)

Memo

To: Managing Director   From: Accounting Technician

Subject: Performance Indicators

Gross profit margin

Operating profit margin

Return on capital employed (ROCE)

Current ratio

Interest cover

---

3 Improving Financial Performance

Financial performance indicators enable managers to make informed decisions about the business. The types of decisions that could be made are:

- Control decisions to improve the performance of the organisation
- Analysis of options to grow the business

Assessment focus point

You may be asked to explain or describe the impact that certain control actions have on financial performance indicators. It is therefore essential that, and that you are able to explain these impacts in a clear and concise way.

Activity 2: Improvements at LNG Ltd

At LNG Ltd, a management meeting was held to discuss the annual results. In a bid to increase profits and be more competitive, the following improvements were identified:

- Average advertising revenue per advertising transaction could be increased by 5%

- Wastage of paper could be reduced which would result in a saving of 3% in total materials costs

- A credit controller could be employed at an annual cost of £25,000. As a result, receivables would be reduced to £850,000

Required

(a) Recalculate the following ratios. Give your answer to 1 decimal place if rounding is required.

    (i)   Gross profit margin
    (ii) Operating profit margin
    (iii) Return on capital employed
    (iv) Receivables age in months

(b) Write a memo to the managing director explaining the impact that these decisions have had on each ratio.

(a)

Ratio	Revised result
Gross profit margin	
Operating profit margin	
Return on capital employed	
Receivables age in months	

(b)

Memo	
To: Managing Director	From: Accounting Technician
Subject: Revised performance Indicators	

Gross profit margin

Operating profit margin

Return on capital employed (ROCE)

Aged receivables in months

Assessment focus point

A task in the assessment may ask for you to suggest improvements that an organisation can make to improve a financial indicator. You therefore need to be comfortable with what affects a financial performance indicator in order to suggest suitable improvements.

Activity 3: Seat Co

The actual and budgeted operating results for the sales and production of leather chairs at Seat Co for the year ended 31 December 20X2 are as follows:

	Actual £	Budget £
Revenue	2,750,000	3,000,000
Cost of sales		
Opening finished goods inventory	200,000	200,000
Cost of production	2,329,600	2,400,000
Closing finished goods inventory	(240,000)	(200,000)
	2,289,600	2,400,000
Gross profit	**460,400**	**600,000**
Distribution and administration costs	345,000	360,000
Profit from operations	**115,400**	**240,000**
Net assets	£1,075,400	£1,200,000

Required

(a) Calculate the following performance indicators:

    (i)   Gross profit margin
    (ii)   Operating profit margin
    (iii) Return on capital employed (ROCE)
    (iv) Inventory turnover (in months)

(b) Write a memo to the Finance Director. Your memo should include one course of action the company could take to improve each performance indicator.

(a)

	Actual	Budget
Gross profit margin		
Operating profit margin		
ROCE		
Inventory turnover		

(b)

Memo	
To: Finance Director	From: Accounting Technician
Subject: Performance Indicators	Date: xx/xx/xxxx

Gross profit margin

Operating profit margin

Return on capital employed (ROCE)

Inventory turnover

Assessment focus point

An assessment task may require you to make recommendations about options to grow the business. To answer these types of task you need to be able to discuss the ratios given and make a clear recommendation as to which option the business will take. Be authoritative when giving a recommendation – don't sit on the fence!

Activity 4: Grippit

Grippit manufacturers domestic wind turbines. A colleague has prepared forecast information based upon two scenarios. The forecast profit and loss account and balance sheet for both scenarios are shown below.

- Scenario 1 is to set the price at £1,250 per unit with sales of 10,000 units per year.
- Scenario 2 is to set the price at £1,000 per unit with sales of 14,000 units per year.

The following information has been provided for each scenario:

	Scenario 1	Scenario 2
Gross profit margin	36.00%	28.57%
Net profit margin	17.20%	11.79%
Direct materials cost per unit	£300	£300
Direct labour cost per unit	£200	£200
Fixed production cost per unit	£300	£214.29
Gearing	58.82%	57.36%
Interest cover	4.58	3.75

Required

Draft an email for the Finance Director covering the following:

(i) **An explanation of why the gross profit margin is different in each scenario. Your answer** should refer to the following:

- **Sales price per unit**
- **Materials, labour and fixed cost per unit**

(ii) **An assessment of the level of gearing and interest cover under each scenario**

(iii) **A recommendation of which scenario the managers should choose**

Email	
Email	
To: Finance Director	Date: xx/xx/20xx
From: Accounting Technician	Subject: Analysis of scenarios

(i)   Why are the gross profit margins different?

- Sales price per unit

- Materials

- Labour

- Fixed costs

(ii)   Assessment of level of gearing and interest cover

(iii)   Recommendation

4 Value added

Value added is the extra value that an organisation has created through its employees. It is the difference between the purchase costs of external materials and services, and the selling prices of an organisation's own goods or services. It can be calculated as follows:

 Formula to learn

Value added = Sales value – cost of purchased materials and bought-in services

Total value added can be converted into a measure of productivity by calculating value added per employee.

Illustration 1: Value Added

You are given the following information about a small manufacturing business for the year ending 30 June.

Sales revenue	£835,400
Cost of materials used	£466,700
Cost of bought-in services	£265,000
Number of employees	12

Required

What is the total value added and the value added per employee in the month?

Value added	=	Sales revenue – (cost of materials and bought-in services)
	=	£835,400 – (466,700 + 265,000)
	=	£103,700
Value added per employee in the month	=	£103,700/12
	=	£8,642

5 Backwards ratios

As well as calculating various ratios, you may need to work backwards through a ratio.

Activity 5: Backwards Ratios

A company has current assets of £650,000 capital employed of £2.25m.

Required

Calculate:

(a) **the revenue required to give an asset turnover of 4.**

(b) **the operating profit required to give a ROCE of 20%.**

(c) **the amount of current liabilities required to give a current ratio of 2.3.**

Give your answer to the nearest whole £.

(a) Revenue needs to be £ [   ] to give an asset turnover of 4.

(b) Operating profit needs to be £ [   ] to give a ROCE of 20%.

(c) The amount of current liabilities to give a current ratio of 2.3 is £ [   ] .

6 Limitations and strengths of financial performance indicators

Limitations of financial performance indicators include:

- They are **not useful on their own** – they need to be analysed against a comparator, eg the previous year or a competitor.

- Comparing over time can be difficult due to the impact of **inflation**.

- Comparing between companies can be difficult due to the **different accounting policies** of organisations.

- They are **based on year end figures** which may not be representative of future costs.

- They **do not convey the full picture** of the organisation as they ignore other important factors that relate to organisational success, e.g. customer satisfaction and quality.

- As they are mostly profit based there is excessive **focus on the short term**.

Strengths of financial performance indicators include:

- Percentages are **easier to understand** than absolute measures.

- **Patterns** over time can be easily identified.

- They can be **used as performance targets** to motivate staff.

- They **provide a summary** that can be put on a dashboard report to managers.

7 Behavioural aspects

Another limitation of financial performance indicators is that they can encourage managers to act in a dysfunctional way. They may take actions for the good of one area or their division but that are not in the interests of the company as a whole. This is known as acting in a **non goal congruent manner.**

Illustration 2: ABC

The key performance indicator for the production department of ABC is ROCE.

Results for the production department for the year 20X9 were:

	£
Profits	90,000
Net assets	500,000

The company is now considering investing in a new labour-saving piece of equipment which will cost £10,000 and have an annual profit of £1,200. This piece of equipment will not only save labour, but will also ensure a more consistent product and should help increase quality and therefore customer satisfaction.

Required

(a) Explain whether the manager will choose to invest in the new machinery

(b) Explain the goal congruence implications of the manager's decision

(a)   Current ROCE = 90,000 / 500,000 = 18%

ROCE of equipment = 1,200 / 10,000 = 12%

As the ROCE of the new equipment is below that of current departmental ROCE the manager will choose not to invest. This is because ROCE is likely to be the manager's key performance target. Investing in the new machinery will drag down the department's ROCE, making it appear like the manager is making poor operating decisions.

(b)   If the manager chooses not to invest in the machinery this is not goal congruent. This is because the machinery will drive future efficiency improvements within ABC, as well as improving product quality attracting more customers and driving more revenue. The investment in the machine is therefore a good long term investment for ABC which will drive long term profit improvements.

Assessment focus point

You may be asked to explain ethical issues in the assessment. This will form the basis of part of a written question. Manipulating variances is one example of an ethical conflict that could arise.

Activity 6: Blossom

Blossom Ltd manufactures and sells garden statues. The managers receive a profit based bonus – if their department's ROCE 5% or more above their target ROCS, then that manager receives a bonus equal to 2% of total department profit.

Required

Explain the ethical and goal congruence consequences of that may arise as a result of the bonus scheme in Blossom.

8 Non-financial performance indicators

Non-financial performance indicators are required in a business to explain its financial performance.

There are two groupings of non-financial performance indictors: effectiveness and productivity.

Effectiveness measures whether the **objectives were achieved**. This measures the extent to which the organisation is achieving its overall strategy.

Productivity measures how productive the workforce is. Productivity is closely related to efficiency, but efficiency is measured in financial terms.

Activity 7: Baker's Biscuits

Baker's Biscuits is a premium biscuit manufacturer. It aims to provide good quality biscuits to the market whist maintaining efficiency in the production process.

Required

Suggest a range of non-financial performance measures to measure effectiveness and productivity with Baker's Biscuits.

8.1 Labour control ratios

In order to control the productivity of the workforce the following **control ratios** can also be calculated.

Formula to learn

Labour activity ratio (or Production volume ratio)

$$= \frac{\text{Standard hours to make output}}{\text{Hours budgeted}} \times 100\%$$

The activity ratio measures how actual output compares to budgeted output.

Formula to learn

Labour efficiency ratio (or productivity ratio) $= \dfrac{\text{Standard hours to make output}}{\text{Actual hours taken}}$

$\times \ 100\%$

The efficiency ratio measures how efficiently the workforce has operated during the period.

Formula to learn

Capacity ratio $= \dfrac{\text{Actual hours worked}}{\text{Hours budgeted}} \times 100\%$

The capacity ratio measures whether the workforce has worked more or fewer hours than budgeted. If it the outcome is more than 100% then the workforce worked more hours overall than expected.

The three ratios are related to each other as follows:

Activity/Production volume ratio	=	Efficiency ratio	×	Capacity ratio

Activity 8: Barnes

Barnes Ltd budgeted to make 12,000 standard units of output during a budget period of 36,000 hours (each unit should take 3 hours each).

During the period, the company actually made 14,000 units which took 40,000 hours.

Required

Calculate the following labour ratios to the nearest whole number:

(i) Efficiency
(ii) Capacity
(iii) Activity

(i) [ ]

(ii) [ ]

(iii) [ ]

8.2 Other performance indicators

Assessment focus point

You may be asked to calculate other ratios in the assessment which apply specifically to the business referred to. The calculation will either be obvious or the formula for the indicator will be provided.

9 The Balanced Scorecard

The **balanced scorecard** is a framework that can be used to determine a number of different performance indicators that are important to a business.

The balanced scorecard recognises that there is not just one perspective of performance – financial performance – but four different perspectives of a business, all of which must be monitored.

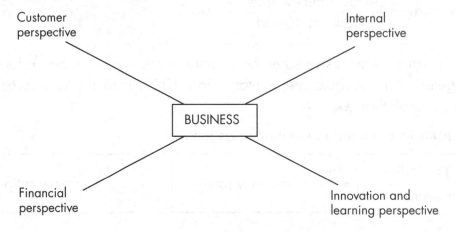

(Kaplan and Norton, 1996)

Perspective	Concerned with:
Customer	What do existing and new customers value from us? This perspective gives rise to targets that matter to customers such as price, quality and customer service.
Internal	What processes must we excel at to achieve our financial and customer objectives? This perspective aims to improve internal processes and decision-making.

Perspective	Concerned with:
Innovation & Learning	Can we continue to improve and create future value? This perspective considers the business's capacity to maintain its competitive position by acquiring new skills and developing new products
Financial	How do we create value for our shareholders? This perspective covers traditional measures, such as profitability, liquidity and gearing.

Activity 9: The Balanced Scorecard

Suggest a range of possible indicators that an organisation could use in each area of the balanced scorecard.

10 Benchmarking

A business will attempt to seek the best available performance against which it can measure its own performance. By adopting what is regarded as best practice as a target, the business attempts to improve its own performance. In this way, the business can be as good as, or better than, the best in the world in the most important areas of operation.

Benchmarking is a comparison exercise that an organisation can perform in order to adopt best practice. It uses a realistic target for improving the operations of the business.

Chapter Summary

- Performance indicators can be calculated to summarise productivity, profitability and resource utilisation – some of the performance indicators are financial measures and some are non-financial measures.

- The gross profit margin measures the profitability of the trading element of a business and the operating and net profit margins give a measure of profitability after deduction of expenses.

- The return on capital employed relates the operating profit to the amount of capital invested in the business to give an overall return to the providers of that capital – the return on capital employed is made up of the asset turnover multiplied by the operating profit margin.

- Return on net assets (also known as return on shareholders' funds) is a similar measure to ROCE and assesses the efficiency with which shareholders' funds have been used by the business to generate profits.

- Asset turnover which shows the amount of revenue earned for each £1 investment.

- The liquidity of a business is its ability to make payments to payables when these are due. Liquidity can be monitored by means of the current ratio and the quick ratio. Individual elements of working capital can be controlled by monitoring and managing inventory days, the receivables' collection period and the payables' payment period.

- The gearing level (amount of debt finance) can be measured using the gearing ratio and the interest cover ratio. Gearing considers the ability of a business to service its debt.

- Productivity can be measured as units produced per hour or units produced per employee. Productivity can also be measured by considering the value added per employee.

- A further method of measuring productivity is to use the three control ratios – efficiency, capacity and activity ratios.

- Performance indicators must also be interpreted. In order to do this comparative figures (or benchmarks) are required.

Keywords

- **Activity ratio:** an indicator of how the actual output compares to budgeted output

- **Asset turnover:** the amount of sales revenue earned for each £1 invested in the capital of the business

- **Benchmarking:** comparison of actual figures to a predetermined target or industry best practice (a 'benchmark' for performance)

- **Capacity ratio:** a measure comparing actual hours worked with budgeted hours

- **Control ratios:** the productivity measures of efficiency, capacity and activity

- **Current ratio:** ratio of current assets to current liabilities

- **Efficiency ratio:** a measure of how efficiently the employees have worked compared to standard efficiency

- **Gearing:** a measure of the percentage of total debt (long- and short-term loan capital) in the capital structure

- **Gross profit margin:** gross profit as a percentage of sales

- **Interest cover:** the number of times that the annual interest charge is covered by the annual profit before interest

- **Inventory turnover days:** number of days inventory is held (on average)

- **Liquidity:** how much cash the business has or can access within a fairly short time

- **Operating profit margin:** operating profit as a percentage of sales

- **Non-current asset turnover:** the amount of sales revenue earned for each £1 invested in non-current assets

- **Operating profit margin:** operating profit as a percentage of sales

- **Payables' payment period:** the number of days before suppliers are paid (on average)

- **Performance indicators:** ways of summarising elements of performance using a formula

- **Productivity:** a measure of how efficiently employees are working

- **Quick ratio:** ratio of current assets less inventory to current liabilities

- **Receivables' collection period:** the number of days it takes customers to pay (on average)

- **Return on capital employed:** operating profit as a percentage of total capital (shareholders' capital plus debt capital)

- **Return on net assets:** net profit as a percentage of net assets (shareholders' funds)

- **Value added:** sales value less the cost of materials and bought-in services
- **Working capital:** current assets less current liabilities

Activity answers

Activity 1: LNG Ltd

(a)

Gross profit margin	23.6%
Operating profit margin	5.0%
Administration costs as a percentage of sales	5.7%
Return on capital employed	5.5%
Average advertising revenue per newspaper produced	£0.56
Advertising revenue per employee	£60,000
Average advertising revenue per advertising transaction	£105
Current ratio	1.89
Average age of receivables in months	3 months
Average age of payables in months	2.2 months
Interest cover	3.5 times

Workings

(i) Gross profit margin $\dfrac{990}{4,200} \times 100$ = 23.6%

(ii) Operating profit margin $\dfrac{210}{4,200} \times 100$ = 5.0%

(iii) Administration costs as a % of sales $\dfrac{240}{4,200} \times 100$ = 5.7%

(iv) Return on capital employed (ROCE) $\dfrac{210}{3,800} \times 100$ = 5.5%

(v) Average advertising revenue per newspaper produced $\dfrac{4,200}{7,500}$ = £0.56

(vi) Advertising revenue per employee $\dfrac{4,200,000}{70}$ = £60,000.00

(vii) Average advertising revenue per advertising transaction $\dfrac{4,200}{40}$ = £105

(viii)	Current ratio	$\dfrac{1,135}{600}$	=	1.89
(ix)	Average age of receivables in months	$\dfrac{1,050}{4,200} \times 12$	=	3 months
(x)	Average age of payables in months	$\dfrac{600}{3,210} \times 12$	=	2.2 months
	Interest cover	$\dfrac{210}{60}$	=	3.5 times

(b)

Memo

To: Managing Director

From: Accounting Technician

Subject: Performance Indicators

Date: xx/xx/xxxx

Gross profit margin

LNG's gross margin is nearly 10% below that of its competitor. This is because of advertising selling prices being lower, as the advertising price per advertising transaction is £15 lower than Ads.

LNG are also not generating revenue as efficiently as Ads, as the average advertising revenue per newspaper produced is 19p lower than Ads, and revenue per employee is £28,500 lower.

The combined effect of lower prices and lower efficiency has reduced the gross profit margin for LNG in comparison to Ads.

Operating profit margin

LNG's operating profit margin is half that of Ads. This is due to a reduced gross profit margin and administration costs as a percentage of sales being 1.7% higher than Ads. This indicates reduced efficiency, which has reduced LNG's operating profit margin compared to Ads.

Return on capital employed (ROCE)

LNG's ROCE is 10% below that of its competitor. This is due to the lower operating profit margin, indicating that LNG is not using capital employed as efficiently as Ads to generate profit. More information is needed on each company's capital employed figure to provide a fuller assessment.

> ### Current ratio
>
> LNG's ratio is below that of Ads. This means that Ads has a slightly better liquidity position than LNG. Although LNG take almost a month longer to pay their suppliers, it also takes them an extra month to collect its income from customers. The combined effect is a lower current ratio and a lower liquidity position.
>
> ### Interest cover
>
> The interest cover of the two companies is the same. This indicates that LNG and Ads have the same ability to service its debt. A similar level of financial risk is therefore apparent within both companies.

Activity 2: Improvements at LNG Ltd

Ratio	Revised result
Gross profit margin	28.5%
Operating profit margin	4.2%
Return on capital employed	5.1%
Receivables age in months	2.3 months

Ratio	Revised result
Gross profit margin	Revised revenue: $4,200 \times 1.05 = £4,410$ Revised cost = $(1,900 \times 0.97 + 430 + 880) = £3,153$ Revised gross profit margin: $\frac{(4,410-3,153)}{4,410} \times 100 = 28.5\%$
Operating profit margin	Revised profit: $210 - 25 = £185$ Revised operating profit margin: $\frac{185}{4,410} \times 100 = 4.2\%$
ROCE	Revised net assets = $3,800 - (1,050 - 850) = £3,600$ Revised ROCE: $\frac{185}{3,600} \times 100 = 5.1\%$

Ratio	Revised result
Receivables age	$\dfrac{850}{4,410} \times 12 = 2.3$ months

(b)

Memo

To: Managing Director   From: Accounting Technician

Subject: Revised performance Indicators

Gross profit margin

LNG's gross profit margin has improved. This is due to the increase in advertising revenue coupled with the decrease in paper costs. LNG's gross profit margin is now more in line with Ads, but further improvements need to be sought to improve it further.

Operating profit margin

The net profit margin has deteriorated. This is due to the cost of the credit controller adding further overheads to LNG. This has moved the operating profit margin further away from Ads.

Return on capital employed (ROCE)

LNG's ROCE has also worsened. This is primarily due to the reduced operating profit, but the reduced receivables has also had an impact as the ratio of assets to liabilities has reduced. This has moved LNG's ROCE further away from that of Ads.

Aged receivables in months

The recruitment of a credit controller has improved the receivables months ratio even though revenue has also increased by 5%. This improves LNG's liquidity position bringing it more in line to that of Ads.

Activity 3: Seat Co

(a)

	Actual	Budget
Gross profit margin	16.7%	20.0%
Operating profit margin	4.2%	8.0%
Return on capital employed	10.7%	20.0%
Inventory turnover (in months)	1.2	1.0

(b)

Memo	
To: Finance Director	Date: xx/xx/xxxx
From: Accounting Technician	Subject: Performance Indicators

Gross profit margin

An increase in the selling price of a chair will result in an increase in the gross margin. At present, however, the company is achieving the budgeted price of £250 per chair and it may not be possible to increase the price. If this is the case, efforts should be made to reduce the cost of production.

Operating profit margin

The net operating margin will increase if the company is able to reduce its distribution and administration costs. It would appear from the actual results that a reduction has already taken place since distribution and administration costs are £15,000 below budget.

Return on capital employed (ROCE)

The return on capital employed will improve if operating profits improve with no increase in capital employed. The measures detailed above will, therefore, have the effect of improving the return. An alternative, however, would be to examine whether all the assets employed are required for use in the business. If not, an asset disposal programme could be implemented and the proceeds distributed to shareholders. This would have the effect of reducing capital employed and improving the return on capital employed.

Inventory turnover

The current inventory represents 1.2 months' production. An increase in sales volumes may lead to a reduction in the number of chairs held in inventory and will consequently improve this indicator.

Activity 4: Grippit

Email

To: Finance Director   From: Accounting Technician

Subject: Analysis of scenarios   Date: xx/xx/20xx

(i) **Gross profit margin**

The gross profit margin for scenario 1 is 36% and scenario 2 is 28.57%. This is mainly driven by sales price per unit rather than the costs under each scenario.

Sales price per unit

Sales price per unit is higher under scenario 1 than scenario 2. This will increase contribution generated per unit within scenario 1, which has driven the gross profit margin to be higher than that of scenario 2.

Materials and labour cost

The materials and labour costs are exactly the same within both scenarios. However because the sales price in scenario 2 has not been set to recover these direct costs at the same rate as in scenario 1, contribution per unit is therefore lower. This has driven a lower gross profit margin in scenario 2.

Fixed costs per unit

Fixed costs per unit are higher in scenario 1 than scenario 2. The reason for this is because of the increased volumes within scenario 2, meaning that total fixed costs are spread over more units. Indeed, the total fixed costs are the same in both scenarios. This has had no impact on the gross profit margins in either scenario.

(ii) **Gearing and interest cover**

The level of gearing for both scenarios is at a similar level. This implies that a similar level of debt will be incurred in each scenario, and therefore the same level of financial risk is evident.

The level of interest cover in scenario 1 the profit is higher than that in scenario 2. This can be attributed to the fall in profits rather than increased debt, as the gearing ratio is broadly similar between both scenarios, meaning that a similar level of interest will be incurred.

(iii) **Recommendation**

It is recommended that scenario 1 is chosen. This is because it has a higher gross profit margin, driving greater profits throughout Grippit, and there is slightly less risk of default on long term debt as gearing is lower and interest cover is higher.

Activity 5: Backwards Ratios

(a) Revenue needs to be £9,000,000 to give an asset turnover of 4.

(b) Operating profit needs to be £450,000 to give a ROCE of 20%.

(c) The amount of current liabilities to give a current ratio of 2.3 is £282,609 .

(a) Asset turnover $= \dfrac{\text{Revenue}}{\text{Capital employed}}$

$= \dfrac{\text{Revenue}}{2.25m} = 4$

$= 2.25m \times 4 \quad = £9m$

(b) ROCE $= \dfrac{\text{Profit from operations}}{\text{Capital employed}}$

$= \dfrac{\text{Profit from operations}}{2.25m} = 0.2$

$= 2.25m \times 0.2 = £450,000$

(c) Current ratio $= \dfrac{\text{Current assets}}{\text{Current liabilities}}$

$= \dfrac{650,000}{\text{Current liabilities}} = 2.3$

$= \dfrac{650,000}{2.3} = £282,609$

Activity 6: Blossom

The bonus system at Blossom makes it tempting for managers to manipulate the profit figures for their department. This represents a **threat of self-interest** for each manager.

If a manager chooses to manipulate their department's profit figures, then their results will not be showing a true picture of what is actually happening within their department. This will **undermine the manager's integrity**.

Managers may also **choose to not invest in new machinery.** This is because new machinery will likely drag down the department's ROCE as capital employed increases, and due to a higher depreciation charge which will suppress the profit. This is also not goal-congruent, as new machines can improve the efficiency of Blossom in the long term.

Managers may also choose to **keep other costs low** in order to keep their operating profit high. For example, managers may choose to use a lower quality supplier in order to reduce materials cost. This is also non-goal congruent as it is likely that the garden statues produced will be of lower quality, impacting on Blossom's reputation.

Activity 7: Baker's Biscuits

Effectiveness indicators:

- Number of customer complaints
- Number of customer recommendations
- Reworked biscuits as a percentage of total production
- Market share
- Industry awards won

Productivity indicators:

- Average batches of biscuits per employee
- Average number of batches produced per labour hour
- Average number of batches per machine hour
- Percentage of labour time spent in production

Activity 8: Barnes

(i) Efficiency ratio = $\dfrac{(14,000 \times 3)\,\text{hours}}{40,000\,\text{hours}} \times 100\% = 105\%$

(ii) Capacity ratio = $\dfrac{40,000\,\text{hours}}{36,000\,\text{hours}} \times 100\% = 111\%$

(iii) Activity ratio = $\dfrac{(14,000 \times 3)\,\text{hours}}{36,000\,\text{hours}} \times 100\% = 117\%$

E × C = A ie 105% × 111% = 117%

The activity ratio of 117% (more output than budgeted and more standard hours produced than budgeted) is explained by the 111% capacity working, and by good efficiency of 105%.

Activity 9: The Balanced Scorecard

Financial Perspective

- Gross profit margin
- Operating profit margin
- Return on Capital Employed
- Asset turnover
- Working capital cycle

Customer perspective

- Number of customer complaints
- Customer satisfaction scores
- Market share
- Number of repeat purchases

Internal

- Labour hours per unit
- Machine hours per unit
- Order processing time
- Average time per customer
- Average queue lengths
- Value added per employee

Innovation and Learning

- Percentage of sales from new products
- Average training cost per employee
- Percentage of employee time spent in training

1   Given below are the production figures for a factory for the last three months.

	April	May	June
Production costs	£418,300	£424,500	£430,500
Production wages	£83,700	£86,000	£86,300
Output in units	121,700	123,500	128,000
Hours worked	11,200	11,500	11,500
Budgeted output	120,000	125,000	125,000
Sales revenue	£625,000	£634,000	£656,000
Number of employees	81	83	83

Production costs are made up of the materials for production and the bought-in services required in the month. It is estimated that 11 units should be produced each hour.

Required

Calculate the following performance indicators:

(a) **Productivity per labour hour**
(b) **Efficiency ratio**
(c) **Capacity ratio**
(d) **Activity ratio**
(e) **Value added per employee**

	April	May	June	Total
Productivity per labour hour				
Efficiency ratio				
Capacity ratio				
Activity ratio				
Value added per employee				

2   Given below is a summary of a business's performance for the last three months:

	Mar £000	Apr £000	May £000
Revenue	450	510	560
Cost of sales	260	320	340
Expenses	141	136	157
Total assets	396	413	467
Current liabilities	69	85	99

Required

(a) For each month of the year, complete the table to calculate the following performance indicators:

  (i)   Gross profit margin
  (ii) Operating profit margin
  (iii) Percentage of expenses to revenue
  (iv) Return on capital employed
  (v)   Asset turnover

	Mar	Apr	May
Gross profit margin			
Net profit margin			
% expenses to revenue			
Return on capital employed			
Asset turnover			

(b) Comment on the movement in the gross profit margin and return on capital employed by referring to the following:

  (i)   Sales revenue
  (ii) Cost of sales
  (iii) Total assets

3   Given below is a summary of the performance of a business for the last three years:

	20X6 £000	20X7 £000	20X8 £000
Revenue	820	850	900
Cost of sales	440	445	500
Expenses	290	305	315
Interest	–	3	3
Capital and reserves	500	560	620
Long-term loan	–	50	50
Non-current assets	385	453	498
Receivables	85	112	128
Inventory	50	55	67
Payables	30	34	41
Bank balance	10	24	18

For each of the three years complete the table to calculate the following performance measures and comment on what the measures indicate about the performance of the business over the period:

(a)   **Gross profit margin**
(b)   **Operating profit margin**
(c)   **Return on capital employed**
(d)   **Asset turnover**
(e)   **Non-current asset turnover**
(f)   **Current ratio**
(g)   **Quick ratio**
(h)   **Receivables' collection period**
(i)   **Inventory days**
(j)   **Payables' payment period**
(k)   **Interest cover**
(l)   **Gearing ratio**

	20X6	20X7	20X8
Gross profit margin			
Operating profit margin			
Return on capital employed			
Asset turnover			
Non-current asset turnover			
Current ratio			
Quick ratio			
Receivables' collection period			
Inventory days			
Payables' payment period			
Interest cover			
Gearing ratio			

4 A retail business has two small department stores in Firmwell and Hartfield. The figures for the first six months of 20X8 are given below:

	Firmwell £	Hartfield £
Financial details		
Revenue	540,000	370,000
Inventory	53,500	47,500
Direct costs	210,000	165,000
Expenses	270,000	175,000
Net assets	550,000	410,000
Payables	25,800	27,500
Non-financial details		
Floor area	2,400 sq m	1,700 sq m
Employees	28	13
Hours worked	30,500	14,100

(a) **Complete the table to calculate the following performance indicators for each store:**

- **(i)** **Gross profit margin**
- **(ii)** **Operating profit margin**
- **(iii)** **Return on net assets**
- **(iv)** **Inventory days**
- **(v)** **Payables' payment period**
- **(vi)** **Sales per square metre of floor area**
- **(vii)** **Sales per employee**
- **(viii)** **Sales per hour worked**

	Firmwell	Hartfield
Gross profit margin		
Operating profit margin		
Return on net assets		
Inventory days		
Payables' payment period		
Sales per sq m		
Sales per employee		
Sales per hour worked		

(b) **Write a report to the sales director of the chain comparing the performances of the two stores for the six-month period.**

5 **Explain the limitations of financial performance indicators.**

6 **Calculate the following:**

(a) A business operates on a gross profit margin of 44% and sales for the period were £106,500. What is the gross profit?

£ [ ]

(b) A business operates on a gross profit margin of 37.5% and the gross profit made in the period was £105,000. What was the figure for revenue for the period?

£ [ ]

(c) A business had revenue of £256,000 in a month, with a gross profit margin of 41% and an operating profit margin of 13.5%. What were the expenses for the month?

£ [ ]

(d) A business has a return on capital employed of 12.8% and made an operating profit for the period of £50,000. What is the capital employed?

£ [   ]

(e) A business has an operating profit percentage of 10% and a return on capital employed of 15%. What is the asset turnover of the business?

[   ] times

(f) A business has opening inventory and closing inventory of £118,000 and £104,000 respectively and made purchases during the year totalling £465,000. How many times did inventory turn over during the year?

[   ] times

(g) A business has a receivables' collection period of 64 days and the closing receivables figure is £64,000. What is the figure for revenue for the year?

£ [   ]

7 **Identify the four perspectives of the Balanced Scorecard.**

Cost management

8

Learning outcomes

5.1	**Use lifecycle cost to aid decision making**
	On completion of this chapter you should be able to:
	• Identify the components of the lifecycle cost of a product, machine or business unit
	• Calculate the discounted and non-discounted lifecycle cost of a product, machine or business unit
	• Interpret the results of calculations of life cycle costs
5.2	**Use target costing to aid decision making**
	On completion of this chapter you should be able to:
	• Analyse and evaluate target costs
	• Identify the components of a target cost
	• Explain how target costing aids value analysis and value engineering
5.4	**Evaluate the commercial factors that underpin the life cycle of a product**
	On completion of this chapter you should be able to:
	• Explain how costs change throughout the product life cycle
	• Explain the concepts of economies of scale, mechanisation and how costs can switch between variable and fixed through the stages of the product life cycle
	• The stages of the product life cycle
5.5	**Take account of ethical considerations in the decision making process**
	On completion of this chapter you should be able to:
	• Explain the ethical considerations that need to be included in the design of a product, its packaging, and the value analysis/engineering of the product in order to promote good corporate citizenship

Assessment context

Cost management will form part of a task in the assessment. It will take the form of either a numeric or written question.

Business context

Modern business is radically different from that of 80 years ago. As such new techniques have emerged, many coming from Japanese companies, such as Toyota, which are more appropriate for today's environment.

Product lifecycles are becoming shorter and shorter. Organisations increasingly reassess product lifecycle costs and revenues as the time available to sell the product and recover the investment shrinks.

Target costing was developed in Japan in response to the problems of controlling and reducing costs over a product's lifecycle.

Chapter overview

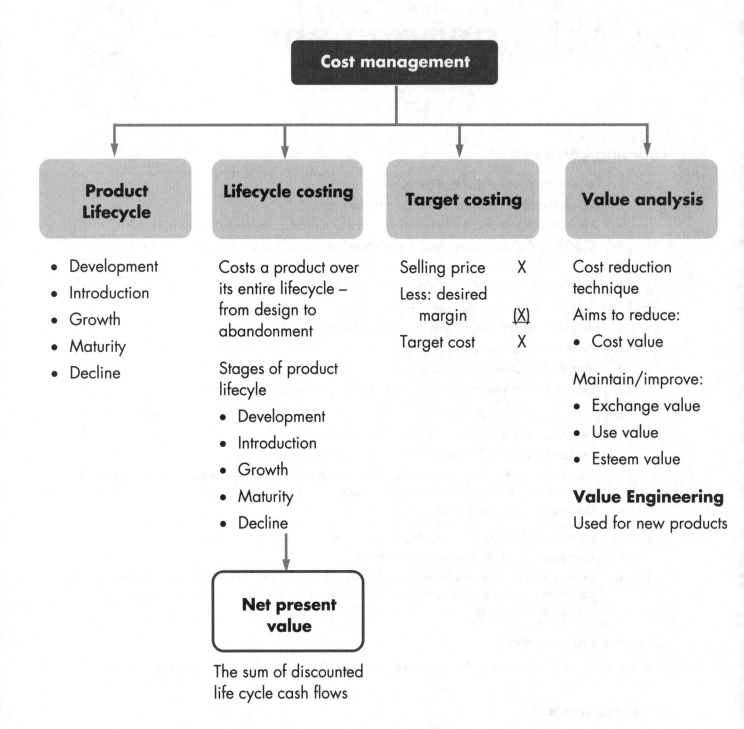

Cost management

Product Lifecycle

- Development
- Introduction
- Growth
- Maturity
- Decline

Lifecycle costing

Costs a product over its entire lifecycle – from design to abandonment

Stages of product lifecyle

- Development
- Introduction
- Growth
- Maturity
- Decline

Net present value

The sum of discounted life cycle cash flows

Target costing

Selling price	X
Less: desired margin	(X)
Target cost	X

Value analysis

Cost reduction technique

Aims to reduce:

- Cost value

Maintain/improve:

- Exchange value
- Use value
- Esteem value

Value Engineering

Used for new products

1 Introduction

Managing costs effectively is important to an organisation in order to control its profitability. Managers can therefore adopt a range of techniques in order for them to manage costs effectively, in particular:

- Being aware of how costs change within the product life cycle, and ensuring that all costs have been considered in the life cycle of products and services

- Considering cost reductions in products using target costing, value analysis and value engineering

2 Product Lifecycle

A product lifecycle consists of different phases or stages in the commercial life of the product. At each stage sales volumes, costs and profitability are different.

2.1 Stages of the product lifecycle

The stages of the product lifecycle are detailed on the below graph:

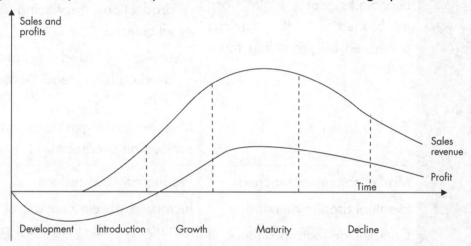

The nature of the market and costs incurred will change as the product progresses through the product lifecycle as demonstrated in the below table

Stage	Nature of market	Costs
Development	No external market.	High level of capital development costs, eg purchase of non-current assets.
Introduction	Little to no competition. Customers have few alternative products to switch to.	Advertising and promotion and continuing development costs. Direct costs (materials, labour and overheads) start to be incurred.

Stage	Nature of market	Costs
Growth	Demand for the product increases. New competitors enter the market.	Fixed promotion cost can remain high to combat the new entrants into the market. Direct material, labour and overheads become biggest proportion of cost as production is increased to satisfy demand.
Maturity	Demand peaks then becomes stagnant. New entrants are not evident, but competition is fierce between established, large organisations. Economies of scale are established (cost savings generated by producing more units).	Costs of production are driven down by: • Mechanisation of the production process • Bulk buying discounts • Staff being more skilled in production producing greater efficiencies • Lower fixed production overheads spread over more units Mechanisation generates more fixed production overheads.
Decline	Market saturation reached. Eventual drop in demand. Competition can be fierce if costs to exit the industry are high.	Production costs reduce. Increased obsolescence cost (eg lost contribution on discounted products, wastage costs of unsold inventory)

Activity 1: Product lifecycle costs

At each stage of the product lifecycle, explain whether the costs incurred will be mostly fixed or variable.

BPP
LEARNING MEDIA

It is important to note that the product lifecycle varies from industry to industry. For example, a chocolate cake may not ever reach the decline phase unless social tastes for chocolate change. In contrast, a tablet computer can have a very short life cycle due to rapid changes in technology.

Activity 2: Co X

Co X is in a high tech industry and is often first to market with new technological advances. It has recently spent £500,000 designing and developing a new product. The new product is expected to have an 18-month life cycle. Advertising spend immediately after the product's launch was £1.1m.

The anticipated performance of this product is as follows:

	Introduction	Growth	Maturity	Decline
Sales volume (units)	4,000	15,000	30,000	10,000
Per unit (£)				
Selling price	600	550	450	350
Variable cost	250	250	200	150
Overhead	100	100	60	75

Required

Calculate the profitability of the new product.

	Development	Introduction	Growth	Maturity	Decline	Total
Sales volume (units)		4,000	15,000	30,000	10,000	
£000						
Revenue						
Variable cost						
Overhead						
Development cost						
Advertising cost						
Profit						

3 Lifecycle costing

Lifecycle costing (LCC) aims to cost a product, service, customer or project over its entire lifecycle with the aim of maximising the return over the total life while minimising costs.

LCC therefore considers **all** the costs that will be incurred from design to abandonment of a new product, and compares these to the revenues that can be generated from selling this product at different target prices throughout the product's life.

In an LCC exercise the costs consist of present and future costs. Therefore, in order to arrive at a better picture of the life cycle costs, these may be discounted to their present value, and a **net present value** calculated.

4 Net present value

The **net present value (NPV)** is the sum of discounted cash flows, and shows the cash increase/decrease generated by a product/project in today's terms.

This is to take into account the **time value of money** – the assumption that cash flows received in the future are worth less than if we received them today due to inflation and interest rates.

4.1 Steps to calculate NPV

(1) Calculate/list the expected cash flows (per year) arising from the investment or decision.

(2) Discount each cash flow at the cost of capital.

(3) Total up the cash flows adding cash inflows and subtracting cash outflows, to arrive at the NPV.

4.2 Net present cost

Sometimes a project will not generate any cash inflows. The net present value method can still be used, but the outcome will be known as **net present cost**.

Illustration 1: JLK

JLK is looking to purchase a new machine which would cost £600,000 incurring annual running costs of £90,000. The machine would be scrapped for £100,000 at the end of 5 years.

Required

Calculate the discounted life cycle cost of the machine using the following 10% discount factors.

Year	Discount factor 10%
0	1.000
1	0.909
2	0.826
3	0.751
4	0.683
5	0.621

The present value of cash flows and the net present value can be calculated as follows:

Time	0	1	2	3	4	5
Cash flow	(600,000)	(90,000)	(90,000)	(90,000)	(90,000)	10,000
Discount factor	1.000	0.909	0.826	0.751	0.683	0.621
Present value	(600,000) × 1.000 = (600,000)	(90,000) × 0.909 = (81,810)	(90,000) × 0.826 = (74,340)	(90,000) × 0.751 = (67,590)	(90,000) × 0.683 = (61,470)	(10,000) × 0.621 = 6,210
Net present cost	(600,000) + (81,810) + (74,340) + (67,590) + (61,470) + 6,210 = (879,000)					

Assessment focus point

When deciding between two different projects always accept the one with the higher NPV as this more fully maximises shareholder wealth.

Activity 3: Caston Foods

Caston Foods Ltd is considering introducing a new type of oven-ready meal, and has produced the following estimates of capital expenditure, revenue and costs. This new product is expected to have a three-year lifecycle.

Year 0 development costs will be £600,000

Other cash flows (£000):

	Year 1	Year 2	Year 3
Revenue	760	920	1,060
Operating costs	456	542	612

The company's cost of capital is 14%.

Present value (PV) factors for a 14% discount rate are:

	Year 0	Year 1	Year 2	Year 3
PV factor	1.000	0.877	0.769	0.675

Required

(a) Calculate the net present value

	Year 0	Year 1	Year 2	Year 3
Revenue				
Operating costs				
Capital expenditure				
Net cash flows				
PV factor				
Discounted cash flows				
NPV				

(b) Complete the following sentence:

The new type of meal [＿＿＿＿＿] be launched.

Picklist:

should
should not

5 Target costing

> **Target costing** A method whereby the company has to take a given market price for its product. The target cost is calculated by taking the market price of the product and deducting the desired profit margin.

Target costing would be an appropriate technique for a new product for which the selling price has been set by the market. It is aimed at reducing the lifecycle costs of new products.

> **Formula to learn**
>
> **Target cost is calculated as:**
>
> | | £ |
> |---|---|
> | Target selling price/market price | X |
> | Less target profit | (X) |
> | Target cost | X |

5.1 Deriving a target cost

Traditionally an organisation establishes the cost of producing a product and the profit margin they want to achieve from the product. The organisation therefore establishes the cost of the product first, then considers the profit they want to make on the product. A mark-up is then applied to the cost to generate the selling price needed to achieve the required profit margin.

Therefore **total cost + required profit = selling price.**

In a target costing situation, this approach is reversed. The selling price is set first, followed by the profit margin that the company wishes to achieve. The target cost is then set as follows:

Selling price – required profit = target cost

Managers can then make incremental improvements to products and processes to ensure that the target cost is met.

Activity 4: Lata A

Lata Ltd is looking to manufacture a new product, the Boom. The market is very competitive and the company has established that to sell 10,000 units a year it should set the selling price at £24.

Required

Calculate the target cost to achieve a profit margin of 20%

The target cost is ☐ .

5.2 Fixed costs within the target cost

Some costs may already be fixed. For example, it may not be possible to change the time taken to produce a unit or the hourly rate of pay for employees. These are costs that the company is unlikely to be able to influence in terms of making savings and therefore they are deducted from the target cost.

Activity 5: Lata B

Each Boom requires 2 hours of labour, at a rate of £6 per hour. In addition, the total fixed production costs have been estimated as £30,000.

Required

Using this information and the information from Activity 4: Lata A, calculate the cost per unit that is available to be spent of materials.

Available for materials is ☐ .

Activity 6: Lata C

Each Boom requires 3 kg of material.

Required

Calculate the maximum cost the company can pay for 1 kg of material.

Max cost per kg: [   ] .

If required, the same process can be applied to calculate the maximum rate per labour hour or the maximum value of fixed costs for a period.

Any difference between the expected cost and the target cost is known as a **cost gap**.

6 Value analysis and value engineering

Value analysis and value engineering are key techniques that an organisation can use to close a cost gap.

Value analysis is a planned, scientific approach to cost reduction that reviews the material composition of a product and production design. It identifies modifications and improvements that can be made without reducing the value of the product to the customer or user of the product.

Value engineering is value analysis but applied to new products. When designing a product each element is assessed to determine whether it adds value to the product and, if it does, that the element is included at the lowest possible cost.

Four aspects of value should be considered:

(a) Cost value   **reduce**

(b) Exchange value ⎫

(c) Use value   ⎬   **maintain or improve**

(d) Esteem value ⎭

6.1 Value adding and non value adding activities

Only value adding activities should take place, ie those activities which create, or enhance, the quality of saleable products.

Non value adding activities should be eliminated, for example:

- Reworking of defective products
- Storage of materials
- Costs associated with staff turnover
- Movement costs (if sub-assemblies between production stages)
- Complex mix of components in products

The need to remove non value adding activities may mean that managers take decisions that negatively impact other parties. The ethics of the value analysis and value engineering exercise therefore needs to be taken into account when making decisions about non value adding activities.

6.2 Sustainability and corporate social responsibility considerations

Sustainability refers to the need of organisations having enough resource to meet their current needs, without compromising the ability of the both the organisation, and other parties, to meet their future needs.

Sustainability considerations can be split into two broad categories:

- **Environmental sustainability** – This considers the organisation's use of natural resources and the impact its operations has on the natural environment. Examples of environmentally sustainable practices include replenishing natural resources and reducing emissions.

- **Economic sustainability** – This considers the impact the organisation has on both the local and national economy that it operates within. Examples of economical sustainable practices include ensuring job security, paying a fair wage to employees, providing a suitable product to customers at a reasonable price, and providing sufficient returns to shareholders.

Corporate social responsibility (CSR) is the responsibility that the organisation has to groups and individuals that are external to it. Examples of CSR practices include:

- Supporting local community activities, for example local fetes and litter picks/graffiti cleaning

- Donating profits to local and national charities

- Supporting disadvantaged groups within the local community

- Paying compensation to groups that have been negatively impacted by the organisation's actions, eg injury caused by an unsafe product

Activity 7: SF Ltd

SF Ltd are a premium food manufacturer. They are currently developing a new range of ready-made lasagnes.

Currently there is a substantial cost gap on the new lasagnes. In order to reduce this cost gap, the management have decided on the following actions

- Use a lower grade of packaging to reduce the materials cost. The packaging selected will be non-recyclable, in contrast to the recyclable packaging they use on their other products.

- Moving production from their factory in Aton to a factory in Beaton. A lower grade of labour, and cheaper machinery, will be used as a result. The Beaton factory has been criticised for its heavy emissions from its production line.

Required

Explain the sustainability implications of the decisions the management have taken.

Chapter summary

- Most products have a limited lifecycle which involves the stages of development and launch, growth, maturity and decline. The position of the product within its lifecycle will affect sales and profitability patterns and be an important factor in cost management.

- The aim of lifecycle costing is to ensure that all the costs of a product (including development costs) are accumulated over the whole of its lifecycle, with or without discounting, in order to ensure that all costs are covered by revenue from the product.

- Target costing involves setting a target for the cost of a product or service by deducting the desired profit margin from the market selling price. The target cost represents the maximum amount of cost that the organisation can incur and still make the desired level of profit.

- Value analysis is a method of analysing the constituent elements of a product or service in order to try to reduce the cost with no loss in value to the customer. This method of analysis applied to new product design is known as value engineering.

Keywords

- **Corporate social responsibility:** the responsibility that the organisation has to groups and individuals that are external to it

- **Product lifecycle:** model to show different sales and profitability patterns at different stages of a product's life

- **Sustainability:** the need of organisations having enough resource to meet their current needs, without compromising the ability of the both the organisation, and other parties, to meet their future needs

- **Target cost:** the desired cost of a product which the designers must achieve, based on deducting the desirable profit margin from the target selling price

- **Value analysis:** analysis of every aspect of existing products/services in order to reduce the cost with no reduction in value to the customer

- **Value engineering:** value analysis in the design stage of a product or planning stage of a service

Activity answers

Activity 1: Product lifecycle costs

Development – Research and development costs will be mostly fixed. Few direct variable overheads are incurred.

Introduction – Advertising and promotion costs, alongside continuing recovery of research and development costs will mean that fixed costs are still the highest proportion of overall cost

Growth – Direct material and labour costs become the biggest proportion of overall cost, so costs switch from fixed to variable.

Maturity – Economies of scale reduce the level of variable cost. Mechanisation will mean that more fixed overheads are incurred. Costs switch from variable to fixed.

Decline – Increased obsolescence costs increase the proportion of variable cost incurred.

Activity 2: Co X

	Development	Introduction	Growth	Maturity	Decline	Total
Sales volume (units)		4,000	15,000	30,000	10,000	
£000						
Revenue		2,400	8,250	13,500	3,500	27,650
Variable cost		(1,000)	(3,750)	(6,000)	(1,500)	(12,250)
Overhead		(400)	(1,500)	(1,800)	(750)	(4,450)
Development cost	(500)	–	–	–	–	(500)
Advertising cost	–	(1,100)	–	–	–	(1,100)
Profit	(500)	(100)	3,000	5,700	1,250	9,350

Activity 3: Caston Foods

(a)

	Year 0	Year 1	Year 2	Year 3
Revenue		760,000	920,000	1,060,000
Operating costs		(456,000)	(542,000)	(612,000)
Capital expenditure	(600,000)			
Net cash flows	**(600,000)**	**304,000**	**378,000**	**448,000**
PV factors	1.000	0.877	0.769	0.675
Discounted cash flows	**(600,000)**	**266,608**	**290,682**	**302,400**
Net present value 259,690				

(b)   The new type of meal   **should**   be launched.

This is because it produces a positive NPV, therefore generating additional wealth to the owners of the business.

Activity 4: Lata A

(a)   The target cost is   £19.20 .

	£
Selling price	24
Profit margin (20%)	(4.8)
Target cost	19.20

Activity 5: Lata B

Available to spend on materials   £4.20 .

	£
Target cost (a)	19.20
Labour (2 hrs × £6)	(12)
Fixed costs (30,000/10,000)	(3)
Available to spend on material	4.20

Activity 6: Lata C

(c) Max cost per kg £1.40

£4.20/3 = £1.40

Activity 7: SF Ltd

Using non-recyclable packaging will mean that more of SF's packaging will end up in landfills. This will have a damaging effect on the environment as it contributes to the destruction of wildlife habitats as well as generating excess methane which is unpleasant to local populations.

The lower grade of packaging also detracts from the quality perception that SF wants to portray on its premium lasagne range. This could have a damaging effect on profit and shareholder returns as a result.

The move towards using a lower grade of labour in Beaton will have a damaging effect on staff in the factory in Aton. It is likely that the staff in the Aton factory will have reduced working hours or be made redundant. This will have a negative impact on the Aton local economy as the local population will have less disposable income and skills levels will reduce.

The machinery used in the Beaton factory has been criticised for heavy emissions. Moving production will see these emissions increasing as more production units are produced, damaging the Beaton local natural environment. SF also may contravene emissions regulation, incurring fines that will impact profits and returns to shareholders.

1   **Identify types of cost that could be incurred in each stage of the product life cycle.**

2   A business is considering investment in new machinery at a cost of £340,000 on 1 April 20X4. This machinery will be used to produce a new product which will give rise to the following net cash inflows:

31 March 20X5	£80,000
31 March 20X6	£70,000
31 March 20X7	£90,000
31 March 20X8	£120,000
31 March 20X9	£60,000

The cost of capital is 7%.

Complete the table below to calculate the net present value of this project.

Year	Cash flows £	Discount factor at 7%	Present value £
0		1.000	
1		0.935	
2		0.873	
3		0.816	
4		0.763	
5		0.713	
Net present value			

3   A business is considering investment in new plant and machinery on 1 January 20X6 at a cost of £90,000. The company has a cost of capital of 11%. The cash cost savings are estimated to be:

31 December 20X6	£23,000
31 December 20X7	£31,000
31 December 20X8	£40,000
31 December 20X9	£18,000

(a) Complete the table below to calculate the net present value of the plant and machinery.

Year	Cash flows £	Discount factor at 11%	Present value £
0		1.000	
1		0.901	
2		0.812	
3		0.731	
4		0.659	
Net present value			

(b) Complete the following sentence:

The organisation ⬚ invest in the plant and machinery.

Picklist:

should
should not

4   Fox Ltd are about to start developing a new product. It is anticipated that it will have a 5 year lifecycle.

Development costs are expected to be £400,000. It is anticipated that the product will have a 5 year lifecycle, at the end of which the machinery used to develop the product will be decommissioned at a cost of £60,000.

The expected cash flows from the product are expected to be as follows:

	Introduction	Growth	Maturity	Decline
Sales volume (units)	5,000	13,000	25,000	10,000
Selling price per unit	250	250	200	150
Variable cost per unit	150	130	70	85
Fixed Overhead (£000)	800	650	450	460

Calculate the profitability of the new product.

	Development	Introduction	Growth	Maturity	Decline	Total
Sales volume (units)		5,000	13,000	25,000	10,000	
£000						
Revenue						
Variable cost						
Fixed Overhead						
Development cost						
Scrap cost						
Profit						

5 Jess Co are developing a product, the Catflap. Jess wants to achieve a profit margin of 20%, and needs to set the selling price at £90 per unit.

Calculate the target cost per unit.

The target cost per unit is £ ☐ .

6 **Explain the terms value analysis and value engineering.**

Activity based costing (ABC)

9

Learning outcomes

5.3	**Calculate Activity Based Costing information**
	On completion of this chapter you should be able to:
	• Calculate activity based costs for a product
	• Understand the principles underpinning ABC

Assessment context

Calculation of various absorption rates using activity based costing (ABC) may be required in one question in the assessment.

Business context

The concepts of ABC were developed in the manufacturing sector of the US during the 1970s and 1980s. Absorption costing has become outdated for many businesses due to the diversity of product ranges and high level of overheads. As such ABC is becoming a much more appropriate tool for businesses to use when costing their products.

An example of an organisation that has used ABC successfully is the Chinese electricity firm Xu Ji. ABC was adopted by them in 2001, and analysis of their direct and variable costs into their respective activities helped them to standardise their processes. This enabled them to set more competitive prices to their customers.

Chapter overview

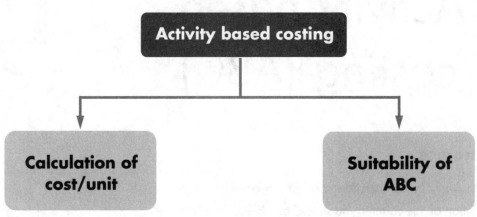

Activity based costing

Calculation of cost/unit

- Overheads are grouped into activities **(cost pools)**
- Identify the item which causes cost to be incurred **(cost driver)**
- Calculate a cost per unit for **each** cost driver

$$\frac{\text{Cost pool}}{\text{Cost driver}} = \text{OAR}$$

- Absorb costs into production based on actual usage if cost drivers

Suitability of ABC

Better analysis of costs leads to better:

- Cost control
- Pricing decisions
- Profitability analysis

Criticisms:

- Time consuming
- Costly
- Some arbitrary apportionment may still exist
- Limited benefit if products have similar cost structures

1 Introduction

> ## Assessment focus point
>
> ABC is an extension of absorption costing specifically considering what causes each type of overhead category to occur. Each type of overhead is absorbed using a different basis depending on the cause of the overhead. The objective of ABC is to arrive at a more realistic product cost.

Traditional absorption costing uses a single basis for absorbing all overheads into cost units for a particular production department cost centre. It assumes that overheads are volume related (ie as more units are produced, more of that activity is consumed).

A business will choose the basis that best reflects the way in which overheads are being incurred, e.g. in an automated business much of the overhead cost will be related to maintenance and repair of the machinery. It is likely that this will vary to some extent with machine hours worked so we would use a machine hour overhead absorption rate (OAR).

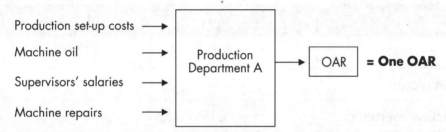

ABC recognises that production overheads are by no means all volume related and hence a single basis for absorption would not adequately reflect the complexity of producing certain products/cost units as opposed to others.

As a result, ABC calculates multiple OARs depending on the cause of the overhead (known as **cost drivers**).

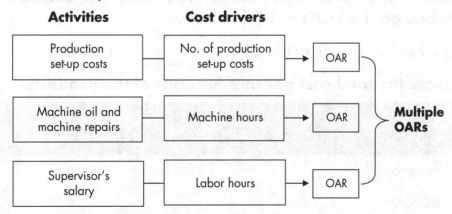

1.1 Steps to take in ABC

(1) Group overheads into activities, according to how they are driven. These are known as **cost pools**.

(2) Identify what causes each cost pool to be incurred, ie the cost drivers

(3) Calculate a **cost per unit of cost driver**:

$$\frac{\text{Total cost pool}}{\text{Total cost driver}}$$

(4) Calculate **total activity cost** for each unit:

Cost per unit of cost driver × **Total cost driver per unit**

(5) **Absorb** activity costs into production based on usage of cost drivers:

$$\frac{\text{Total activity cost per unit}}{\text{No of units}}$$

Activity 1: Dodo

Dodo Ltd manufactures three products, A, B and C. Data for the period just ended is as follows.

	A	B	C
Output (units)	20,000	25,000	2,000
	£/unit	**£/unit**	**£/unit**
Sales price	20	20	20
Direct material cost	5	10	10
Total production overheads	£190,000		
Labour hours/unit	2	1	1
Wages paid at £5/hr			

Required

(a) **Calculate the overhead absorption rate if overheads are absorbed on the basis of labour hours.**

The overhead absorption rate is £ ☐ per labour hour.

(b) **Calculate the total cost per unit for each of the products.**

	A £/unit	B £/unit	C £/unit
Direct materials			
Direct labour			
Production overheads			
Total cost			

You have now been given the following breakdown of overheads and cost driver information for Dodo:

	£
Machining	55,000
Quality control and Set-up costs	90,000
Receiving	30,000
Packing	15,000
	190,000

Cost driver data	A	B	C
Labour hours/unit	2	1	1
Machine hours/unit	2	2	2
No. of production runs	10	13	2
No. of component receipts	10	10	2
No. of customer orders	20	20	20
Output (units)	20,000	25,000	2,000

(c) Calculate the following overhead absorption rates (cost driver rates):

(i)   Machining
(ii) Quality control and Set-up costs
(iii) Receiving
(iv) Packing

(i)   [   ] per [   ]

(ii) [   ] per [   ]

(iii) [   ] per [   ]

(iv) [   ] per [   ]

(d) Calculate the total overhead cost for each of the products.

	A £	B £	C £	Total £
Machining				
Quality control and set-up costs				
Receiving				
Packing				
Total				

(e) Calculate the overhead cost per unit for each of the products.

	A £	B £	C £
Total overhead costs			
Units produced			
Overhead cost per unit			

(f) Calculate the total cost per unit for each of the products.

	A £/unit	B £/unit	C £/unit
Direct materials	5.00	10.00	10.00
Direct labour	10.00	5.00	5.00
Production overheads			
Total cost			

Assessment focus point

An assessment task may ask you to explain why products with smaller production runs may have more overhead absorbed per unit.

A product that is made in small batches will incur more set-up cost than a product made in larger batches. This is because producing in smaller batches will need more production

2 A critique of ABC

2.1 When ABC should be used

General environments where ABC would be more useful than traditional absorption costing include:

- When **production overheads are high** relative to prime costs (eg service sector). This is particularly important if production overheads are mainly fixed.

- When there is a **diversity of product range** meaning there are considerable **differences in the use of resources** by products

- Where consumption of **resources** is **not driven by volume** (ie as more units are produced more overhead is incurred as a result, meaning the overheads are largely variable).

2.2 Benefits of ABC

The use of ABC provides opportunities for:

- **Improved decision making:** A more realistic estimate of costs and profits which can be used in performance appraisal, meaning that more relevant and realistic decisions can be taken about products – for example whether to discontinue a product line.

- **Improved cost control and reduction:** Having visibility of the different cost drivers means that managers understand how costs are being incurred. Improvements can then be sought to reduce the usage of those cost drivers.

- **Improved pricing:** Better costing information means that better pricing structures for products can be sought to improve their overall profitability and the profitability of the business.

2.3 Criticisms of ABC

- Breaking down overheads into cost pools and ascertaining cost drivers takes a lot of time. ABC is therefore **time consuming and expensive.**

- If overheads are mainly driven by the fact that more cost units are produced – ie if **overheads are mainly volume driven** – then ABC provides a similar outcome to traditional absorption costing. It is therefore not appropriate in these situations.

- If the organisation is producing only one product, or several products that use overheads in very similar ways, then ABC has little benefit. This is because the product will absorb a similar amount of overheads, so the time and effort spent on providing the ABC information is wasted.

- In a complex environment it can be hard to establish reasons why overheads are incurred. Therefore **identification of cost drivers can be difficult in complex situations.**

- As with traditional absorption costing, matching the cost pool to the cost driver can sometimes rely on guesswork. Therefore there is **still some arbitrary apportionment** associated with ABC.

BPP
LEARNING MEDIA

Chapter summary

- Activity based costing (ABC) considers the activities that cause overheads to be incurred and the factors that give rise to these activity costs (cost drivers).

- It is a method of absorbing overheads into products on the basis of the amount of each activity that the particular product is expected to use in the period.

- ABC may be more suitable than traditional absorption costing in manufacturing businesses where overhead costs are much larger than direct production costs.

Keywords

- **Activity based costing (ABC):** a more complex approach to absorption of overheads, based upon an analysis of the detailed causes of the overheads

Activity 1: Dodo

(a) Under traditional absorption costing

OAR = £190,000 ÷ 67,000(w) = £2.836/hr

(W) total hours

	A	B	C	Total
Units	20,000	25,000	2,000	
Hrs/unit	2	1	1	
Total hours required	40,000	25,000	2,000	67,000

(b)

	A £/unit	B £/unit	C £/unit
Direct materials	5.00	10.00	10.00
Direct labour	10.00	5.00	5.00
Production overheads	5.67	2.84	2.84
Total cost	20.67	17.84	17.84

(c) (i) Machine costs $\dfrac{£55,000}{40,000+50,000+4,000}$ = $\boxed{£0.585}$ per $\boxed{\text{machine hour}}$

(ii) QC and set-up $\dfrac{90,000}{10+13+2}$ = $\boxed{£3,600}$ per $\boxed{\text{production run}}$

(iii) Receiving $\dfrac{£30,000}{10+10+2}$ = $\boxed{£1,363.64}$ per $\boxed{\text{component receipt}}$

(iv) Packing $\dfrac{£15,000}{20+20+20}$ = $\boxed{£250}$ per $\boxed{\text{customer order}}$

(d)

	A £	B £	C £	Total £
Machining costs (20:25:2)	23,404	29,255	2,341	55,000
Quality control and set-up (10:13:2)	36,000	46,800	7,200	90,000
Receiving (10:10:2)	13,636	13,636	2,728	30,000
Packing (20:20:20)	5,000	5,000	5,000	15,000
Total overhead costs	78,040	94,691	17,269	190,000

(e)

	A £	B £	C £
Total overhead costs	78,040	94,691	17,269
Units produced	20,000	25,000	2,000
Overhead cost/unit	£3.90	£3.79	£8.63

(f)

	A £/unit	B £/unit	C £/unit
Direct materials	5.00	10.00	10.00
Direct labour	10.00	5.00	5.00
Production overheads	3.90	3.79	8.63
Total cost	18.90	18.79	23.63

1 **Explain how activity based costing differs from traditional absorption costing.**

2 A business produces two products, the LM and the NP. The direct costs of the two products are:

	LM	NP
Direct materials	£2.60	£3.90
Direct labour	£3.50	£2.70

The total overhead cost is made up as follows:

	£
Stores costs	140,000
Production set-up costs	280,000
Quality control inspection costs	180,000
	600,000

The budgeted production is for 50,000 units of LM and 20,000 units of NP.

Each product is expected to make the following use of the service activities:

	LM	NP	Total
Materials requisitions from stores	100	220	320
Production set-ups	80	200	280
Quality control inspections	30	60	90

Complete the following table to show the budgeted cost per unit for each product using activity based costing and how much total budgeted overhead is included in the unit cost for each product.

Product	Budgeted cost per unit £	Budgeted overhead per unit £
LM		
NP		

3 **Explain the benefits of activity based costing.**

4 **Explain the disadvantages of activity based costing.**

Decision making techniques 10

Learning outcomes

1.3	Recognise and calculate measures of profitability and contribution
	On completion of this chapter you should be able to:
	• Identify when to use contribution analysis as a decision making tool
	• Calculate the contribution per unit and per £ of turnover
4.3	Make recommendations using decision making techniques
	On completion of this chapter you should be able to:
	• Calculate the optimal production mix when resources are limited
	• Calculate the breakeven point and margin of safety
	• Analyse whether an organisation should make a product or buy it in from a third party
	• Analyse whether the organisation should close down an area of the business
	• Analyse whether mechanisation will aid the business
	• Make use of relevant and non-relevant costing information to aid decision making

Assessment context

The concepts contained in this chapter will be tested in one task in the assessment. You won't be tested on all of these concepts in the same assessment – it depends on the variant of the assessment you are allocated as to which one you get.

Regardless of which decision you are asked to make, you must use contribution instead of profit to make them.

Business context

The tools demonstrated in this chapter are widely used by businesses. This is to ensure that risk has been adequately assessed, and that the most profitable option is adopted by the organisation.

Chapter overview

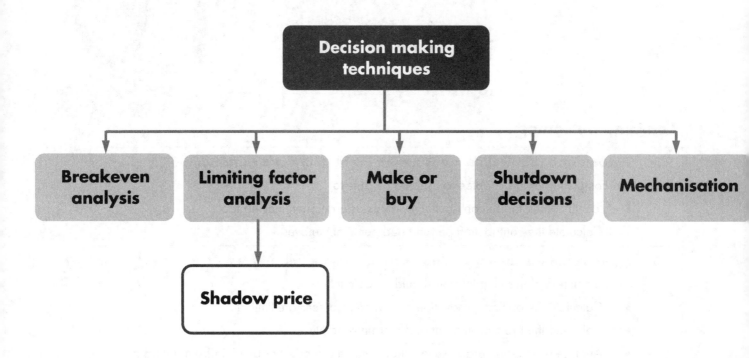

1 Introduction

When making short term decisions profit should not be the basis of the decision made. Profit includes fixed overheads which are likely to still be incurred at the same rate regardless of the decision that is made. Instead **contribution** is the tool that should be used for decision making purposes.

Remember that contribution is defined as selling price less all variable costs per unit.

When using contribution as a decision making tool the following assumptions are made:

(a) Contribution per unit is a constant figure at each level of activity; but
(b) Total contribution increases directly with increases in output and sales.

Fixed costs are different. As the volume of output and sales increases:

(a) Total fixed costs are unchanged; but

(b) The fixed costs per unit fall with increases in output and sales (because the fixed costs are spread over more units).

2 Breakeven analysis

Breakeven analysis helps the business to determine the breakeven point for business operations. It is sometimes referred to as **cost-volume-profit analysis** (CVP analysis) as it considers the relationship between activity levels, costs and profit. It is based on contribution analysis.

2.1 Breakeven point (BEP)

Assessment focus point

The **breakeven point (BEP)** for a company is the sales volume which will give the company a profit of £0. This means that all costs are covered by sales revenue.

	£	
Sales	15,000	
Less VCs	(5,000)	
Contribution	10,000	Must be
Fixed costs	(10,000)	**equal**
Profit	0	

The BEP is an important point for managers of a business to be aware of, because if the activity level falls below the BEP then there will be a loss. The breakeven volume of sales is therefore the minimum amount of sales needed to avoid a loss.

2.2 Calculating the BEP

Breakeven occurs when

Total contribution = Fixed costs

Or   Contribution per unit × Sales units = Fixed costs

Sales units will therefore be the amount of units to sell to make neither a profit nor a loss, ie the BEP. Therefore:

Formula to learn

$$BEP = \frac{\text{Fixed costs}}{\text{Cont'n/unit}}$$

Activity 1: Widget A

Financial data for the Widget is as follows:

Per unit:	£
Materials	12
Labour	30
Variable production overhead	13
Variable distribution cost	5
Total variable cost	60
Selling price	100

	£
Factory cost	100,000
Administration costs	50,000
Total fixed costs	150,000

Required

What is the breakeven point in units?

2.3 Breakeven revenue

The breakeven revenue can be calculated as follows:

Formula to learn

Breakeven revenue = Breakeven point (units) × Selling price per unit

An alternative method of finding the breakeven revenue is to use the **contribution to sales (C/S) ratio** rather than the selling price per unit.

Formula to learn

$$\text{C/S ratio} = \frac{\text{Contribution}}{\text{Sales}}$$

The C/S ratio gives the **amount of contribution earned per pound of sales**. The breakeven revenue can then be calculated as follows:

Formula to learn

$$\text{Breakeven revenue (£)} = \frac{\text{Fixed costs}}{\text{C/S ratio}}$$

Activity 2: Widget B

Required

Using the information from Activity 1: Widget A, calculate:

(a) The C/S ratio.

The C/S ratio is [   ].

(b) The breakeven revenue for the Widget.

The breakeven revenue is [   ].

2.4 Margin of safety

The **margin of safety (MOS)** is a measure of the amount by which sales could fall before a loss is made.

In units, the MOS can be calculated as:

Formula to learn

MOS (in units) = Budgeted sales volume – breakeven sales volume

Alternatively the MOS can be calculated as a percentage as follows:

Formula to learn

$$\text{MOS (as \%)} = \frac{\text{Budgeted sales volume} - \text{breakeven sales volume}}{\text{Budgeted sales volume}} \times 100$$

Assessment focus point

A common error in the assessment is candidates calculating the MOS as a percentage of breakeven units rather than budgeted units. Be careful to **ensure that budgeted units is always on the bottom of the fraction** in your calculation

Activity 3: Widget C

Budgeted sales of the Widget are 5,000 units.

Required

Using the information above and from Activity 1: Widget A, calculate

(a)   The margin of safety in units

    [   ] units

(b)   The margin of safety as a % of budgeted sales

    [   ] %

2.5 Required profit level

The approach used to find the breakeven sales volumes can be extended to find the volume needed to attain a required profit level.

Formula to learn

$$\text{Sales volume to reach required profit level} = \frac{\text{Fixed costs} + \text{required profit}}{\text{Contribution per unit}}$$

The required profit is like an additional fixed cost which must be covered before the company 'breaks even'.

Alternatively the C/S ratio can be used to find the sales revenue required for a target profit as follows:

$$\text{Sales revenue required} = \frac{\text{Target contribution}}{\text{C/S ratio}}$$

Activity 4: Widget D

Required

Using the information from Activity 1: Widget A, calculate the sales volume required to make a profit of £30,000.

| units

2.6 Cost changes and impact on risk

When the costs of a business change this will impact the breakeven analysis.

An increase in costs will cause the BEP to rise whereas an increase in selling price will lower the BEP.

The greater the proportion of fixed costs in a business, the greater the risk in that business. These costs need to be paid regardless of the volume of units produced and sold. Variable costs on the other hand are only incurred when units are produced.

An organisation that has high fixed costs as a proportion of its total costs is known to have high operational gearing.

Activity 5: Widget E

It is now expected that the fixed costs will rise by 10%, variable costs by 5% and the selling price by 6%.

Required

(a) Using the information from Activity 1: Widget A, calculate the revised breakeven point.

The revised breakeven point is [   ] units.

(b) Explain how this impacts on the risk associated with selling the Widget.

Assessment focus point

A written assessment task may ask you to compare the breakeven point and margin of safety of two products. You may therefore need to describe how each is calculated, and explain how each can be improved in order to reduce risk within the organisation.

Activity 6: Chuck

Chuck Limited has two departments, Lob and Throw. Each department manufactures separate products.

It has supplied the following information for last month:

	Lob	Throw
Sales volume (units)	35,000	30,000
Selling price (£ per unit)	6	6
Variable production costs (£ per unit)	3.50	1.00
Fixed overheads (£)	43,750	120,000
Contribution per unit (£)	2.50	5.00
Breakeven point (units)	175,000	24,000
Margin of safety (%)	50	20

Required

Draft a report in which you provide analysis of these figures under the given section headings.

Implications of the differences in breakeven point between the two departments.

Which department has the better margin of safety and why?

Comment on the results from a risk perspective and suggest any potential ways of reducing it.

3 Limiting factor analysis

The production and sales plans of a business may be limited by a **limiting factor**/scarce resource. There are a number of potential limiting factors.

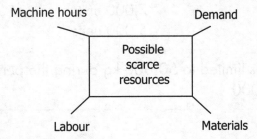

The plans of the business must be built around the limiting factor.

Optimal production plan

Normally the limiting factor is sales demand. However, if materials, labour or machine hours are limited then the business will need to find a production plan that

makes the most profitable use of that scarce resource. This is known as the optimal production plan, which is especially important if the business makes more than one product.

In order to maximise overall profit, contribution per unit of scarce resource must be maximised.

This is done using the following approach:

(1) Identify the limiting factor.

(2) Calculate contribution per unit.

(3) Calculate contribution per unit of limiting factor by making the following calculation:

$$\frac{\textbf{Contribution per unit}}{\textbf{Limiting factor per unit}}$$

(4) Rank products by contribution per unit of limiting factor.

(5) Prepare the optimal production plan.

Illustration 1: Farnham Engineering

Farnham Engineering makes three products, A, B and C. The costs and selling prices of the three products are:

	A	B	C
	£	£	£
Direct materials @ £4 per kg	8	16	12
Direct labour @ £7 per hour	7	21	14
Variable overheads	3	9	6
Marginal cost	18	46	32
Selling price	22	54	39

Sales demand for the coming period is expected to be as follows:

Product A	3,000 units
Product B	7,000 units
Product C	5,000 units

The supply of materials is limited to 50,000 kg during the period and the labour hours available are 28,000.

Required

Calculate the optimal production plan for Farnham Engineering

This can be done be following the above steps:

Step 1: Identify the limiting factor

The following calculations can be done to identify the limiting factor:

	A	B	C	Total required
Materials (2/4/3 kg)	6,000 kg	28,000 kg	15,000 kg	49,000 kg
Labour (1/3/2 hrs)	3,000 hours	21,000 hours	10,000 hours	34,000 hours

From the above table we can see that labour hours are the limiting factor (28,000 labour hours are available whereas 34,000 hours are required to meet total sales demand).

Step 2: Calculate contribution per unit

Using the above table, the contribution per unit of each of products A, B & C is as follows (remember that contribution per unit = selling price – marginal cost):

A: £22 - £18 = £4 per unit

B: £54 - £46 = £8 per unit

C: £39 - £32 = £7 per unit

Step 3: Calculate contribution per unit of limiting factor

As labour hours is the limiting factor, the contribution earned per labour hour needs to be calculated. This will ensure that we are maximising contribution for every labour hour that is worked.

The calculations needed are as follows:

	A	B	C
Contribution	£4	£8	£7
Labour hours per unit	1 hour	3 hours	2 hours
Contribution per labour hour:			
£4/1	£4.00		
£8/3		£2.67	
£7/2			£3.50

Step 4: Rank products by contribution per unit of limiting factor

Once the above calculation has been complete, the products are ranked in order of contribution per labour hour. This ensures that production priority is given to the most profitable product.

Product A makes the most contribution per unit of limiting factor (labour hours) and therefore, in order to maximise contribution, we must concentrate first on production of A up to its maximum sales demand. Then we can concentrate on producing C, and finally, if there are any remaining hours available, on B.

Step 5: Calculate the optimal production plan

The optimal production plan can now be calculated as per the below table:

	Units produced	Labour hours required
A	3,000	3,000
C	5,000	10,000
		13,000
B (balance)	5,000 (15,000 hrs / 3 hrs per unit)	15,000 (balancing figure)
		28,000

Activity 7: LF

LF is trying to work out its optimal production plan.

Machine time available is 300 hours.

Labour time available is 200 hours.

	A £/unit	B £/unit	C £/unit
Selling price	150	120	100
Variable costs	100	80	70
Fixed costs	20	20	20
Profit	30	20	10
Machine time	5 hrs	2 hrs	1 hr
Labour time	2 hrs	1 hr	0.5 hrs
Demand	50	50	50

Required

(a) Identify the limiting factor.

The limiting factor is [   ].

Picklist:

labour hours
machine hours

(b) Calculate the contribution per unit of limiting factor for each product.

The contribution per limiting factor for:

A is [ ]

B is [ ]

C is [ ]

(c) Calculate the optimal production plan.

The optimum number of units to be produced of:

A is [ ] units

B is [ ] units

C is [ ] units

3.1 Shadow price

The contribution per unit of limiting factor will help the organisation decide how much extra should be paid for additional units of that scarce resource.

Ideally the organisation would not want to pay more than the contribution generated by each unit of limiting factor as it would find itself in a loss making situation.

The resources obtained will be used to produce any units that remain outstanding. Therefore the **shadow price** is the **contribution per unit of limiting factor on the product that has not been maximised.**

Activity 8: LF Shadow Price

LF is deciding how much extra it should pay for additional resources.

Required

Using the information from Activity 7, calculate the maximum price that LF should pay for each of the following:

(a) 100 hours of additional labour: £ [ ] .

(b) 100 hours of additional machine time: £ [ ] .

4 Make or buy decisions

A company may want to consider whether it is best to manufacture a unit itself or whether it would be better to outsource the production. Some examples include:

(a) Whether a company should manufacture its own components, or buy the components from an outside supplier

(b) Whether a construction company should do some work with its own employees, or whether it should sub-contract the work to another company

(c) Whether a service should be carried out by an internal department or whether an external organisation should be employed

4.1 Relevant costs in make or buy decisions

To numerically analyse the make or buy decision, the **relevant costs** need to be considered. These are costs that will be incurred or saved purely as a result of making a decision.

In make or buy decisions, the following costs would be deemed relevant:

- **All variable cost** savings

- **Fixed cost savings if that cost saving is directly attributable to the decision being made**. For example, by choosing to buy component A, the rental cost of a machine used to make that component would be saved. This wouldn't be the case for factory rent – as other components will still need to be made, the factory would still need to be kept on.

Activity 9: Dolphin

Dolphin makes three components. Details for the following year are as follows:

	A	J	H
Production (units)	5,000	4,000	3,000
	£	£	£
Direct material/unit	15	6	18
Direct labour/unit	15	20	22
Variable production overheads/unit	5	4	4
Directly attributable fixed costs	2,000	3,000	6,000

Other general fixed costs are £20,000.

A subcontractor has quoted a price per unit of	30	39	50

Required

Indicate whether the components should be made or bought in.

Dolphin should buy in [   ].

Picklist:

all of the components
none of the components
some of the components

4.2 Non-financial considerations

Assessment focus point

Such a decision should not be taken purely on financial grounds. In the assessment you may have to explain other factors that need to be considered before making an outsourcing decision. Some ideas are given in the below table.

Advantages of outsourcing	Disadvantages of outsourcing
Cost savings due to the flexibility provided by the outsource partner	Control of the operations is lost
Expertise that the organisation may have difficulty accessing themselves	Quality of the product could be impacted as the organisation is reliant on the processes of the outsourced partner
Capital can be released from the department or product to maximise opportunities	The outsourced partner will have other customers to service, so reliability could drop
Resources can be diverted to more value adding activities	Confidential information will need to be provided to the outsource partner, and there is potential that this could be misappropriated
	Skills are lost in-house, making it difficult to bring operations back in-house if required
	Employees are likely to be made redundant, negatively impacting morale and motivation

5 Shutdown decisions

Shutdown decisions will include the following:

(a) Whether or not to close down a product line, department or other activity, either because it is making losses or because it is too expensive to run

(b) If the decision is to shut down, whether the closure should be permanent or temporary

5.1 Relevant costs in shutdown decisions

The same relevant costing principles need to be applied as per make or buy decisions when numerically evaluating a shutdown position.

Activity 10: Duo

Duo Ltd owns two factories, A and B. The forecasts for both factories for the year ending 31 December 20X5 are below:

	A		**B**	
	£000		£000	
Revenue	2,200		2,850	
Direct materials	660		784	
Direct labour	440		448	
Fixed production overheads	220		420	
Cost of sales	1,320		1,652	
Gross profit	880	40%	1,198	42%
Sales and distribution costs	520		640	
Administration costs	210		250	
Profit from operations	150	6.8%	308	10.8%

Other information:

Inventories are of raw materials and will remain unchanged throughout the year.

Sales and distribution costs are variable with turnover from each factory.

Administration costs are fixed.

The Managing Director has proposed closing factory A. The impact to Factory B's results will be as follows:

- Revenue would increase by 40%

- Materials, labour and sales and distribution costs are all variable with sales revenue

- Fixed production overheads will increase by £100,000

- Administration costs will increase by £60,000

- It is forecast that purchasing costs will decrease by 5% as a result of the closure

BPP
LEARNING MEDIA

Required

(a) Prepare a revised statement of profit or loss for factory B, assuming factory A is closed.

	Factory B £	
Revenue		
Materials		
Direct labour		
Fixed production overheads		
Cost of sales		
Gross profit		%
Sales and distribution costs		
Administration costs		
Profit from operations		%

(b) Indicate whether factory A should be closed.

Factory A [   ] be closed.

Picklist:

should
should not

5.2 Non-financial considerations of shutdown decisions

The decision again should not be judged purely on financial analysis. Some other factors to consider are:

- **Staff morale** – Staff will be made redundant, which negatively impacts morale and motivation.

- **Customers** – Market share could be lost if customers choose to source the discontinued product from a competitor.

- **Suppliers** – Some suppliers may be reliant on the organisation to stay in business. If the organisation chooses to stop making the product this could have severe consequences on these suppliers.

6 Mechanisation decisions

Management may face a decision about changing the technology that is used in production. For example, as technology plays a greater part in manufacturing, a business may be considering changing from a labour-intensive production process to a machine-intensive one.

6.1 Relevant costs in mechanisation decisions

Relevant costs can also be used to assess profit impacts on whether to mechanise part of the organisation.

Relevant costs in mechanisation decisions include:

- Labour cost savings
- The capital cost of acquiring the machine
- Increased fixed overheads due to running of the machine
- Increased revenue due to increased sales volumes

Activity 11: Hill Ltd

Hill Ltd is considering replacing one of its current machines with a new machine.

The table below shows how having the new equipment compares with the current situation:

	Current situation	Proposed situation with new equipment
Direct material	3 kg @ £5	Usage down by 10%
Direct labour	6 hrs @ £10	Time down by 25%
Sales	4,000 units at £125 each	No change
Fixed costs	£180,000	Up by £47,500

Required

Calculate the profit figures for the current and proposed situations, and indicate whether the machine should be acquired.

	Current situation	Proposed situation
Profit		

It [   ] be better to acquire the new equipment.

Picklist:

would
would not

Assessment focus point

Instead of being asked to calculate the difference in profit in a mechanisation decision, you could instead be asked to calculate the net present value of the decision. The net present value is covered in an earlier chapter of this Course Book.

6.2 Other considerations in mechanisation decisions

Other factors to consider in mechanisation decisions include:

- **Increased operational gearing** – If the level of fixed costs in the business increases as a proportion of total cost, the profits of the business will become more sensitive to changes in sales volumes. This is because when sales volumes fall, the cost base remains largely the same and as a result there is a bigger impact on profits.

- **Qualitative factors** – These will include the effect on the morale of the remaining workforce and any environmental issues involved in the mechanisation process, such as increased emissions.

Chapter summary

- For short-term decision making we concentrate on marginal costing and contribution – total fixed costs are assumed to be constant for the period.

- The breakeven point in units is found by dividing the fixed costs by the contribution per unit.

- The unit sales to achieve a target profit can be found by dividing the fixed costs plus target profit by the contribution per unit.

- The difference between budgeted or actual sales and the breakeven point is the margin of safety. This is often expressed as a percentage of budgeted sales or actual sales.

- The contribution to sales ratio can be used to find the breakeven point in terms of sales revenue:

  Breakeven point (sales revenue £) = Fixed costs ÷ C/S ratio

- Normally output in any period is limited by sales demand. However, occasionally a factor of production such as the availability of material, labour hours or machine hours may be a limiting factor on output and profitability.

- Where there is more than one product and a limiting factor, overall profit is maximised by concentrating production on the products with the highest contribution per limiting factor unit.

- In a make or buy decisions, the relevant costs are any variable costs incurred/saved as a result of the decision and any savings in attributable fixed costs.

- Qualitative aspects of make or buy, shutdown and mechanisation need to be considered alongside the financial analysis.

- Whether or not to move from a labour-intensive production process to a machine-intensive production process will also have many short- and some long-term effects.

Keywords

- **Breakeven analysis:** calculations to determine the breakeven point

- **Breakeven point:** level of sales where sales revenue and total costs are equal, so that there is no profit and no loss

- **Contribution:** sales revenue less variable costs

- **Contribution to sales (C/S) ratio:** ratio of contribution to sales revenue

- **Cost-volume-profit analysis:** analysis of the relationships between activity levels, costs and profits using marginal costing

- **Limiting factor:** a factor that limits the amount of a product that can be produced or sold: it is often sales demand but may be a production factor in limited supply

- **Margin of safety:** excess of budgeted sales or actual sales over the breakeven point sales, which may be measured as a percentage of budgeted or actual sales

- **Profit volume (P/V) ratio:** alternative name for the contribution to sales ratio

Activity 1: Widget A

Breakeven point = fixed cost/contribution per unit = £150,000/£40 = 3,750.

Activity 2: Widget B

(a)   40/100 = 0.4 or 40%

(b)   £150,000/0.4 = £375,000

Activity 3: Widget C

(a)   Margin of safety = budgeted volume – breakeven volume = 1,250 units

(b)   Margin of safety = (budgeted volume – breakeven volume)/budgeted volume
×100

= (5,000 – 3,750)/5,000 × 100 = 25%.

Activity 4: Widget D

Fixed costs + required profit = £(150,000 + 30,000) = £180,000.

Contribution per unit = £40

Sales volume   = £180,000/£40 = 4,500 units.

Activity 5: Widget E

(a)   Fixed costs rise by 10% = 165,000

Variable costs rise by 5% = £63 per unit

Selling price rises by 6% = £106 per unit

Therefore contribution per unit = £43

Breakeven point = $\dfrac{165,000}{43} = 3,838$ units

(b)   The breakeven point rises by 88 units.

This reduces the margin of safety to: 23.24%.

The breakeven point should still be achieved; the margin of safety falls but only marginally. There is a greater risk that the fixed costs will not be covered but this risk has only been impacted slightly by the change.

Activity 6: Chuck

Implications of the differences in breakeven point between the two departments

The breakeven point of Lob is much higher than that of Throw, despite having a lower contribution per unit. This is because Lob has much lower fixed costs, so the contribution generated per unit has less fixed cost to cover.

As a consequence Lob needs to sell much fewer units to cover its fixed cost base than Throw does in order to recover its fixed costs.

Which department has the better margin of safety and why?

Lob has a much higher margin of safety than Throw. This is because the proportion of budgeted sales to breakeven point is much lower than that of Throw. Indeed Lob can drop 17,500 units before it starts making a loss compared to Throw's 6,000 units.

The main reason for this is not only because of the lower fixed costs generating a low breakeven point, but because there is more demand for Lob's product, generating higher sales volumes.

Comment on the results from a risk perspective and suggest any potential ways of reducing it.

Throw is the more risky department as its operational gearing is much higher than that of Lob. To reduce the risk within Throw the following improvements could be made:

Sales volumes could be increased. This will generate more contribution towards fixed costs. However there will be an impact on fixed costs as advertising spend will increase which, if the sales volume increase didn't materialise, would further increase breakeven point and reduce margin of safety.

Alternatively sales prices could increase. This would increase contribution without any impact on fixed costs. Care must be taken here as a substantial increase in price could impact on sales volumes, which may cancel out the price increase.

Automation of the production process in Throw may improve efficiency. This will reduce variable production costs, especially labour, and will improve contribution per unit. The breakeven point will reduce in turn.

Throw could also analyse their fixed costs and work towards reducing these. This will improve Throw's breakeven point as contribution generated will be covering fewer fixed costs.

Activity 7: LF

(a) The limiting factor is ⟨ machine hours ⟩.

Labour time required = (50 × 2 hr) + (50 × 1 hr) + (50 × 0.5 hr) = 175 hrs

Labour time available = 200 hrs

Machine time required = (50 × 5 hr) + (50 × 2 hr) + (50 × 1 hr) = 400 hrs

Machine time available = 300 hrs

(b) A is £10

B is £20

C is £30

(c) A is 30 units

B is 50 units

C is 50 units

Workings

	A	B	C
Contribution/unit	£50	£40	£30
Contribution/machine hour	£10	£20	£30
Rank	3rd	2nd	1st

Production schedule	Hrs used
(1) Produce maximum 50 of C	50
(2) Produce maximum 50 of B	100
(3) Produce A with remaining hours	
$\dfrac{150}{5}$ = 30 units	150
	300

Activity 8: LF Shadow Price

(a) 100 hours of additional labour: £0

There are enough labour hours available to make all require units so no additional labour hours need to be obtained.

(b) 100 hours of additional machine time: £1000 (£10 per hour × 100 hours)

The additional hours will be used to make the maximum amount of A.

The shadow price is therefore the contribution per machine hour on production of A.

Activity 9: Dolphin

Dolphin should buy in | some of the components |.

The company would save £27,000 by buying in A, but would lose a total of £45,000 if they bought in J & H. This is demonstrated in the below table:

	A	J	H
Cost of making			
Direct material/unit	15	6	18
Direct labour/unit	15	20	22
Variable production overheads/unit	5	4	4
Variable cost of making/unit	35	30	44
Production (units)	5,000	4,000	3,000
Total variable production cost	175,000	120,000	132,000
Incremental fixed costs	2,000	3,000	6,000
Total cost of making	177,000	123,000	138,000
Cost of buying			
Cost per unit	30	39	50
Production (units)	5,000	4,000	3,000
Total cost of buying	150,000	156,000	150,000
Benefit/(additional cost) of buying the units	27,000	(33,000)	(12,000)

Activity 10: Duo

(a)

	Factory B £000	
Revenue (2,850 + (2,200 × 40%))	3,730.0	
Materials (784 + (660 × 40%)) × 95%	995.6	
Direct labour (448 + (440 × 40%))	624.0	
Fixed production overheads (420 + 100)	520.0	
Cost of sales	2,139.6	
Gross profit	1,590.4	42.6%
Sales and distribution costs (640/2,850) × 3,730	837.6	
Administration costs (250 + 60)	310.0	
Profit from operations	442.8	11.9%

(b) Factory A | should not | be closed down.

This is because the company will be less profitable:

Current profit = 150 + 308 = £458

New profit = £442.8

Activity 11: Hill Ltd

	Current situation £	Proposed situation £
Sales	4,000 units × £125 = 500,000	500,000
Direct materials	3 kg × £5 × 4,000 units = (60,000)	3 kg × £5 × 4,000 units × 90% = (54,000)
Direct labour	6 hrs × £10 × 4,000 units = (240,000)	6 hrs × £10 × 4,000 units × 75% = (180,000)
Fixed costs	(180,000)	180,000 + 47,500 = (227,500)
Profit	**20,000**	**38,500**

It | would | be better to acquire the new equipment.

Test your learning

1. A business making a single product has budgeted sales of 38,000 units. The selling price per unit is £57 and the variable costs per unit of production are £45. The fixed costs of the business are £360,000.

   Required

   Calculate

   (a) The breakeven point in units

   (b) The margin of safety as a percentage

   The breakeven point is ⬚ units.

   The margin of safety is ⬚ %.

2. A business has fixed costs of £910,000. It sells a single product at a selling price of £24 and the variable costs of production and sales are £17 per unit.

   Required

   Calculate the amount of units that need to be sold to make a profit of £500,000.

   The amount of units that need to be sold is ⬚ units.

3. A business sells its single product for £40. The variable costs of this product total £32 per unit. The fixed costs of the business are £100,000.

   Required

   Calculate the sales revenue required to make a profit of £200,000.

   The sales revenue required in order to make a profit of £200,000 is £ ⬚

4. A business produces three products, the production and sales details of which are given below:

	Product		
	R	**S**	**T**
Direct materials @ £2 per kg	£16	£12	£10
Direct labour @ £9 per hour	£18	£36	£9
Selling price	£40	£60	£25
Machine hours per unit	6	4	3
Maximum sales demand	10,000 units	20,000 units	5,000 units

   During the next period the supply of materials is limited to 250,000 kg, the labour hours available are 120,000 and the machine hours available are also 120,000. Fixed costs are £50,000 per period.

Required

(a) Identify the limiting factor.

(b) Calculate the optimal production plan.

(c) Calculate the profit earned under the optimal production plan.

(a)   The limiting factor is [   ].

Picklist:

labour hours
machine hours
materials

(b)

Product	Units produced

(c)   The profit that will be earned under this production plan is £ [   ].

5   A business has two products, X and Y, with the following costs per unit.

	X Cost per unit	Y Cost per unit
	£	£
Direct materials	2.50	3.00
Direct labour	8.00	6.00
Fixed overheads	3.00	1.50

The business could buy in X from an external supplier at a cost of £11 per unit, and it could buy in Y at £10 per unit.

Fixed overheads are not directly attributable and will be incurred regardless of whether the products will be bought in or not.

Required

Which product(s) should be bought in?

The business should buy in [   ].

Picklist:

both products
neither product

X
Y

6   Timmy Co is short on labour hours meaning that it can't meet maximum sales demand.

Labour hours available to Timmy Co are 20,000 hours.

It has produced the following optimal production plan for its products Badger and Pelican:

	Badger	Pelican
Sales demand (units)	5,000	10,000
Labour hours per unit (Hrs)	1	2
Contribution per unit (£)	5.00	7.00
Contribution per unit of limiting factor (£)	5.00	3.50
Optimal production plan	5,000	7,500

How much should Timmy Co pay for 5,000 additional labour hours?

£ [   ].

Test your learning: Answers

Chapter 1   Costing Techniques

1

True ☑

10,000 units   Cost per unit £43,600/10,000 =   £4.36

12,000 units   Cost per unit £52,320/12,000 =   £4.36

As the cost per unit is the same at each level of production this would appear to be a purely variable cost.

2

Activity level	Total fixed cost £	Fixed cost per unit £
3,000 units	64,000	21.33
10,000 units	64,000	6.40
16,000 units	64,000	4.00

Working

3,000 units   £64,000/3,000 = £21.33

10,000 units   £64,000/10,000 = £6.40

16,000 units   £64,000/16,000 = £4.00

3   The marginal cost per month is

£52,500 .

The full production cost per month is

£70,000 .

Workings

	Production cost £
Direct material costs (£5 × 3,500)	17,500
Direct labour costs (£10 × 3,500)	35,000
Marginal cost	52,500
Rent	10,000
Supervisor cost	7,500
Full production cost	70,000

4   (a)   The variable element of the production cost is

£3 per unit

The fixed element of the production cost is

£169,000

(b)

Level of production	Production cost £
120,000 units	529,000
150,000 units	619,000

Workings

(a)

		£
Highest level	126,000	547,000
Lowest level	101,000	472,000
Increase	25,000	75,000

$$\text{Variable rate} = \frac{£75,000}{25,000} = £3 \text{ per unit}$$

Using highest level:

	£
Variable cost 126,000 × £3	378,000
Fixed costs (balancing figure)	169,000
Total cost	547,000

(b)   (i)

120,000 units	£
Variable cost 120,000 × £3	360,000
Fixed cost	169,000
Total forecast cost	529,000

(ii)

150,000 units	£
Variable cost 150,000 × £3	450,000
Fixed cost	169,000
Total forecast cost	619,000

5 (a) The correct answer is £20.00.
   (b) The correct answer is £15.00.

Workings

Department P1 = $\dfrac{£50,000}{2,500\,h}$

= £20 per direct labour hour

Department P2 = $\dfrac{£60,000}{4,000\,h}$

= £15 per machine hour

6

	Amount of under-/over-absorption £	Under- or over-absorption	Add or subtract in statement of profit or loss (income statement)
An overhead absorption rate of £3 per unit, based on expected production levels of 500 units. Actual overheads turn out to be £1,600, and actual production is 650 units.	350.00	Over-absorption	Add
The budget is set at 1,000 units, with £9,000 overheads recovered on the basis of 600 direct labour hours. At the end of the period, overheads amounted to £8,600, production achieved was only 950 units and 590 direct labour hours had been worked.	250.00	Over-absorption	Add

Workings

(a)

	£
Actual overheads	1,600
Absorbed overheads (650 units @ £3 per unit)	1,950
Over-absorption	350

The over-absorption of £350 would be added to profit in the statement of profit or loss (income statement).

(b)

	£
Actual overheads	8,600
Absorbed overheads (590 hrs × £15* per hr)	8,850
Over-absorption	250

$$* \text{ Overhead absorption rate} = \frac{£9,000}{600 \text{ direct labour hours}}$$

=£15 per direct labour hour

The over-absorption of £250 would be added to profit in the statement or profit or loss (income statement).

7   (a)

Department	Overhead absorption rate
X	£2.60 per machine hour
Y	£3.17 per direct labour hour

Workings

$$X = \frac{£260,000}{100,000}$$

= £2.60 per machine hour

As X is a highly mechanised department, most of the overhead will relate to the machinery therefore machine hours have been used to absorb the overhead.

$$Y = \frac{£380,000}{120,000}$$

= £3.17 per direct labour hour

As Y is a highly labour-intensive department, most of the overhead will relate to the hours that are worked by the labour force therefore labour hours are used to absorb the overhead.

(b)   The overhead to be included in the cost of product A is £25.68.

Workings

Product A – department X overhead	£2.60 × 5	= £13.00
Product A – department Y overhead	£3.17 × 4	= £12.68
		£25.68

8   In an absorption costing system all fixed production overheads are absorbed into the cost of the products and are included in unit cost. In a marginal costing system the fixed production overheads are written off in the statement or profit or loss (income statement) as a period cost.

9

Method of costing	Budgeted cost £
Absorption costing	59.70
Marginal costing	57.11

Workings

Absorption costing – unit cost

	£
Direct materials	12.50
Direct labour assembly (4 × £8.40)	33.60
Finishing (1 × £6.60)	6.60
Assembly overheads (£336,000/60,000)	5.60
Finishing overheads (£84,000/60,000)	1.40
	59.70

Marginal costing – unit cost

		£
Direct materials		12.50
Direct labour assembly	(4 × £8.40)	33.60
Finishing	(1 × £6.60)	6.60
Assembly overheads	$\dfrac{£336,000 \times 60\%}{60,000}$	3.36
Finishing overheads	$\dfrac{£84,000 \times 75\%}{60,000}$	1.05
		57.11

10   Unit cost

	£
Direct materials	12.00
Direct labour	8.00
Variable overhead (£237,000/15,000)	15.80
Marginal costing unit cost	35.80
Fixed overhead (£390,000/15,000)	26.00
Absorption costing unit cost	61.80

(a) (i) Absorption costing – statement of profit or loss (income statement)

	November		December	
	£	£	£	£
Sales				
(12,500/18,000 × £75)		937,500		1,350,000
Less cost of sales				
Opening inventory				
(2,000 × £61.80)	123,600			
(4,500 × £61.80)			278,100	
Production costs				
(15,000 × £61.80)	<u>927,000</u>		<u>927,000</u>	
	1,050,600		1,205,100	
Less closing inventory				
(4,500 × £61.80)	<u>278,100</u>			
(1,500 × £61.80)			<u>92,700</u>	
		<u>772,500</u>		<u>1,112,400</u>
Profit		<u>165,000</u>		<u>237,600</u>

(ii) **Marginal costing – statement of profit or loss (income statement)**

	November £	November £	December £	December £
Sales				
(12,500/18,000 × £75)		937,500		1,350,000
Less cost of sales				
Opening inventory				
(2,000 × £35.80)	71,600			
(4,500 × £35.80)			161,100	
Production costs				
(15,000 × £35.80)	537,000		537,000	
	608,600		698,100	
Less closing inventory				
(4,500 × £35.80)	161,100			
(1,500 × £35.80)			53,700	
		447,500		644,400
Contribution		490,000		705,600
Less fixed overheads		390,000		390,000
Profit		100,000		315,600

(b)

	November £	December £
Absorption costing profit	165,000	237,600
Inventory changes	(65,000)	78,000
Marginal costing profit	100,000	315,600

Workings

	November £	December £
Increase in inventory × fixed cost per unit ((4,500 – 2,000) × £26)	(65,000)	
Decrease in inventory × fixed cost per unit ((4,500 – 1,500) × £26)		78,000

Chapter 2 Statistical techniques

1

	Actual £	Three-month moving average £
July	397,500	
August	403,800	400,300
September	399,600	402,900
October	405,300	403,667
November	406,100	406,633
December	408,500	407,500
January	407,900	408,933
February	410,400	411,433
March	416,000	413,167
April	413,100	415,533
May	417,500	417,467
June	421,800	

2

		Actual £	Four-quarter moving average £	Centred moving average = TREND £	Seasonal variations £
20X5	Quarter 1	383,600			
	Quarter 2	387,600			
			365,400		
	Quarter 3	361,800		365,688	−3,888
			365,975		
	Quarter 4	328,600		366,575	−37,975
			367,175		
20X6	Quarter 1	385,900		366,013	+19,887
			364,850		
	Quarter 2	392,400		366,125	+26,275
			367,400		
	Quarter 3	352,500		368,225	−15,725
			369,050		
	Quarter 4	338,800		371,288	−32,488
			373,525		
20X7	Quarter 1	392,500		375,575	+16,925
			377,625		
	Quarter 2	410,300		378,325	+31,975
			379,025		
	Quarter 3	368,900		379,750	−10,850
			380,475		
	Quarter 4	344,400		382,388	−37,988
			384,300		
20X8	Quarter 1	398,300			
	Quarter 2	425,600			

3

	Cost £	Index
January	59,700	100.0
February	62,300	104.4
March	56,900	95.3
April	60,400	101.2
May	62,400	104.5
June	66,700	111.7

Workings

January	59,700/59,700 = 100.0
February	62,300/59,700 = 104.4
March	56,900/59,700 = 95.3
April	60,400/59,700 = 101.2
May	62,400/59,700 = 104.5
June	66,700/59,700 = 111.7

4   (a)

	Wages cost £	RPI	Adjusted cost £
January	126,700	171.1	126,848
February	129,700	172.0	129,172
March	130,400	172.2	129,718
April	131,600	173.0	130,307
May	130,500	172.1	129,893
June	131,600	171.3	131,600

Workings

	Wages cost £	Adjusted cost £
January	126,700 × 171.3/171.1	126,848
February	129,700 × 171.3/172.0	129,172
March	130,400 × 171.3/172.2	129,718
April	131,600 × 171.3/173.0	130,307
May	130,500 × 171.3/172.1	129,893
June	131,600 × 171.3/171.3	131,600

(b)

	Adjusted cost £	Working	Index
January	126,848	126,848/126,848	100.0
February	129,172	129,172/126,848	101.8
March	129,718	129,718/126,848	102.3
April	130,307	130,307/126,848	102.7
May	129,893	129,893/126,848	102.4
June	131,600	131,600/126,848	103.7

5    $y = 5,000 + 10 x$

Production cost of 1,400 units = £19,000

Workings

£15,000 = a + (1,000 × b)

£25,000 = a + (2,000 × b)

£(25,000 – 15,000) = (a + (2,000 × b)) – (a + (1,000 × b))

£10,000 = a +2,000b – a – 1,000b

£10,000 = 1,000 × b

b = £10,000/1,000 = £10

£15,000 = a + (1,000 × 10)

a = £15,000 – £10,000

a = £5,000

so the regression line is y = 5,000 + 10 b

Production cost of 1,400 units = 5,000 + (10 × 1,400) = £19,000

6

	Production Units	Costs £
January	5,400	17,320
February	5,600	17,480
March	5,700	17,560
April	6,000	17,800
May	5,500	17,400
June	6,100	17,880

Workings

Stores costs:

January	13,000 + (0.8 × 5,400)	17,320
February	13,000 + (0.8 × 5,600)	17,480
March	13,000 + (0.8 × 5,700)	17,560
April	13,000 + (0.8 × 6,000)	17,800
May	13,000 + (0.8 × 5,500)	17,400
June	13,000 + (0.8 × 6,100)	17,880

7

	Value of x	Trend	Seasonal variation	Forecast sales
Quarter 1 20X9	13	2,785	–200	2,585
Quarter 2 20X9	14	2,830	+500	3,330
Quarter 3 20X9	15	2,875	+350	3,225
Quarter 4 20X9	16	2,920	–650	2,270

Workings

Value of x for Quarter 1, 20X9

Quarter 1 20X6   =   1

Add 3 years of 4 quarters $\underline{12}$

 = $\underline{13}$

Trend for Quarter 1, 20X9: 2,200 + (45 × 13) = 2,785

Trend for Quarter 2, 20X9: 2,200 + (45 × 14) = 2,830

Trend for Quarter 3, 20X9: 2,200 + (45 × 15) = 2,875

Trend for Quarter 4, 20X9: 2,200 + (45 × 16) = 2,920

Chapter 3   Standard costing

1   The information for the amount of labour time for each cost unit would come from payroll records such as time sheets or from physical observations such as time and motion studies. Factors that should be taken into account include:

- The level of skill or training of the labour grade to be used on the product
- Any anticipated changes on the grade of labour used on the product
- Any anticipated changes in work methods or productivity levels
- The effect of any bonus scheme on productivity

The hourly rate for the direct labour can be found from payroll records but the following factors should be considered:

- Anticipated pay rises
- Anticipated changes in grade of labour
- Effect of any bonus scheme on the labour rate
- Whether any anticipated overtime is built into the hourly rate

2   The information for the amount of material required for each unit of a product can be found from the original product specification – the amount originally considered necessary for each unit. Factors that should be taken into account include:

- The level of skill of the labour to be used on the product

- Any anticipated changes to the quality of material sourced

- Any anticipated changes in work methods/equipment used to work the material

However, this figure may be amended over time as the actual amount used in production is monitored.

The basic price of the material can be found from suppliers' quotations or invoices. However, when setting the standard, the following should also be taken into account:

- General inflation rates

- Any foreseen increases in the price of this particular material

- Any seasonality in the price

- Any discounts available for bulk purchases

- Any anticipated scarcity of the material which may mean paying a higher price

3   Ideal standards are set on the basis of perfect working conditions. No allowance is made for normal wastage or inefficiencies.

Target standards are standards that are set on the basis of normal working conditions by building in some element to reflect normal wastage or inefficiencies. Target standards are capable of being met by efficient operations.

Basic standards are the original historical standards based upon the original expectations of cost for the product.

4   Ideal standards assume perfect operating conditions exist at all times, making them very difficult to achieve. As a result, staff performance is controlled on very tight targets, putting them under extreme pressure. This can therefore result in demotivated staff.

Chapter 4 Variance Analysis

1   (a)   Total materials cost variance

	£
Standard cost of actual production	
1,800 units should have cost (× 7 kg × £6.00)	75,600
But did cost	70,800
	4,800 (F)

(b) Materials price variance

	£
12,000 kg should have cost (× £6.00)	72,000
But did cost	70,800
	1,200 (F)

(c) Materials usage variance

1,800 units should have used (× 7 kg)	12,600
But did use	12,000
Variance in kg	600 (F)
× standard price per kg	× £6
Material usage variance in £	£3,600 (F)

2 (a) Total labour cost variance

	£
Standard cost of actual production	
15,400 units should have cost (× 2.5 hours × £6.80)	261,800
But did cost	265,200
	3,400 (A)

(b) Labour rate variance

Actual hours at standard rate	
41,000 hrs should cost (× £6.80)	278,800
But did cost	265,200
	13,600 (F)

(c) Labour efficiency variance

Standard hours for actual production at standard rate	
15,400 units should have taken (× 2.5 hrs)	38,500
But did take	41,000
	2,500 (A)
× standard rate per hour	× £6.80
	£17,000 (A)

3 (a) Standard materials for 6,400 units:

6,400 units × 5,500 kg/7,000 units = 5,029 kg

(b) Standard labour hours for 6,400 units:

6,400 units × 10,000 hrs/7,000 units = 9,143 hrs

(c) Standard machine hours for 6,400 units:

6,400 units × 21,000 hrs/7,000 units = 19,200 hrs

4   (a)   Fixed overhead expenditure variance

	£
Budgeted fixed overhead	52,500
Actual fixed overhead expenditure	56,000
Fixed overhead expenditure variance	3,500 (A)

(b)   Fixed overhead volume variance

	Units
Budgeted output	7,000
Actual output	6,400
Volume variance in units	600 (A)
Standard fixed overhead cost per unit	£7.50
Fixed overhead volume variance in £	4,500 Adv

(c)   Fixed overhead efficiency variance

6,400 units should take (× 3 hrs)	19,200 hrs
But did take	20,000 hrs
Efficiency variance in hours	800 hrs (A)
× Standard absorption rate per hour	× £2.50
Fixed overhead efficiency variance	£2,000 Adv

(d)   Fixed overhead capacity variance

Budgeted hours of work (7,000 × 3 hrs)	21,000 hrs
Actual hours of work	20,000 hrs
Capacity variance in hours	1,000 hrs (A)
× Standard absorption rate per hour	× £2.50
Capacity variance in £	2,500 (A)

Chapter 5 Operating Statements

1   (a)   Materials price variance

		£
7,500 kg should have cost (× £3.60)		27,000
But did cost		25,900
		1,100 (F)

Materials usage variance

		£
1,750 units should have used (× 4.2 kg)		7,350 kg
But did use		7,500 kg
Materials usage variance in kg		150 kg (A)
× Standard price per kg		× £3.60
Materials usage variance in £		540 (A)

(b)   Labour rate variance

2,580 hrs should have cost (× £7.80)		20,124
But did cost		20,600
		476 (A)

Labour efficiency variance

1,750 units should have taken (× 1.5 hrs)		2,625 hrs
But did take		2,580 hrs
Efficiency variance in hrs		45 hrs (F)
× Standard rate per hour		× £7.80
Labour efficiency variance in £		351 (F)

(c)   Fixed overhead expenditure variance

Budgeted fixed overhead 1,800 × £4.20		7,560
Actual fixed overhead		8,100
Fixed overhead expenditure variance		540 (A)

Fixed overhead efficiency variance

Efficiency variance in hours (same as labour efficiency)		45 hrs (F)
× Standard fixed overhead absorption rate per hour		£2.80
Fixed overhead efficiency variance in £		£126 (F)

Fixed overhead capacity variance

Budgeted hours of work (1,800 × 1.5)		2,700 hrs
Actual hours of work		2,580 hrs
Capacity variance in hours		120 hrs (A)
× Standard fixed overhead absorption rate per hour		× £2.80
Capacity variance in £		£336 (A)

(d) Standard cost of actual production

Direct materials 1,750 × 4.2 × £3.60	26,460
Direct labour 1,750 × 1.5 × £7.80	20,475
Fixed overhead 1,750 × £4.20	7,350
Total cost 1,750 × £31.02	54,285

Operating statement – Absorption costing

	Favourable variances	Adverse variances	£
Variances:			
Materials price	1,100		
Materials usage		540	
Labour rate		476	
Labour efficiency	351		
Fixed overhead expenditure		540	
Fixed overhead efficiency	126		
Fixed overhead capacity		336	
	1,577	1,892	315 (A)
Actual cost of production			54,600

2   (a) Total direct materials cost variance

	£
Standard cost of actual production 2,400 × 12 × £4.80	138,240
Actual cost of actual production	145,000
	6,760 (A)

Materials price variance

	£
Actual quantity should have cost 29,600 × £4.80	142,080
But did cost	145,000
	2,920 (A)

Materials usage variance

Actual production should have used (2,400 × 12)	28,800 kg
But did use	29,600 kg
Materials usage variance in kg	800 kg (A)

× Standard price per kg	£4.80
Materials usage variance in £	3,840 (A)

(b) Total direct labour variance

Standard labour cost of actual production	
2,400 × 3 × £8.00	57,600
Actual labour cost of actual production	56,200
	1,400 (F)

Labour rate variance

Actual hours should have cost	
6,900 × £8.00	55,200
But did cost	56,200
Labour rate variance	1,000 (A)

Labour efficiency variance

Actual production should have taken	Hours
2,400 × 3 × £8.00	7,200
But did take	6,900
Labour efficiency variance in hours	300 hrs (F)

× Standard rate per hour	£8
Labour efficiency variance in £	2,400 (F)

(c) Fixed overhead expenditure variance

Actual fixed overhead	92,000
Budgeted fixed overhead	95,000
	3,000 (F)

(d) Standard cost of production

	£
Direct materials 2,400 × 12 × £4.80	138,240
Direct labour 2,400 × 3 × £8.00	57,600
Standard variable cost (2,400 × 81.60)	195,840

			£
Standard variable cost of actual production			195,840
Budgeted fixed overhead			95,000
Variances	**Favourable variances**	**Adverse variances**	
Materials price		2,920	
Materials usage		3,840	
Labour rate		1,000	
Labour efficiency	2,400		
Fixed overhead expenditure	3,000	—	
	5,400	7,760	2,360 (A)
Total actual cost			293,200

Chapter 6   Standard costing – further aspects

1   REPORT

To: Managing Director
From: Accountant
Date: xx.xx.xx
Subject: November production cost variances

The November production cost is 5% more than the standard cost for the actual production, due to a number of fairly significant adverse variances.

The main cause appears to have been the labour that was used in production for the month which was a more junior grade than normal due to staff shortages. Although this has given a favourable labour rate variance, it has also caused adverse labour efficiency and materials usage variances due to inefficiencies and wastage from the staff. This inefficiency in labour hours has also led to the fixed overhead efficiency adverse variance.

For future months we should either ensure that we have enough of the normal grade of labour for production of this product or train the junior staff in the production process.

There is also an adverse materials price variance which has been due to an increase in the price of our materials. As it is believed that this is a permanent price increase by all suppliers, we should consider altering the direct materials standard cost to reflect this, otherwise each month we will have adverse materials price variances.

The factory now has an additional rent cost which has presumably caused the adverse fixed overhead expenditure variance. If the additional inventory requirement and hence the additional rent is a permanent change then this should be built into the budgeted fixed overhead figure.

Due to the labour inefficiency, more hours have been worked than were budgeted for, leading to the favourable capacity variance. This indicates that the factory has more capacity than we have been making use of which, if the inefficiencies are sorted out, could be used to increase monthly production if required.

2

Scenario	Possible effects
A business replaces machinery with new equipment	• Favourable materials usage variance, if new machinery leads to less waste • Alternatively, adverse materials usage variance, if workers have to adapt to using new machinery • Adverse fixed overheads expenditure variance (higher depreciation charged, although overheads may decrease leading to favourable variance if more power-efficient) • Favourable labour efficiency if workers can work faster (and so favourable overhead efficiency variance)
A company has supply issues with a raw material	• Adverse materials price variance • Possible adverse materials usage variance, if can only source inferior material • Adverse labour efficiency variance (idle time) if no material for production • Possible adverse labour rate efficiency, if must use overtime to catch up, when material does become available

3   Materials price variance

	£
Actual kg should cost (1000 + 268)	1,268
Actual kg did cost	1,000
	268 F

The actual quantity of materials purchased = £1,268/£22 = $\boxed{58}$ kg

Labour rate variance

	£
768 hours should cost (22,560 – 636)	21,924
768 hours did cost	22,560
	636 A

The standard labour rate = £21,924/768 hrs = £ 28.55

4   Fixed overhead expenditure variance

	£
Budgeted overheads	78,000
Actual overheads (78,000 – 8,500)	69,500
	8,500 F

Fixed overhead total variance

	£
Overheads absorbed (69,500 – 4,400)	65,100
Actual overheads	69,500
Under-absorbed overhead (8,500 – 12,900)	4,400

The standard labour hours for the period = $\frac{65,100}{4.2}$ = 15,500 hours

5   Uncontrollable variance

	£
800 hours should cost (800 × £5.00)	4,000
800 hours should now cost (800 × £6.50)	5,200
	1,200 A

Controllable variance

	£
800 hours should now cost	5,200
800 hours did cost	4,900
	300 F

Chapter 7 Performance indicators

1

	April	May	June	Total
Productivity per labour hour	10.9 units	10.7 units	11.1 units	10.9 units
Efficiency ratio	98.8%	97.6%	101.2%	99.2%
Capacity ratio	102.7%	101.2%	101.2%	101.7%
Activity ratio	101.4%	98.8%	102.4%	100.9%
Value added per employee	£2,552	£2,524	£2,717	£2,598

Workings

	April	May	June	Total

(a) Productivity per labour hour

$$\frac{121,700}{11,200} \qquad \frac{123,500}{11,500} \qquad \frac{128,000}{11,500} \qquad \frac{373,200}{34,200}$$

$$= 10.9 \text{ units} \quad = 10.7 \text{ units} \quad = 11.1 \text{ units} \quad = 10.9 \text{ units}$$

(b) Standard hours for actual production

$$\frac{121,700}{11} \qquad \frac{123,500}{11} \qquad \frac{128,000}{11} \qquad \frac{373,200}{11}$$

$$= 11,064 \qquad = 11,227 \qquad = 11,636 \qquad = 33,927$$

Efficiency ratio

$$\frac{11,064}{11,200}\times100 \quad \frac{11,227}{11,500}\times100 \quad \frac{11,636}{11,500}\times100 \quad \frac{33,927}{34,200}\times100$$

$$=98.8\% \qquad =97.6\% \qquad =101.2\% \qquad =99.2\%$$

(c) Budgeted hours

$$\frac{120,000}{11} \qquad \frac{125,000}{11} \qquad \frac{125,000}{11} \qquad \frac{370,000}{11}$$

$$= 10,909 \qquad = 11,364 \qquad = 11,363 \qquad = 33,636$$

Capacity ratio

$$\frac{11,200}{10,909}\times100 \quad \frac{11,500}{11,364}\times100 \quad \frac{11,500}{11,363}\times100 \quad \frac{34,200}{33,636}\times100$$

$$= 102.7\% \qquad = 101.2\% \qquad = 101.2\% \qquad = 101.7\%$$

(d) Activity ratio

$$\frac{11,064}{10,909}\times100 \quad \frac{11,227}{11,364}\times100 \quad \frac{11,636}{11,363}\times100 \quad \frac{33,927}{33,636}\times100$$

$$= 101.4\% \qquad = 98.8\% \qquad = 102.4\% \qquad = 100.9\%$$

(e) Value added

£625,000 – £418,300	£206,700	
£634,000 – £424,500	£209,500	
£656,000 – £430,500		£225,500	£641,700

	Mar	Apr	May	
Value added per employee	$\frac{206,700}{81}$	$\frac{209,500}{83}$	$\frac{225,500}{83}$	$\frac{641,700}{247}$
	= £2,552	= £2,524	= £2,717	= £2,598

2

	Mar	Apr	May
Gross profit margin	42.2%	37.3%	39.3%
Net profit margin	10.9%	10.6%	11.3%
% expenses to revenue	31.3%	26.7%	28.0%
Return on capital employed	15.0%	16.5%	17.1%
Asset turnover	1.38	1.55	1.52

Workings

(a)

		Mar	Apr	May
(i)	Gross profit margin	$\frac{190}{450}$ 42.2%	$\frac{190}{510}$ 37.3%	$\frac{220}{560}$ 39.3%
(ii)	Operating profit margin	$\frac{49}{450}$ 10.9%	$\frac{54}{510}$ 10.6%	$\frac{63}{560}$ 11.3%
(iii)	Expenses to revenue	$\frac{141}{450}$ 31.3%	$\frac{136}{510}$ 26.7%	$\frac{157}{560}$ 28.0%
(iv)	Return on capital employed	$\frac{49}{(396-69)}$ 15.0%	$\frac{54}{(413-85)}$ 16.5%	$\frac{63}{(467-99)}$ 17.1%
(v)	Asset turnover	$\frac{450}{(396-69)}$ 1.38	$\frac{510}{(413-85)}$ 1.55	$\frac{560}{(467-99)}$ 1.52

(b) Gross profit margin

The decrease in the gross profit margin in April has mainly been driven by increasing cost of sales. Although revenue has increased between the two months, cost in sales did not increase in line with it. This has worsened the gross profit margin between March and April.

The increase in May is predominantly due to good cost control within cost of sales. Once again cost of sales have not increased in line with revenue – they have increased only marginally. This has led to an improved gross profit margin.

Return on capital employed

The increase of return on capital employed between March and April can be attributed to improving asset turnover and operating profit margin. Assets are being used more efficiently to generate revenue whereas the expense as a percentage of revenue has dropped. This has enabled more profit to be made, hence a greater return being generated.

Between April and May asset turnover has dropped, meaning the business is using assets less efficiently to generate revenue. However even better cost control has been managed, helping to improve the operating profit margin. The increase in ROCE can therefore be attributed more to good cost control rather than good revenue performance.

3

	20X6	20X7	20X8
Gross profit margin	46.3%	47.6%	44.4%
Operating profit margin	11.0%	11.8%	9.4%
Return on capital employed	18.0%	16.4%	12.7%
Asset turnover	1.64	1.39	1.34
Non-current asset turnover	2.13	1.88	1.81
Current ratio	4.8:1	5.6:1	5.2:1
Quick ratio	3.2:1	4.0:1	3.6:1
Receivables' collection period	38 days	48 days	52 days
Inventory days	41 days	45 days	49 days
Payables' payment period	25 days	28 days	30 days
Interest cover	N/A	33.3	28.3
Gearing ratio	N/A	8.9%	8.1%

Workings

		20X6	20X7	20X8
(a)	Gross profit margin	$\frac{380}{820} \times 100$	$\frac{405}{850} \times 100$	$\frac{400}{900} \times 100$
		46.3%	47.6%	44.4%
(b)	Operating profit margin	$\frac{90}{820} \times 100$	$\frac{100}{850} \times 100$	$\frac{85}{900} \times 100$
		11.0%	11.8%	9.4%
(c)	Return on capital employed	$\frac{90}{500} \times 100$	$\frac{100}{610} \times 100$	$\frac{85}{670} \times 100$
		18.0%	16.4%	12.7%
(d)	Asset turnover	$\frac{820}{500}$	$\frac{850}{610}$	$\frac{900}{670}$
		1.64	1.39	1.34
(e)	Non-current asset turnover	$\frac{820}{385}$	$\frac{850}{453}$	$\frac{900}{498}$
		2.13	1.88	1.81
(f)	Current ratio	$\frac{145}{30}$	$\frac{191}{34}$	$\frac{213}{41}$
		4.8	5.6	5.2
(g)	Quick ratio	$\frac{95}{30}$	$\frac{136}{34}$	$\frac{146}{41}$
		3.2	4.0	3.6
(h)	Receivables' collection period	$\frac{85}{820} \times 365$	$\frac{112}{850} \times 365$	$\frac{128}{900} \times 365$
		38 days	48 days	52 days
(i)	Inventory days	$\frac{50}{440} \times 365$	$\frac{55}{445} \times 365$	$\frac{67}{500} \times 365$
		41 days	45 days	49 days
(j)	Payables' payment period	$\frac{30}{440} \times 365$	$\frac{34}{445} \times 365$	$\frac{41}{500} \times 365$
		25 days	28 days	30 days
(k)	Interest cover	N/A	100/3	85/3
			= 33.3	= 28.3
(l)	Gearing ratio	N/A	50/560 × 100	50/620 × 100
			= 8.9%	= 8.1%

4

		Firmwell	Hartfield
	Cost of sales	51 + 210 − 56	45 + 165 − 50
		= £205,000	= £160,000
(i)	Gross profit margin	$\dfrac{335,000}{540,000}\times100$	$\dfrac{210,000}{370,000}\times100$
		62.0%	56.8%
(ii)	Operating profit margin	$\dfrac{65,000}{540,000}\times100$	$\dfrac{35,000}{370,000}\times100$
		12.0%	9.5%
(iii)	Return on net assets	$\dfrac{65,000}{550,000}\times100$	$\dfrac{35,000}{410,000}\times100$
		11.8%	8.5%
(iv)	Net asset turnover	$\dfrac{540,000}{550,000}$	$\dfrac{370,000}{410,000}$
		0.98	0.90
(v)	Average inventory	$\dfrac{51+56}{2}$	$\dfrac{45+50}{2}$
		£53,500	£47,500
	Inventory days	$\dfrac{53,500}{205,000}\times365$	$\dfrac{47,500}{160,000}\times365$
		95 days	108 days
(vi)	Payables' payment period	$\dfrac{25,800}{210,000}\times365$	$\dfrac{27,500}{165,000}\times365$
		45 days	61 days
(vii)	Sales per sq m	$\dfrac{540,000}{2,400}$	$\dfrac{370,000}{1,700}$
		£225	£218
(viii)	Sales per employee	$\dfrac{540,000}{28}$	$\dfrac{370,000}{13}$
		£19,286	£28,462
(ix)	Sales per hour worked	$\dfrac{540,000}{30,500}$	$\dfrac{370,000}{14,100}$
		£17.70	£26.24

(b) REPORT

To:	Sales Director
From:	Accounts Assistant
Date:	xx.xx.xx
Subject:	Performance of stores

I have considered the performance figures for our two stores in Flimwell and Hartfield for the first six months of the year. The key factors that have appeared from these figures are addressed below.

Firmwell has a higher gross profit margin than Hartfield. This could be because sales volumes are not as high in Hartfield, as its inventory days are higher than that of Firmwell. This implies that revenue is not being generated as efficiently in Hartfield, having a negative impact on their gross profit revenue. Hartfield could try and emulate Firmwell's revenue per square metre by looking at their store layout. This should help to drive up the gross profit margin in the future.

Hartfield, however, does have the highest productivity as sales per employee and sales per hour worked as these are higher than Firmwell. This implies that the lower gross profit margin is not due to inefficient use of staff – indeed its direct costs are much lower than that of Firmwell.

Firmwell has the net profit margin and return on net assets. Firmwell therefore has better control of its expenses than Hartfield. If the Firmwell practices can be emulated in Hartfield this could improve Hartfield's profitability.

Hartfield does have the better liquidity position as, despite having longer inventory days. This is because it has a longer payables period, meaning its working capital cycle is lower. Both stores can learn from each other to improve their liquidity – Firmwell can emulate Hartfield's payables control, and Hartfield can emulate Firmwell's inventory control.

5   Financial performance indictors are **not useful on their own.** They need to be assessed to a comparator, either a previous financial indicator or a financial indicator of a competitor

Financial performance indictors are an **historic measurement.** They therefore give little reassurance to the future performance of an organisation.

Financial performance indictors **do not convey the full picture** of what is happening within an organisation. A range of non-financial indicators is therefore useful to the organisation to put their financial performance into context.

As financial indicators are mostly based around profit they encourage managers to **focus on the short-term**. Managers may therefore be discouraged to take decisions for the long-term benefit of the organisation.

6

(a) Gross profit margin $= \dfrac{\text{Gross profit}}{\text{Revenue}}$

44% $= \dfrac{\text{Gross profit}}{£106,500}$

44% × £106,500 = Gross profit

Gross profit = £46,860

(b) Gross profit margin $= \dfrac{\text{Gross profit}}{\text{Revenue}}$

37.5% $= \dfrac{£105,000}{\text{Revenue}}$

Revenue $= \dfrac{£105,000}{0.375}$

Revenue = £280,000

(c) Gross profit = £256,000 × 41%

= £104,960

Operating profit = £256,000 × 13.5%

= £34,560

Expenses = £104,960 – 34,560

= £70,400

(d) ROCE $= \dfrac{\text{Operating profit}}{\text{Capital employed}}$

12.8% $= \dfrac{£50,000}{\text{Capital employed}}$

Capital employed $= \dfrac{£50,000}{0.128}$

= £390,625

(e) ROCE = Operating profit margin × Asset turnover

15% = 10% × Asset turnover

$\dfrac{15\%}{10\%}$ = Asset turnover

Asset turnover = 1.5

(f) Average inventory $= \dfrac{118,000+104,000}{2}$

= £111,000

Inventory turnover $= \dfrac{\text{Cost of sales}}{\text{Average inventory}}$

$= \dfrac{£118,000+465,000-104,000}{£111,000}$

= 4.3 times

(g) Receivables' collection period $= \dfrac{\text{Receivables}}{\text{Revenue}} \times 365$

64 days $= \dfrac{64,000}{\text{Revenue}} \times 365$

Revenue $= \dfrac{64,000}{64 \text{ days}} \times 365$

$= £365,000$

7   Financial
Customer
Innovation and learning
Internal

Chapter 8 Cost management

1   **Development** – Fixed research and development costs

Introductory – Continuing research and development costs, fixed advertising expenditure, low level direct materials and labour costs

Growth – Continuing advertising and promotion expenditure, high level of direct materials and labour costs, high fixed and variable production overheads

Maturity – Lower level of direct materials and labour costs due to economies of scale, higher level of production overheads due to mechanisation

Decline – Low level of direct materials and labour, production overheads low, decommissioning and opportunity costs high due to wastage of obsolete stock

2

Year	Cash flows £	Discount factor at 7%	Present value £
0	(340,000)	1.000	(340,000)
1	80,000	0.935	74,800
2	70,000	0.873	61,110
3	90,000	0.816	73,440
4	120,000	0.763	91,560
5	60,000	0.713	42,780
Net present value			3,690

Remember that depreciation is not a cash flow and is therefore excluded from the net present value calculations.

3 (a)

Year	Cash flows £	Discount factor at 11%	Present value £
0	(90,000)	1.000	(90,000)
1	23,000	0.901	20,723
2	31,000	0.812	25,172
3	40,000	0.731	29,240
4	18,000	0.659	11,862
Net present value			(3,003)

(b) The organisation | should not | invest in the plant and machinery

4

	Develop-ment	Introduction	Growth	Maturity	Decline	Total
Sales volume (units)		5,000	13,000	25,000	10,000	
£000						
Revenue		£250 × 5 1,250	£250 × 13 3,250	£200 × 25 5,000	£150 × 10 1,500	11,000
Variable cost		£150 × 5 (750)	£130 × 13 (1,690)	£70 × 25 (1,750)	£85 × 10 (850)	(5,040)
Fixed Overhead		(800)	(650)	(450)	(460)	(2,360)
Development cost	(400)					(400)
Scrap cost					(60)	(60)
Profit	(400)	(300)	910	2,800	130	3,140

5

	£
Target selling price	90
Target profit margin (90 × 20%)	(18)
Target cost	72

6 **Value analysis** assesses the composition of a product that is currently in production, and its associated production process. Improvements are then sought to both the product and the process. This reduces the cost of production, resulting in a lower cost per unit.

Value engineering assesses the composition of a product that is not currently in production and is currently in its design stage. It looks at elements of the proposed product and assess whether each element adds value to the overall product. Elements that don't add value are subsequently eliminated, reducing the production cost of the product once it goes into production.

Chapter 9 Activity Based Costing

1 Activity based costing absorbs costs using **multiple bases,** and therefore establishes different reasons why overheads are incurred. This differs to absorption costing which assumes that overheads are incurred for one reason and therefore uses one base, such as labour or machine hours.

Due to the fact the activity based costing recognises there are different reasons for overheads to be incurred it therefore absorbs overhead using **multiple overhead absorption rate.** This differs from absorption costing that absorbs overhead using a single overhead absorption rate.

Activity based costing assumes that overheads are **not volume related,** ie if more units are produced the overhead remains unaffected. This differs from absorption costing which assumes that as more units are produced more overheads are incurred as a result.

2

Product	Budgeted cost per unit £	Budgeted overhead per unit £
LM	9.78	3.68
NP	27.41	20.81

Workings

Stores cost $= \dfrac{£140,000}{320}$

$= £437.50$ per materials requisition

Production set-up costs $= \dfrac{£280,000}{280}$

$= £1,000$ per set-up

Quality control costs $= \dfrac{£180,000}{90}$

$= £2,000$ per inspection

Product costs		LM £	NP £
Direct materials	50,000 × £2.60	130,000	
	20,000 × £3.90		78,000
Direct labour	50,000 × £3.50	175,000	
	20,000 × £2.70		54,000
Stores costs	100 × £437.50	43,750	
	220 × £437.50		96,250
Production set-up costs	80 × £1,000	80,000	
	200 × £1,000		200,000
Quality control costs	30 × £2,000	60,000	
	60 × £2,000		120,000
Total cost		488,750	548,250

Cost per unit		$\dfrac{488{,}750}{50{,}000}$	$\dfrac{548{,}250}{20{,}000}$
		= £9.78	= £27.41

Analysis of total unit cost

Direct costs	(2.60 + 3.50)	6.10	
	(3.90 + 2.70)		6.60
Overheads	$\dfrac{(43{,}750+80{,}000+60{,}000)}{50{,}000}$	3.68	
	$\dfrac{(96{,}250+200{,}000+120{,}000)}{20{,}000}$		20.81
		9.78	27.41

3   Activity based costing gives a **more realistic estimate** of cost usage by products. This in turn gives a more accurate reflection of profits, meaning a more realistic price can be set to recover those costs.

Activity based costing aids better **cost control and reduction** as cost drivers are more visible. This helps managers to find methods to reduce usage of cost drivers that are generating high overheads.

Activity based costing aids better **profitability analysis** of products as a more realistic profit is calculated. This will enhance the organisation's performance reporting.

Activity based costing recognises the **complexity and diversity** of the production process. It therefore enables managers to establish the true reasons why costs are incurred rather than assuming that overheads are incurred simply because more units have been produced.

4   Activity based costing is **time consuming** and therefore expensive, as it relies on collection and interpretation of a vast array of data.

Activity based costing has **limited use if only one product is produced** as the production overheads incurred tend to be more complex if a diverse product range is produced.

Activity based costing will still need some **arbitrary apportionment** as it is sometimes not obvious which cost driver is related to which cost pool.

The **amount of overhead absorption rates** calculated can be vast. It therefore makes standard cost cards complicated and difficult to interpret.

Chapter 10　　Decision making techniques

1　The breakeven point is ⎡ 30,000 ⎤ units.

　The margin of safety is ⎡ 21 ⎤ %.

Workings

Breakeven point $=$ $\dfrac{£360,000}{£57 - £45}$

　　　　　$=$　　30,000 units

Margin of safety　$=$　$\dfrac{38,000 - 30,000}{38,000}$

　　　　　$=$　　21%

2　The amount of units that needs to be sold is ⎡ 201,429 ⎤ units.

Target profit sales　$=$　$\dfrac{£910,000 + £500,000}{£24 - £17}$

　　　　　$=$　　201,429 units

3　The sales revenue required in order to make a profit of £200,000 is £ ⎡ 1,500,000 ⎤ .

Workings

Profit volume ratio　　$=$　$\dfrac{£(40 - 32)}{£40} \times 100$

　　　　　　$=$　　20%

Target profit sales revenue　$=$　$\dfrac{£100,000 + £200,000}{0.20}$

　　　　　　$=$　　£1,500,000

4　(a)　The limiting factor of production resources is ⎡ machine hours ⎤ .

Working

Resource requirements for maximum demand

	R	S	T	Total
Materials	80,000 kg	120,000 kg	25,000 kg	225,000 kg
Labour hours	20,000 hours	80,000 hours	5,000 hours	105,000 hours
Machine hours	60,000 hours	80,000 hours	15,000 hours	155,000 hours

The limiting factor is machine hours.

(b)

Product	Units produced
S	20,000
T	5,000
R	4,166

Workings

Contribution per machine hour

	R	S	T
Contribution	£6	£12	£6
Machine hours	6	4	3
Contribution/machine hour	£1.00	£3.00	£2.00
Ranking	3	1	2

Production plan

Product	Units produced	Machine hours used
S	20,000	80,000
T	5,000	15,000
R (balance 25,000/6 = 4,166.67 = 4,166 complete units))	4,166	24,996
		119,996

(c) The profit that will be earned under this production plan is £ 244,996 .

Workings

Product contribution:	£
R (4,166 × £6)	24,996
S (20,000 × £12)	240,000
T (5,000 × £6)	30,000
Total contribution	294,996
Less fixed costs	(50,000)
Profit	244,996

5 The business should buy in neither product .

	X	Y
	£	£
Direct materials	2.50	3.00
Direct labour	8.00	6.00
Variable cost of production	10.50	9.00
External price	11.00	10.00

On the basis of costs alone, neither product should be purchased externally as they are cheaper to make.

6 Timmy should pay £ 17,500 for additional labour hours (£3.50 × 5,000 hours)

Synoptic assessment preparation

The questions below are ones to consider once you have completed and passed your assessment. Thinking these questions through will enable you to consider the topics covered in the *Management Accounting: Decision and Control* syllabus in a 'real world' context. This is a vital skill to develop before you attempt the synoptic assessment.

The questions presented are short-form questions. In the real synoptic assessment they will be attached to a wider case study.

Questions

(1) You are asked to consider the pricing strategy for two new products of a business. You have been given the following information regarding the new products:

	£ per unit	
	P1	**P2**
Direct materials	3.00	7.00
Direct labour	5.00	11.00
Variable production overhead	2.50	5.30
Fixed production overhead	1.45	3.30
Competitor sales price	14.50	32.00

The sales manager has suggested that you should price the products at 20% mark-up over marginal cost.

(a) Calculate the marginal cost of each product.

(b) Calculate the sales price of each product.

(c) Explain the impact that this pricing policy will have on the business.

(2) In order to close a cost gap of a new product, the production manager of JamJar Ltd. has proposed mechanising part of the production process. Alongside reducing the cost of production, mechanisation will also bring the JamJar in line with developments in the wider industry – indeed most of JamJar's competitors have installed this machinery and are seeing improvements in sales volumes as a result.

The costs of mechanising the production line are given below:

	20X1	20X2	20X3	20X4	20X5
Purchase cost	100,000				
Labour cost saving		10,000	8,000	6,400	5,120
Annual running costs		7,500	7,500	7,500	7,500
Increase in sales revenue		25,000	27,500	30,000	33,000

The discount rates for 12% cost of capital are given below:

0	1.000
1	0.893
2	0.797
3	0.712
4	0.636

(a) Calculate the net present value of mechanising the production line.

	Yr 0	Yr 1	Yr 2	Yr 3	Yr 4
Purchase cost					
Labour cost saving					
Annual running costs					
Increase in sales revenue					
Net cash flow					
Discount factor					
Present value					
Net present value					

(b) What are the potential advantages of mechanising the production line?

(c) What are the potential drawbacks of mechanising the production line?

(3) You are analysing resource utilisation for the coming periods and have established that there isn't enough labour hours available to cover production.

   (a) What actions can the business take to access more labour hours?

   (b) What are the potential consequences of the above actions?

(4) HeetMe Ltd has been reviewing the quality of the solar panels and has engineered two new products, the SP2000 and the SP3000.

The SP2000 is a low quality product with an economic life of 5 years. The SP3000 is a high quality product with an economic life of 20 years.

The Sales Director has provided information about the expected demand and price for the SP2000 and SP3000 for the coming year.

- SP2000 will be priced at £200 per panel and demand is expected to be around 9,000 units per year.

- SP3000 will be priced at £300 per panel and demand is expected to be around 5,000 units per year.

Forecast statement of profit or loss

	SP2000	SP3000
Volume	9,000 units	5,000 units
	£	£
Turnover	1,800,000	1,500,000
Cost of production		
Direct materials (glass)	540,000	300,000
Direct labour	126,000	175,000
Fixed production overheads	120,000	120,000
Total cost of sales	786,000	595,000
Gross profit	1,014,000	905,000
Selling and distribution costs	400,000	400,000
Administration costs	200,000	200,000
Operating profit	414,000	305,000
Extracts from the forecast statement of financial position		
	£	£
Material inventory (glass)	60,000	60,000
Finished goods inventory	0	0
Turnover	2,014,000	1,905,000

(a) Calculate the following performance indicators for both products:

- (i) Gross profit margin
- (ii) Operating profit margin
- (iii) Direct materials cost per unit
- (iv) Direct labour cost per unit
- (v) Fixed production overheads cost per unit
- (vi) Return on net assets
- (vii) Raw materials inventory turnover in days

(b) Compare the performance of each product, referring to the following:

- (i) Sales price per unit
- (ii) Materials, labour and fixed cost per unit
- (iii) Return on net assets

Potential answers

(1)

(a)

	£ per unit	
	P1	**P2**
Direct materials	3.00	7.00
Direct labour	5.00	11.00
Variable production overhead	2.50	5.30
Total marginal cost	**10.50**	**23.30**

(b) P1: 10.50 × 1.2 = £12.60

P2: 23.30 × 1.2 = £27.96

(c) The prices set for each product are lower than those of its competitor. It is likely that the business will be able to attract high sales volumes, which will increase sales revenue to the business.

However the price set is not adequate to cover the fixed overhead of the product. If this price is set over the long-term these products are likely to be unprofitable. They therefore will not be generating an adequate return to the owners of the business.

The lack of profit being generated is likely to put more pressure on other profitable products that the business sells. This will mean that cost efficiencies will need to be made elsewhere to support the profitability of the whole business.

(2) (a)

	Yr 0	Yr 1	Yr 2	Yr 3	Yr 4
Purchase cost	(100,000)				
Labour cost saving		10,000	8,000	6,400	5,120
Annual running costs		(7,500)	(7,500)	(7,500)	(7,500)
Increase in sales revenue		25,000	27,500	30,000	33,000
Net cash flow	(100,000)	27,500	28,000	28,900	30,620
Discount factor	1.000	0.893	0.797	0.712	0.636
Present value	(100,000)	24,558	22,316	20,577	19,474
Net present value	(13,075)				

(b) The potential advantages of mechanising the production line are as follows:

JamJar is able to realise cost savings per unit as both labour and material costs will decrease as a result of mechanisation. This will enable JamJar to close the cost gap currently experienced on the product.

JamJar will see potential sales volumes increases as the target price can be set lower. This increase in sales volume will increase sales revenue, boosting profits.

By mechanising the production line, JamJar will be brought in line with its competitors. This will mean that JamJar is able to compete more effectively in the market by using competitive pricing arrangements.

(c) The potential disadvantages of mechanising the production line include:

Mechanisation is likely to cause anxiety amongst the existing workforce due to the threat of redeployment or redundancy. This will cause demotivation within the workforce, meaning that the labour efficiency savings won't be realised.

If staff will be made redundant, the wider community will also be impacted. This is because disposable income levels will be lower, which will threaten other local business and therefore the local economy. The skill set of the local workforce may also decrease, making it difficult for those affected staff to gain other employment.

The machine produces a negative net present value. This indicates that the new machinery will not produce an adequate return to shareholders. They may resist the mechanisation as it is will deteriorate value within JamJar.

The existing machine may not fit the current production process entirely. Extensive re-design of the process may need to be implemented which is time consuming and expensive.

(3) (a) Suitable answers could include:

- Increase overtime working
- Outsource additional hours required
- Access temporary staff
- Reduce amount of production units

(b) Suitable answers could include:

- Overtime working – this will have a negative impact on labour rates being paid, pushing up labour cost and driving an adverse labour rate variance.

- Outsourcing – there is reliance on the supplier to deliver the additional units in time for them to be sold.

- Temporary staff – if these staff are less experienced this will mean more time spent in production and subsequent impacts on wastage levels, affecting the materials usage and labour efficiency variances.

- Reduce production units – will affect sales volumes and therefore will reduce short-term profits. This could also affect long-term profits if customers defect to the competitor.

(4) (a)

		SP2000	SP3000
(i)	Gross profit margin SP2000: 1,014,000/1,800,000 × 100 SP3000: 905,000/1,500,000 × 100	56.3%	60.3%
(ii)	Operating profit margin SP2000: 414,000/1,800,000 × 100 SP3000: 305,000/1,500,000 × 100	23%	20.3%
(iii)	Direct materials cost per unit SP2000: 540,000/9,000 SP3000: 300,000/5,000	£60 per unit	£60 per unit
(iv)	Direct labour cost per unit SP2000: 126,000/9,000 SP3000: 175,000/5,000	£14 per unit	£35 per unit
(v)	Fixed production overhead cost per unit SP2000: 120,000/9,000 SP3000: 120,000/5,000	£13.33 per unit	£24 per unit
(vi)	Return on net assets SP2000: 414,000/2,014,000 × 100 SP3000: 305,000/1,905,000	20.6%	16%
(vii)	Raw materials inventory turnover in days SP2000: 60,000/786,000 × 365 SP3000: 60,000/595,000 × 365	27.9 days	36.8 days

(b) **Sales price per unit**

The sales price per unit is £100 more expensive for SP3000 than SP2000. This is due to the fact that it's higher quality and can therefore command a higher selling price per unit. Although the increased sales revenue has suppressed sales volume for SP3000, the additional revenue generated by selling SP3000 at a higher selling price has pushed

SP3000's gross profit margin above that of SP2000, as more contribution is being generated per unit.

Materials cost per unit

The materials cost per unit is constant between SP2000 and SP3000 despite SP3000 being sold for a higher price. This has had no impact on the gross profit margin as there is no impact on contribution generated per product.

Labour cost per unit

The labour cost per unit is £19 higher for SP3000 than SP2000. This is because the SP3000 is of higher quality, meaning that more labour time needs to be spent producing each unit. However, combined with SP3000's higher selling price, contribution per unit is much higher than on SP2000 (£126 for SP2000 and £206 for SP3000 respectively). This additional contribution earned by SP3000 has had a positive impact on its gross profit generated, pushing its gross profit margin above SP3000.

Fixed overhead cost per unit

The fixed overhead cost per unit is £10.67 higher for SP3000 than SP2000. This is predominantly due to fewer units of SP3000 being produced, as the same level of fixed overhead is being spread over fewer units. Whereas this will have a negative impact on the profitability per unit, there is ultimately no impact on the gross profit margin as, in total, the fixed overheads are constant between each product.

Return on net assets

The return on net assets is lower for SP3000 than SP2000. This is ultimately due to the lower operating profit margin (20.3% for SP3000 compared to 23% for SP2000). The lower operating profit margin performance can be attributed to the selling and distribution costs. Even though fewer units of SP3000 are produced and sold, selling and distribution costs are projected to be incurred at the same rate as that of SP2000. This could be attributed to the quality of the products, and the need to transport them more carefully than SP2000.

Bibliography

Kaplan, R.S. and Norton, D.P. (1996) Using the Balanced Scorecard as a Strategic Management System. Harvard Business Review. 74(1): 75-85.

Index

A
Absorption costing, 28
Activity based costing, 215
Activity ratio, 169
Adverse variance, 96
Asset turnover, 169

B
Balanced scorecard, 166
Base period, 57
Basic standards, 75
Benchmarking, 169
Break-even analysis, 239
Break-even point, 239

C
Capacity ratio, 169
Capital expenditure, 28
Centred moving average, 57
Contribution, 21, 22, 239
Contribution to sales ratio, 239
Control ratios, 169
Controllable variance, 137
Cost centre, 13, 28
Cost unit, 28
Cost-volume-profit analysis, 221, 239
Current ratio, 169

D
Direct cost, 28

E
Efficiency ratio, 169

F
Favourable variance, 96
Fixed costs, 5, 28
Fixed overhead capacity variance, 96
Fixed overhead efficiency variance, 96
Fixed overhead expenditure variance, 96
Fixed overhead volume variance, 96
Forecast, 57
Full production cost, 28

G
Gearing, 169
Gross profit margin, 169

I
Ideal standards, 75
Index, 50
Index number, 57
Indirect cost, 28
Indirect production costs, 11
Interdependence of variances, 137
Interest cover, 169
Inventory days, 169
Investment centres, 14, 28

K
Key budget factor, 57

L
Labour efficiency variance, 86
Labour rate variance, 85, 96
Limiting factor, 239
Linear regression, 57
Linear regression equation, 57
Liquidity, 169

M
Margin of safety, 239
Marginal costing, 21, 28, 36, 37, 38
Material price variance, 82, 96
Material usage variance, 82, 96
Moving average, 57
Multiplicative model, 46

N
Net profit margin, 169
Non-controllable variance, 137
Non-current asset turnover, 169
Normal standards, 75

O
Operating profit margin, 169
Operating statement, 113
Over-absorption, 19